Freshly Minted

MBA Essentials for the First Time Manager

Shreyas Harish

White Falcon Publishing

www.whitefalconpublishing.com

Freshly Minted
Shreyas Harish

www.whitefalconpublishing.com

Requests for permission should be addressed to
mailto:shreyasharish31@gmail.com

ISBN - 978-1-63640-669-5

Table of Contents

To my sister, Smriti

Who introduced me to the first of many books
that would shape my life

Acknowledgement

There is a long list of people to whom I am ever indebted for their support, encouragement, teaching and mentoring. In order to minimise the chance of human error, to which I am particularly prone, I shall try to list the people who have shaped this book in chronological order.

My **grandparents** have ensured that I grew up in a world full of stories. They are uniquely responsible for instilling the belief that I too can write a book, whatever its contents may be.

My **mother**, from as early as I can remember has been responsible for my scientific curiosity and should be given all the credit for my education, from school to date. She is also to thank for the artistic and clean illustration of the cover of this book.

My **father** likes to believe that he sent me to IIT and then IIM. Undeniably, he was the one who got me excited about starting my career as a management trainee at Reckitt. If not for him, I might never have set foot in the world of business management.

My **sister** will claim that I have been following in her footsteps for years. What I will definitely concede is that she got me hooked on Philip Kotler's textbook on marketing, and convinced me to pursue my MBA at IIM-Ahmedabad. These 2 decisions have perhaps had the strongest and most profound impact on this book, and the rest of my career in management.

The entire institution of **IIT-Madras**, including hundreds of the smartest people that I shall ever meet, is due great thanks for anything that I may achieve in life. I strongly believe that I learnt how to think from first principles, how to organise myself and my time, and how to manage my relationships with the people around me in this magical institute.

The organisation of **Reckitt** will always hold a special place in my heart, as the impressive, complex and yet warm and comfortable company where I began my career. Whatever very limited practical understanding of management I have, has been gifted to me by my mentors in **Udayan Dutt**, **Paul Varghese**, **Manish Gupta**, **Akshat Jain**, **Abhishek Jamwal** and **Alok Sinha**.

The person that I am today, this book and all of its contents owe an incalculable debt to the institution of **IIM-Ahmedabad**. It is almost certain that I will miss out on someone who has been instrumental to my personal development over the last 2 years. However, I shall attempt to chronologically give my thanks to everyone who has been a part of my IIM-Ahmedabad journey.

PGP-Office, support staff and all faculty involved in the administration of the 2-year MBA programme.

Everything that I have learnt and tried to capture in this book is thanks to the following professors' tireless efforts:

Prof. Biju Varkkey
Prof. Chirantan Chatterjee
Prof. M P Ram Mohan
Prof. Shailesh Gandhi
Prof. Parvinder Gupta
Prof. Ajay Pandey
Prof. Samrat Gupta
Prof. Rajat Sharma
Prof. Chetan Soman
Prof. Arnab Kumar Laha
Prof. Tathagatha Bandyopadhyay
Prof. Vaibhavi Kulkarni
Prof. Aditya Christopher Moses
Prof. K V Gopakumar
Prof. Abhiman Das
Prof. Sourav Borah
Prof. Naman Desai
Prof. Ankur Sinha
Prof. Saral Mukherjee
Prof. Diptesh Ghosh
Prof. Navdeep Mathur
Prof. Adrija Majumdar
Prof. Avani Desai
Prof. Anish Sugathan
Prof. Akshaya Vijayalakshmi
Prof. Sidharth Sinha

Prof. Sandip Chakrabarti
Prof. Swanand Deodhar
Mr Danesh Gojer
Prof. Arvind Sahay
Prof. Chitra Singla
Prof. Manjari Singh
Prof. Kathan Shukla
Prof. S Manikutty
Prof. Naveen Amblee
Prof. Devasmita Chakraverty
Prof. Sebastian Morris
Prof. Sanjay Verma
Prof. Mohammad Fuad
Mr. Paranjoy Guha Thakurta
Prof. Anuj Kapoor
Prof. Neha Tripathi
Prof. Rajesh Chandwani
Prof. Arun Sreekumar

I would have hardly completed my MBA, much less this book, without the support and friendship of the entire IIM-A batch of 2020-22. In particular, the 2 years of my MBA were made special by those people who chose to make Dorm 12, Room 12 (the dungeon) a part of their home at IIM-A.

Anoushka Pal
Avantika Mathur
Bisweswar Morang
Dhruv Chawla
Jahanavi Bansal
Piyush Kumar
Prakhar Khandelwal
Pratheebha G
Shikhar Budhiraja
Simran Kanodia
Srivarshini S
Tanishq Diddee

Varun Hooda
Vishwas Maheshwari

Chapter 1
Context Setting

I call this chapter context setting. In more real speak this chapter is to ensure that we're on the same page about what will happen throughout the rest of the book. I often find myself picking up a fancy-sounding book in the hope of reading through all of it and becoming a better person for it. I also often find myself putting that book down soon after that. I either lose interest in the book halfway through or realise that it was never going to fulfil all of the unrealistic expectations that I had of it. The hope is that this chapter is going to save some people a lot of time and protect me from some loathsome reviews.

I'm a big fan of using the 6 big question words to set the context or to begin anything new. So, here we go.

What is this book?

This book is a sort of compilation of what I learnt from my MBA at IIM-Ahmedabad. Before I get your hopes up, this is far from a professionally condensed premier MBA textbook. Rather, this is me trying to review and make sense of what I think are some of the key principles of management. To be super clear, **this book is not**:

- A comprehensive guide on management.
- An expert's guide to management.
- Authored or promoted by any authority on management.

But, before you throw the book away and write a horrible review on Amazon (hopefully I can delay this for a few more chapters), **this book is**:

- A reasonable introduction to the subjects taught at business school.
- A walk through my mind and understanding of what I learnt at IIM-Ahmedabad.
- Sprinkled with first-principles-based (intuitive) thinking about key management principles.

Why did I write this book?

This one's a simple question for me to answer. There are broadly 2 reasons why I chose to write and publish this book:

- Writing helps me learn – There's a whole lot of material covered over the course of 2 years in business school. Reviewing, filtering and consolidating all of it helps me solidify whatever it is that I learnt. Forcing myself to put it in the format of a book ensures that I can't cut corners and skip the subjects that I didn't enjoy learning.
- Why not? – Writing this out and publishing it seemed to be a low-risk, high-gain move. Either it's horrible and gets buried in some corner of the internet, or this is actually useful to someone else, and I get some karma points.

Why should you read this book?

This is the 'why' question that you're probably more interested in. The way I see it there are 2 potentially good reasons why you might want to read this book:

- Short-circuit your learning – Maybe you have not yet been to business school. If so, this is a really quick run-through of what some people pay very good money to learn. The frameworks and principles here can help you get a better grip on your career or anything else that you might be working on managing. While I'm not an expert, I have always been a fairly good student. In the first year of my MBA, I had made detailed notes across all subjects, and then shared them with the next batch of students. To the best of my knowledge, these notes have been nearly universally adopted as a supplement, and a few students even prefer them to the prescribed reference books. And so, whatever I have consolidated in this book ought to be at least slightly useful.
- Revise and re-imagine your learning – Maybe you have already been to business school or have a good amount of management experience. This book probably won't be a source of enlightenment for you, but might shine a light on some new ideas. Further, maybe you haven't had the opportunity to take time out of your busy schedule to organise all of your knowledge on management. If so, reading this book is an opportunity to bring some structure to your knowledge and experience, and a chance to brush up on whatever it is that you already know.

Who am I?

Without boring you excessively, let me try and quickly summarise who I am, in the context of writing this book:

- I am an alumnus of IIT-Madras (B.Tech + M.Tech in computer science & engineering, 2013-18). While this is not very useful in the context of this book, a lot of the first-principles-based thinking that I try to bring alive here, I credit to what I learnt in those 5 years.
- I worked with Reckitt Benckiser (now Reckitt) for 2 years, as a sales and marketing management trainee, and then as a part of the national sales development team. As an engineering student in India, I wasn't going to voluntarily work in engineering now, was I? While my work experience was very useful for me in the process of learning at IIM-Ahmedabad, I will try to avoid directly using learnings from work, to keep this book as generic as possible.
- I am an alumnus of IIM-Ahmedabad (batch of 2020-22), where I consistently ranked within the top 10 students, while also working on a start-up and other pet projects. What I learnt in and outside of classrooms over these 2 years is the main motivation behind creating this resource for myself and for anyone else who sees value in it.

Who is this book for?

I have aimed to keep the target audience for this book as broad as possible. Realistically, the people whom I believe would see the most value in this book are:

- Students Entering Business School – If you are just about to or are already enrolled in business school, this is the ideal time to read something like this. You are clearly interested in the topics that I cover in the book. Further, this is a super quick run-through of what I think you would aim to have learnt by the end of school. Finally, this will help get you through the basics, so that you can make the most of the time and money that you will invest in all of those classes.
- Current or Prospective Managers – Unless the people at business school are way off (I'll let you decide), the stuff that they teach there is likely useful for managers on a regular basis. This book should contain at least a couple of insightful ideas, or at least provide you with an opportunity to think through what you know about management and put it in context.

- <u>College Students Anywhere</u> – Independent of what you are studying and how far into your education you are, there is some element of management (of yourself or others) that your work involves. Further, all of our lives are more impacted today by the business in the market than ever before. If either of these statements seems relevant and compelling to you, this book will not be a complete and utter waste of your time.

When should you read this book?

The answer to this question is largely a function of who you are. Assuming that you are going to attend business school at some point in time, reading this book just before joining, while in school or even just after is the ideal time. For anyone else, the sooner the better. I really do believe that what I have learnt at business school, and therefore what I have written in this book are very generically applicable. Therefore, the earlier in life that you read it, the earlier you can take a call on when and how you want to use what you have learnt.

Where should you use what you read in this book?

This to me is the selling point of management education. On the surface, a lot of it sounds like it is meant for and only useful in the context of a business and other large organisations. However, you'll be surprised at how many principles of communication, marketing, economics etc apply to the strangest of everyday scenarios. There is no denying that this book will be most useful for a manager in a business establishment. The point I would like to drive home, however, is that management education can be interesting and live outside of the boundaries of work as well.

How should you read this book?

The simple answer is that you should read it like a little storybook, not even a classic or a novel. You will find that most of what is written here is nothing but common sense dressed up in fancy words and organised in the form of frameworks. There are going to be a lot of frameworks. You have been warned.

I am not an expert on any of these topics and am thinking out loud through this book. So, as you read it, think with me, agree or disagree and keep building your own mental model of how things work. There's a whole lot of information, so try not to bother remembering all of it, but just have fun with the process. If any of these ideas click, you can always remember the intuition behind it and look up the details of the framework as and when you need to.

At the end of this book, if you feel like you have learnt a new thing or two, and more importantly are comfortable navigating hypothetical management situations, I think that's a big win!

Chapter 2
Management: What's It All About?

If you've managed to make it past the cover of this book, you seem to have some sort of interest in management. Maybe you're training to be a manager, maybe you're already a manager yourself, or maybe you want to know why your boss gets paid so much more than you when you're the one doing all of the work.

Now that we have established that we're interested in knowing more about management, let's start with a definition.

"Management is about getting stuff done."

-Shreyas Harish, 2022

This might not be the textbook definition, but this is about the gist of it, without getting too technical. I think that we'll get a little more value from breaking this definition down than we will from learning a textbook definition. So, management seems to involve:

- A Goal – The 'stuff' that we're trying to get done.
  - o Sometimes managers need to begin by figuring out what the goal is in the first place.
  - o Sometimes the goal is given to you, and you need to figure out how to get it done.
- Getting it Done – 'Getting it done' would be easy unless there were some challenges involved.
  - o Challenges may come in the form of the resources you have available. Managers are expected to figure out how to use whatever they have available with them to achieve the goal at hand.
  - o Challenges may also come in the form of the external environment. Things happening in the outside world will often affect your organisation. Managers are expected to plan ahead and figure out how to navigate the complicated world.

Now that we have broken down our definition, management sounds nice and vague once again, and we can justify the high salaries. On a more serious note, we now have a starting point of what we want to understand, and we have broken it down into parts which need to be demystified. We have laid out that we may know the goal ahead of time, or we may need to identify the goal itself, and that we may have to overcome internal or external challenges.

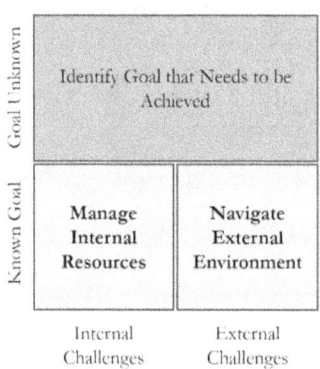

Real-life scenarios are usually pretty complicated, and we will probably need to identify our goal and then achieve it, with a mix of internal and external challenges. But since management is all about getting stuff done, we usually break complex challenges into smaller parts, where each part has only one type of challenge and goal.

This helps us simplify our task of management into just managing the organisation itself and dealing with the world outside of the organisation.

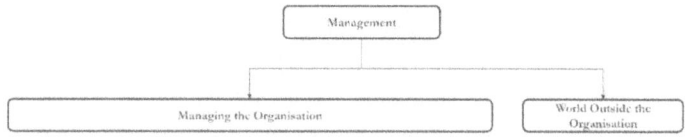

At this stage, we have broken down the mammoth task of management into 2 other large, but marginally more doable tasks. Between these 2 tasks, the first task of "managing the organisation" is usually given more importance in most contexts. To me, this makes sense because in most situations you have a lot more information about and control over your own organisation than you do about the rest of the world. Therefore, while it is important to be able to understand and even predict how the outside world will develop, managers have to be experts in managing their own organisations.

Now that we know that we need to manage the organisation and that it's really tough, we have 2 options. We can give up, get fired and cry. Or we can figure out how to get stuff done, as managers do. If you're still with me, let's try to break down managing the organisation into smaller parts.

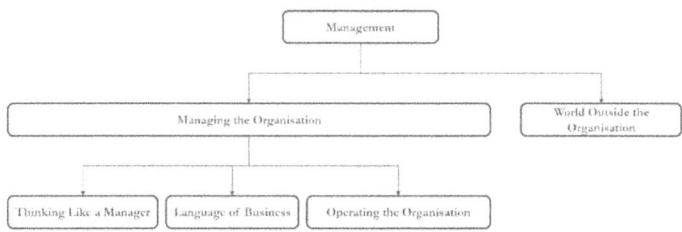

I like to think of managing the organisation as requiring us to complete 3 smaller sub-tasks. For one thing, need to be able to think like a manager (whatever that may mean). To me, this means that once we have understood our situation, we need to be able to process that information, come up with alternatives and make decisions. This really is the cornerstone of management, and a skill we will keep reusing. Secondly, we also need to understand the language of business. If we don't understand the jargon of the organisation and more pertinently, if we don't understand the implications of various metrics that define our situation, we don't understand what is going on at all, and we won't be able to use our thinking. So, we need to understand the language of the business. Finally, we need to be able to handle operations or get stuff done on the ground. This means that it's not enough to understand what's happening and decide what we need to do but to actually make sure that it gets done (operate the organisation). When we put these 3 sub-tasks together, we understand what's happening, decide what needs to be done, and get it done. In a nutshell, we can then manage the organisation.

Now we have broken management down further into smaller tasks. It probably doesn't yet seem like management is easy. But I think we have taken a great step in the direction of understanding what we need to learn.

Before we get down to studying each of these sub-tasks in more detail, one of the sub-tasks seems a bit chunky and big to me. Operating the organisation still seems like the lion's share of work. After all, by definition, this is everything which makes the organisation work, until a manager says that we can do something better. I, therefore, think that this can further be broken down into the hard skills (technical skills) and soft skills (people skills) required to operate a business on the ground.

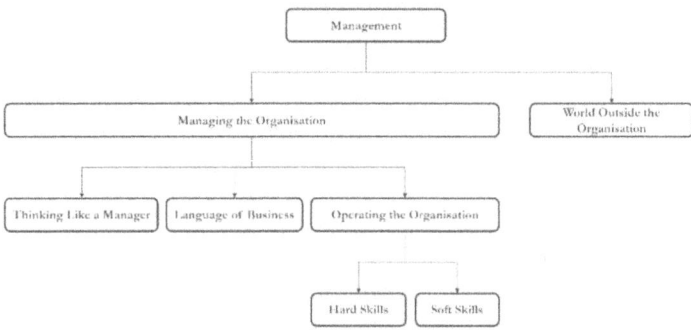

That's it. This flow chart sums up everything that I think goes into management. To the best of my knowledge, there are no textbooks or online resources which will show you the same breakdown of management. But I'm also sure that they won't say something very different either. If many different experts (and this book that you chose to pick up for some reason) can't agree on exactly what makes up management, what's the right answer? What I've been told many a time, and have come to therefore believe is:

"In management, as in life, there are rarely right or wrong answers. There are directionally useful and less useful answers."

- Any professor pushed into a corner

Clearly, I think that this breakdown of management is somehow useful. If you don't believe me, you can skip to the last page, to verify that I don't reveal that this was all just a prank. The reason that I think that breaking management down this way is useful is twofold:

1. Each step of the breakdown makes sense to me. I understand how the sum of the components at each step makes up the larger goal.
2. The experts seem to agree with this breakdown of management. Each of the smaller components coincides with and corresponds to subject areas which we study in business school. Unless all of business school was one big scam (I'll let you decide).

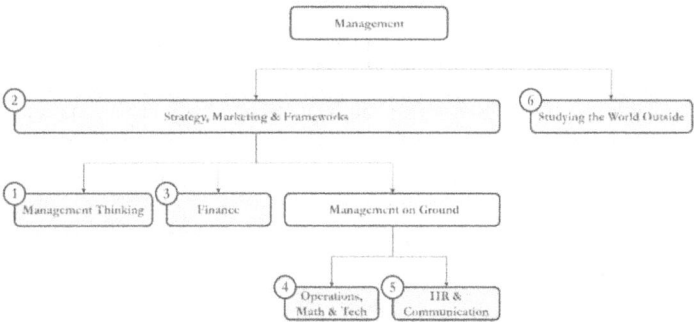

I have now revised the flowchart and renamed each block with the names of the subject groups which I believe help us target the sub-tasks from our earlier breakdown of management. Some of these might make sense to you, and on other points, you might disagree. I don't think it matters too much, because it should still be a directionally useful way of thinking about how each of the subject areas fit together in our grand task of understanding management.

Organisation of the book

From the numbers in the flowchart, you might have guessed that I'm trying to communicate some sort of cryptic message. The numbers suggest the order in which I think it makes sense to learn each subject. In business school, one learns all of these subjects in parallel. That makes sense because they aren't independent of each other, and this perfect ordering that I have tried to provide is impractical. In trying to break down and simplify management, I'm attempting to put pieces together as if they are pieces of a jigsaw puzzle. In reality, they fit together more like the shapes and figures in a Picasso painting, in awkward and complex angles, creating something beautiful. Alas, I am not Picasso, and so we will have to try to get through the mystery of management in an order which still kind of makes sense and fits into a single book.

This book has therefore been divided into 6 sections:

1. <u>Management Thinking</u> – This is the first skill that I believe one should pick up. With this in hand, it becomes much easier to appreciate each of the other subject areas, since one can derive them from first principles.
2. <u>Strategy, Marketing & Frameworks</u> – This juxtaposition of subject areas I believe equips one with top-level models of how an organisation works and can be managed. It, therefore, makes sense to develop this broad level of understanding before diving into the details.
3. <u>Finance</u> – Equipped with an understanding of organisations and how to think about them, it makes sense to start reading into what's happening in one's own organisation. Finance is the language of business, and it helps translate the vague ideas of management into objective and actionable decision criteria and metrics.
4. <u>Operations, Math & Technology</u> – By this point, we would have learnt how to read a situation, what it means for the organisation at large, and how to decide what our actions should be. To bring these top-level management decisions to life, one needs an understanding of operations, one needs to be able to do the math, instead of just following one's gut, and bringing in some efficiency through technology has never hurt anyone.
5. <u>HR & Communication</u> – From a theoretical standpoint, from the first 4 sections, we know how to manage the organisation already. However, at the end of the day, the organisation is made of people. And a manager manages people, not theory. So just to make sure that everything that we have learnt isn't completely useless, we'll learn a little more about managing human resources and communicating within the organisation.
6. <u>Studying the World Outside</u> – If there's anything that one can learn from a newspaper, it's that the world is crazy and anything can happen. So, before we can declare ourselves management experts, we'll have to learn how to get a read on the world outside and how it can impact our organisation.

Chapter 3
Starting Our Business: The Dungeon

Through the first couple of chapters, we have outlined what this book is all about, and the topics that we intend to cover, to become better managers. Before we jump into the 6 major sections of this book, let's discuss how we can make this volume of learning a little more fun, and easy to digest.

The case for the case method

Through this book, we're clearly trying to learn how to manage a business. A useful pre-requisite for this is having a business to manage. Of course, starting an actual business for this purpose is about as useful as it is impractical. This is one of the key reasons that the top business schools adopt the case method of learning. In the case method, we read about all of the details and nitty-gritty of a business situation. We can immerse ourselves in the context of a certain manager who has an important decision to make. And then, from their point of view, with the information that they have available, we try to arrive at the right business decision.

Thus, the case method is a decent proxy for running an actual business, through which you can learn how to manage different business situations.

Secondly, the case method is a lot more fun than just reading through pages of theory. Through the case method, you are usually introduced to a real-world business setting. You might have heard of the company in question, and might already have an outsider's view of what happened. The case method allows you to understand the people, the financials and the dynamics involved. There is often a lot of fun to be had in reading about and roleplaying these situations.

Thirdly, case discussions are a useful vehicle to broaden one's horizons. Each of us has our own experiences and ideas when it comes to tackling a situation. People from different backgrounds, with different kinds of intelligence, will approach the situation differently. Having a well-constructed discussion around cases can help each of us broaden our horizons. Over time, this should enable one to think more inclusively and effectively.

By now you might have guessed that I plan on employing the case method in this book. I don't have years of experience or any insider information through which I can construct cases on industry leaders. Nor is it fair for me to rehash and borrow cases from IIM-A or Harvard. I will therefore transport my learnings from some of the best cases that I have read into a fictional setting, and construct simplified, but effective cases for learning the concepts that I would like to illustrate.

A fictional business

Therefore, we are going to have to start a fictional business of our own, upon which we will build these cases.

We will be covering a very large number of business settings, in our attempt to learn all about management. Therefore, it would be most useful if our fictional business could operate in a wide range of industries and across many different management functions. At the same time, in the interest of keeping things accessible, we don't want to try and study a giant like Amazon. That might be too much of a task for me to embark on.

So, we want our fictional business to be easily relatable, and super flexible in terms of its business operations. Let's, therefore, use a start-up, being run out of a college dorm room as our fictional business throughout all cases. Since it's a college-run start-up, we can on a whim change the business that we're in for each case. I hope that most of the readers are familiar with the context of a college dorm/hostel. In any case, I shall provide some brief information on the specific dorm room (business) that we shall be working with

The Dungeon

On November 11th, 2020, after a full online term from home, I moved into my dorm room in IIM-A. I was in room 12, dorm 12. Dorm 12, I am told is the first dorm to have been built on the IIM-A old campus. I suppose that that number (12) was changed up at some point in time. Most dorms are given a new name each year. The name which our dorm had inherited was 'Purana Qila' (old fort), as a result of its very visible age, and the common red-brick architecture.

A lot of traditions had been lost on our batch (the covid batch). In the absence of seniors to inform us of the dorm's history, within the first few days, my wing-mates and I went on to fondly refer to the dorm and my room in particular as 'the dungeon'. This was in part because of the dingy look of the place. But largely because I intended to give my room an unforgettable name. It was not my first time living in a hostel, and so I had grand plans of how to set my room up so that it could become party central. One part of that plan was giving it a more fun name, creating a google profile for it, and on the whole making it an unforgettable icon. Other parts of the plan included having the best light and sound setup possible, extra mattresses and cushions for comfort, aromatic candles and a good stock of snacks.

Scan the QR code below to have a look at the dungeon. Whimsical fake reviews are appreciated if you'd like to leave your mark on this fictional business that we are building together.

Long story short, the dungeon soon became the standard hangout for me and my friends. This of course is not the sort of introduction one expects for a business venture. But, now that we're all on the same page with regards to the origin of the dungeon, we can begin to define what our fictional business might look like.

Business constraints

Let's assume that we are starting with the very same dungeon that we have described above as our business. We now have a rough idea of what our headquarters looks like and a general sense of our company culture. For most of our business situations, we can assume that this business has been set up by us (the readers and myself). We can also assume that we are college students who are starting this business, and have no real shortage of resources unless it is useful in the context of a given case.

The big question remains what our business is. I shall conveniently avoid answering that question for the time being. Remember, we wanted to have a business which can easily switch fields as and when needed. So, let's assume that we are starry-eyed college students, who are intent on starting a business. But we're trying to hedge our bets, and so now and then we'll completely pivot our business idea, for the sake of the case that we're working on.

I must assure you that this is a horrible business idea. But for the purpose of this book, I hope that it makes the illustration of concepts fun and easy.

Section I

Management Thinking

In this section, we will try to break down how a manager thinks. Or in any case my understanding of a good thought process for a manager to employ. So how does one go about developing management thinking?

Firstly, we acknowledge that we're looking to develop a good thought process. A thought process, much like any process, must have some critical steps as a part of it. So, in the first chapter of this section, we will have a look at what seem to be the 4 critical steps of management thinking.

Secondly, we understand that if these steps are that critical, just knowing what the steps are might not be enough to follow them successfully. One of the critical steps of management thinking is structuring, or breaking the problem down into more manageable parts. Of all the steps, it's the toughest, but most useful to master. In the second chapter of the section, we shall spend some time coming up with a highly effective structure to structure any problem.

Finally, we remember that not all management problems can be solved with a perfectly unidimensional and rational approach. In order to sprinkle some creativity into our management thinking, we explore a process which can force us into a divergent thinking mindset now and then.

Putting these ideas together, by the end of this section, we should be able to employ convergent and divergent thinking as and when needed. We should be able to pick up any management problem and come up with directionally useful approaches to tackle it. And on the whole, we should be able to think like effective managers.

Chapter 4
4 Critical Steps: Manage Any Situation

Thinking like a manager may sound like a loaded statement at first. After all business schools have an incentive to advertise management thinking as a valuable skill which can only be acquired through a specialised programme. Whether it's easy or difficult to do, there seem to be just 4 steps that every effective manager follows. As with most everything else in this book, I can't claim to be an expert. However, everyone from management consultants to strategy professors seem to call out these 4 steps in some permutation and combination as the key to arriving at directionally useful answers. I have therefore noted them down and presented them here. In my limited experience, they work well. And as with most principles of management, it sounds sensible and is, therefore, a rather intuitive idea.

Without further delay, the 4 critical steps to thinking through management situations (in order) are:

1. Objective Orientation

The first step sounds like a no-brainer. It kind of is a no-brainer. But you may sometimes find yourself in a heated discussion at work where no one is on the same page. I'd reckon that the reason is often that we get caught up in our points of view and forget to start from the beginning.

Objective orientation essentially means that as a starting point we need to define what our end goal is. Better yet, if we ensure that everyone involved is on the same page as to what this end goal is. The more specific and detail-oriented that we are about our end goal the easier things get. But of course, this isn't always perfectly possible. So, we settle for a bare minimum of ensuring that we have laid out our objective before we get started with problem-solving.

2. Structured Approach

Most objectives are not trivial. If they were we wouldn't have business problems left to solve. Given that our objectives may be complex to achieve, we thus want to break them down into smaller problems which are more approachable. Most problems are large and very involved. We will thus go through this process of breaking problems into more solvable problems (structuring) repeatedly.

You might have noticed that we similarly broke down the task of management into smaller sub-tasks earlier on. This too involved 'structuring' the problems at hand into smaller sub-tasks. This step, unlike the other 3 steps requires a marginally new way of thinking and isn't just something that we need to remember to do. Structuring can be a tricky step. There is often a big gap between the best (directionally useful) and the worst (less useful) structures. For this reason, I have dedicated an entire chapter to structuring.

3. Hypotheses & Efficiencies

So far, we are clear on what we want to achieve. We have also broken down the singular but complex objective into many much more achievable (but numerous) sub-objectives. On the one hand, we have been thorough so far, which gives us the confidence that we will achieve our main objective (in theory). On the other hand, we have also been super theoretical, meaning that we have created a lot of work (numerous sub-objectives) for ourselves. We probably don't have the resources (time and money) to complete all of the sub-objectives created.

We will therefore now make a clear distinction between management thinking and scientific thinking. In scientific thinking, we usually aim to be perfectly correct 100% of the time. In management thinking, as long as our solution produces pretty good results with minimum resources, we keep moving forward.

Thus, after breaking down a big problem into smaller problems, we sometimes hypothesise that we don't need to solve all of the sub-problems. This planned laziness allows us to spend minimum resources. With a good hypothesis as to which sub-problems matter the most, we can get a pretty good solution, at minimum cost. A hypothesis would be of the form "option X is the best way to achieve objective A". We would then keep going down the structure, making these hypotheses and verifying or invalidating them.

Hypotheses are a useful instrument and become more useful with experience, as our intuition gets sharpened. This is true because we are more likely to make useful hypotheses as opposed to going down the wrong track and having to correct them later on.

This business idea of doing less without loss in return dates back to 1896. The 80:20 rule (Pareto principle) says that we can get 80% of the result for 20% of the effort. And the last 20% of the result requires a whopping 80% of the effort (Investopedia,

2022). The important implication is that we can smartly put in only a small amount of effort and get the bulk of the result. Across our structures, we will often use this rule to efficiently work on only those easy options which help us achieve most of the objective, as opposed to venturing into all branches at excessive cost.

4. Fact-Based

At this stage, we know what we want to achieve. We have laid out all possible paths to achieve it. We have even identified possible clever shortcuts to realistically achieve it. What remains is to do the math and make sure that our clever solutions are backed up by real-world data. To this end, we have to validate all of the hypotheses that we made along the way. It is critical to make sure that this step of hypothesis validation is as fact-based as possible. What this means is that we want to check our assumptions and ensure that we are deriving all of our inferences from hard data wherever possible. Of course, this is not always perfectly doable in a real business setting. In some contexts, we will have to settle for proxies and degrees of confidence. Our aim however in a management setting is to bring in the confidence that we have in a scientific research paper as often as realistically possible, as opposed to just relying on intuition and common sense. Ensuring that our work is factually accurate seems obvious. However, in the confusion of all that happens in the workplace, one might cut a corner or simply forget. It is therefore useful to call out that a key final step is ensuring that all of our derived solutions stem correctly from hard, cold data.

These principles are very simple in theory. However, they require discipline to implement without fail. Therefore, it is important to make a practice of always asking one's self whether they are sure that everything they have done has been:

1. Objective Oriented
2. Structured
3. Hypothesis Driven & Efficient
4. Fact-Based

Case 1

It's soon after placement season at IIM-A. And everyone is just about ready to drop their books, and start partying. There's something about the pleasant December air, which is drawing people out of the library. The time is ripe for the first major Dungeon party!

Of course, Dungeon management hasn't yet decided what business they're in. But an exclusive party, to help develop a reputation on campus never hurt anyone.

Having read a fair bit about management thinking, they decide to apply the process, to ensure that the party is a success.

Objective Orientation

This being the very first party, management doesn't want to do anything too experimental. It has been decided that the invitee list should be restricted to a handful of people that they know well enough. This is an important constraint because they need everyone to fit into the room, lest campus security should be called on them.

The key objective is that those invited have a memorable and positive experience at the party.

Structured Approach

After the dungeon's management recognised that their focus was the experience of the party guests, they tried to break down this qualitative output. They reasoned that one's experience at any point in time is a function of their physical, emotional and mental (intellectual) state of mind. If all 3 of these aspects could be handled, every individual is bound to have a great experience.

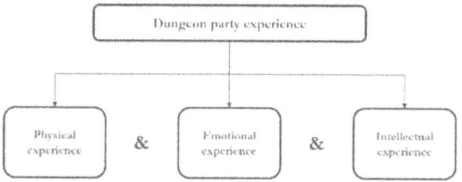

Of these 3 aspects, management believed that the physical experience would be the easiest to control. The physical experience would probably also have the largest impact on one's experience since someone attending a party is likely to already be in the right emotional and intellectual state of mind.

To further break down the physical experience, they used the 5 human senses to map out every aspect of the physical world that one could experience. Thus, the physical experience consisted of taste, sight, hearing, smell and touch.

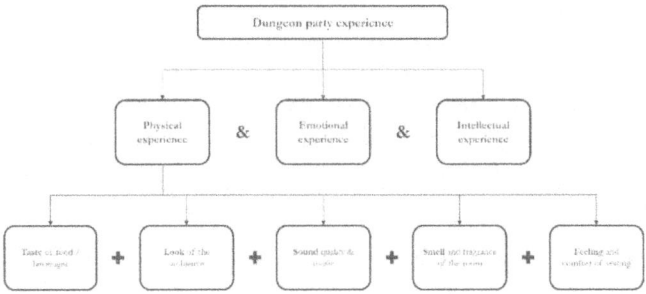

Hypotheses & Efficiencies

At first, dungeon management was tempted to transform the room into the perfect physical, emotional and intellectual experience. They wanted to create a shrine for the mind, body and soul. But they soon realised that this would probably be an overkill, which might work for a cult, but not so much for a party.

Their first hypothesis was that the physical experience is more controllable and matters more than the emotional and intellectual experience at a party.

Their next hypothesis was that the sense of taste and sense of sound matter more than the remaining senses. This means that good-tasting food and the right kind of beverages, paired with great music from powerful speakers would light up the party. The other senses of sight, smell and touch also had to be catered to. However, just making sure that the room looked reasonably nice and clean, had a few scented candles and enough soft seating should suffice. Thus, 2 senses would make the party, by standing out. While the other 3 had to only be satisfactory, so as to not ruin the vibe.

Their final hypothesis was that the emotional and intellectual experience could be controlled through careful selection of the guest list, and ensuring that conversation flowed well. The ideal guest list might include some people who knew each other, with a few new faces to spark conversation. The guest list should have a balanced gender ratio and avoid groups of people between whom there is friction. The hosts of the party should always be prepared with a few games and conversation topics to ensure that the party doesn't get slow or boring.

Fact-Based

Once dungeon management had come up with the above ideas for the party, they wanted to build up some confidence in the plan. They relied mainly on their own past experiences of great and underwhelming parties to decide on whether their plans were likely to succeed. They also googled a few party ideas to check on whether there was enough commonality between the best party plans and their own. Finally, they casually struck up conversations with the potential guests, to understand whether their party plan was in line with what the audience might enjoy.

At this stage, they had a clear goal in mind, as well as a structured plan of how to achieve this goal. The dungeon management was also confident that their plans were on the right track and likely to create the required result.

Case Questions

Assuming that the goal remains the same, "those invited have a memorable and positive experience at the party", what are your thoughts on the ideal:

1. Structure to break down this goal.
2. Hypotheses that help simplify our approach to the goal.
3. Sources of facts to double-check our plan.

Instead of just thinking on your own, I would encourage you to participate in a case discussion on the following Reddit thread. Through case discussion, your ideas may be validated or improved upon. You would also benefit from other people's viewpoints.

Recap

The combined application of these 4 steps makes for great 'convergent thinking'. This means that if you have an end goal in mind, this process is going to help you achieve it. In my mind, the crux of this approach is structuring. While all of the steps are important, structuring, as the name suggests brings some structure to the approach and ensures that we're well organised. It's the step that ensures that when things get complicated, we have a clear map of what to do, and when to do it. In the next chapter, we shall break down how we can structure the complex problems that we face.

Chapter 5
Structuring: The Secret Sauce

As long as you're reading through this book, you already understand where in the process of management thinking structuring is useful (repeatedly in problem-solving). Alternately, maybe you're playing book cricket and landed up on this page at random. I will naively assume that you're convinced that structuring is a useful skill, which can translate big, daunting problems into a list of more solvable, smaller problems.

The question ahead of us then is, "how do we magically structure any problem into smaller, more solvable parts?".

Structuring buzzwords

Let's start by understanding the output that we want:

- Smaller parts which sum up to the whole.
- Solvable parts (more easily solvable).

I'd love to say that this is a piece of cake, but it's actually not. There's a big and crucial difference between cake and these kinds of complex problems. Have you ever tried to break up a problem into smaller parts and ended up with more on your plate than you started with? Have you also realised that try as you may, solving these smaller parts isn't helping you with your original problem? Maybe I'm the only one who struggles like this. But let's pretend that everyone is about as slow as I am. There's something valuable that we can learn from how cakes are cut up. There are 2 properties that pieces of cake have which make our life easier:

- Mutually Exclusive – Every part of the cut-up cake is in one piece or another, never in multiple pieces. This means that there is no overlap between the 2 pieces of cake. Similarly, we want each smaller part of the problem to be mutually exclusive, thus avoiding any overlap with other parts.
- Cumulatively Exhaustive – When you put all of the pieces of the cake back together, it forms the whole cake, without anything missing. Except for that rose made of icing, that someone always steals before the candles are even

blown out. But that's a useful property for our structures to have as well. We want to know that if each part is tackled, the larger problem has necessarily been addressed.

We call this property of our structures being like cake, 'MECE' or Mutually Exclusive & Cumulatively Exhaustive. In business school, you might hear this term being thrown around a lot. As and when you propose structures to break down complex problems, you always want to make sure that your proposed structure is 'MECE'. But wait, that's not enough. MECE structures only ensure that the problem is broken into smaller parts, which sum up to the whole. We also need each of the smaller parts to be more easily solvable. Ideally, we want them to be much more easily solvable, otherwise, we'd be breaking down problems for ages before we arrive at an answer.

An easy way to think about this is how you can slice up a pizza. There are multiple 'MECE' ways of slicing up a pizza. But not all ways of slicing it make it easier to eat a slice (part) of pizza. There is of course the traditional way of slicing along diameters of the circle. It's traditional for a reason, it's easy to cut and easy to eat. You can also cut the pizza through a set of parallel lines. This isn't ideal, because it makes it difficult to eat. I realise that some people reading this might have the strangest preferences, and argue that they actually like the parallel cuts. Just in case, I have illustrated another MECE, but useless way of slicing the pizza, through concentric circles.

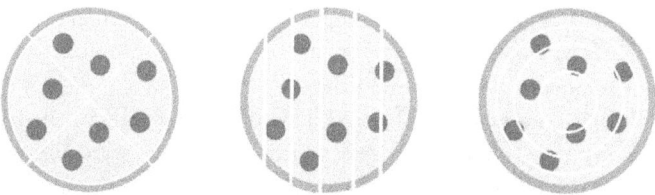

Hopefully, we all now agree that not every MECE structure is a useful structure. So, we have transformed our original question of "how do we magically structure any problem into smaller, more solvable parts?" into "how to convert any problem into a MECE and useful structure?". At this stage, you're probably thinking that all I have done is help you work up an appetite, without shining any light on the problem of structuring. Well yeah, that's kind of true. We have established what makes a good structure, and we have established that they're hard to develop. We are still yet to develop this process through which we can structure any problem.

Management thinking for structuring

But not to worry, we can solve any hard problem with the help of management thinking. So, let's get meta, and use management thinking to develop an approach to structuring, so that we can easily structure any problem, and therefore apply management thinking to any situation later on. If you didn't follow that, it's okay. We're going to come up with a way to break down (structure) any kind of problem.

Objective – Clearly, we want a well-defined process through which we can easily come up with 'good' (MECE & useful) structures to break down any problem.

Structure – A single process to break down any problem might be a bit much. So, let's try to first categorise 'any problem' into a few categories which cover any and all business problems.

In the interest of simplicity and time, I'm not going to run through my structuring thought process. Instead, I will just present the outcome, a structure of 5 different categories under which all business problems fall into. Broadly, I believe that complex business problems may require us to either:

- Identify what the problem is:
    1. Identify an unknown issue(s) with a process.
    2. Identify an unknown issue(s) leading to an incorrect numeric outcome.
    3. Identify an unknown issue(s) leading to a poor-quality outcome.
- Define a solution to a known problem:
    4. A known issue which can be solved by one of a fixed set of alternatives.
    5. A required outcome, for which we must identify the best solution/approach.

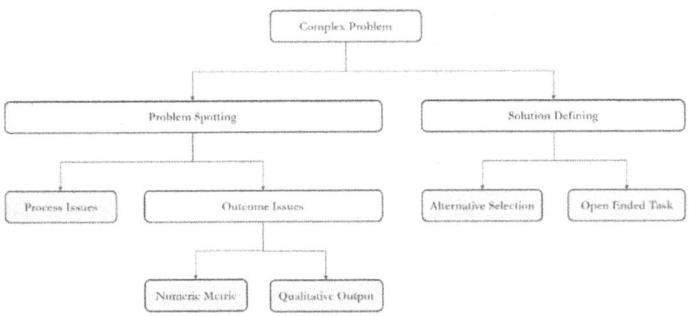

If it's of interest to you, you could work through the exercise of trying to structure 'any problem' into these 5 categories. Maybe you will arrive at a similar solution, or maybe you will arrive at something different, which works better for you. But hopefully, you will agree that the above 5 categories of problems are a MECE and useful way of classifying any complex business problem.

You might at this stage be asking why any of this is useful. Hopefully, my hypothesis will make you feel a little better about the time you spent reading all of this.

Hypothesis – I hypothesise that "all problems belonging to the same class (1 of the 5) can be well structured through a similar pattern". What's more, I will also provide hypotheses as to what structure works best for each class. This is useful, because if my hypotheses are correct (or directionally useful), then for any complex problem, all that we have to do is:

1. Classify the complex problem into the appropriate problem class (1 out of 5).
2. Apply the appropriate pattern of structuring to that problem.
3. The complex problem is broken into easier problems which we can either solve directly or upon which we can repeat the above process.

I will not yet go into the details of what these structuring patterns are for each problem class. At the end of the chapter, we will use a case to illustrate how these structuring patterns can be used.

Fact-Based Reasoning – In theory, we now require facts that suggest that the above approach to structuring is the 'correct' one. But keep in mind that we have already said that there are no right and wrong answers here, just directionally useful ones. Here's how we can test if this approach is directionally useful:

- Apply the approach to structuring to a wide range of problem scenarios.
- Check if the structures help us arrive at correct (directionally useful) answers.
- If yes, this is a good approach to structuring. If not, this is not a good approach.

At this stage, the facts that I can offer you are just empirical evidence from my own experience and that of my friends and batchmates. There may well be better approaches to structuring problems. To the best of my knowledge, there are no other well-publicised approaches to structuring any problem. So, at this stage, my approach to structuring should be a fairly good starting point.

My secret approach to structuring

Let's now put together what we have arrived at through our management thinking process. A well-defined process through which we can easily come up with 'good' (MECE & useful) structures to breakdown any problem is:

1. Classify the complex problem into the appropriate problem class (1 out of 5).
   - Unknown issue(s) with a process.
   - Unknown issue(s) leading to an incorrect numeric outcome.
   - Unknown issue(s) leading to a poor-quality outcome.
   - Known issue to be solved by 1 of a set of alternatives.
   - Known task, unknown best approach.
2. Apply the appropriate pattern of structuring to that problem (described below).
   - Process Issues (draw out the process journey)
   - Numeric Outcome Issues (write the formula)
   - Qualitative Outcome Issues (list the properties)
   - Alternative Selection (list the pre-defined options)
   - Task to Be Completed (inside, neighbourhood & outside)

I will explain the above gibberish through the case. For now, all you need to know is that for each class of problems we have an established pattern through which structuring can be made easier.

3.   The complex problem is broken into easier problems which we can either solve directly or upon which we can repeat the above process.

As long as one can complete step 1 and step 2 of the above process, they should be able to structure just about any business problem. Let's, therefore, run through a case to better understand each problem type.

Case 2

Let's say that the dungeon party from case 1 was a huge success. Let's also say that we had called just the right set of influential people, and now everyone on campus is excited about our dungeon business, even though no one yet knows quite what it is. Since we're saying whatever we want, let's say something nice about this book on social media. Hopefully my subliminal messaging worked.

As a result of this jump in popularity, the dungeon has managed to start dabbling in a wide range of businesses. On the one hand, management has started producing notes for all subjects in IIM-A. On the other hand, they have started consulting for other small businesses on campus. And there are several other small side hustles which have been entered into.

Soon, dungeon management is faced with an assortment of different problems to solve. Unlike the academic workload, this can't be put off until someone else solves it. They, therefore, decide to live up to their role as managers. They plan to tackle each problem one by one. Each problem must be broken down into simpler parts. Once that is done, they plan on delegating the actual work to ground employees.

Process Issues

Management had compiled, collated, begged, borrowed and even hand-written notes for all of the subjects in college. They thought that it would be a good idea to share these notes with the entire batch, free of cost. Monetisation wasn't their immediate concern. They only hoped to ensure that enough students would routinely access these notes. With a loyal audience, they were sure to figure out a complete business model later on.

However, they had a problem at hand. Students didn't seem to be using the notes. And the dungeon management wasn't sure what was going wrong at what stage.

To investigate where along the usage journey there was a break, management mapped out the entire usage journey.

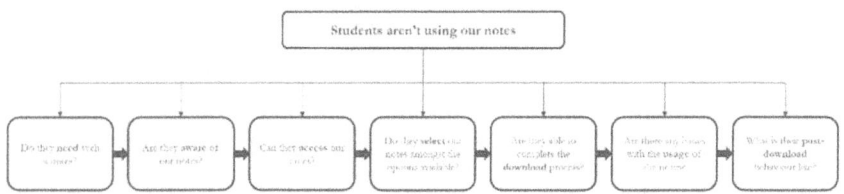

They speculated that at least 1 of the 7 steps involved was not going according to plan. If all 7 stages were on track, students would be using the notes.

First and foremost, students must have some need for notes. If they do not need notes, there's no way that they would waste their time on it.

Second, students must be aware of the notes made by the dungeon. If they are unaware, they will not end up downloading and using them.

Third, students must be able to access these notes. If their Gmail or Microsoft IDs are not provided with access, even if they wished to use the notes, they would be unable to. The students might then switch to notes which they are more easily able to access.

Fourth, students must select the dungeon notes over other competing notes. There are several black books, white books, blue books etc which are made available to the students. If other notes are more comprehensive, easy to follow etc, students would not select the dungeon notes.

Fifth, students must be able to complete the download process. Sometimes online access is insufficient. Thorough usage requires being able to download and print the notes, at least for open notes exams. This is similar to a situation where one can access a product in a store but unable to afford its purchase.

Sixth, students who use the notes once shouldn't have issues with them. In case there are inaccuracies and contradictions in the notes, an existing user might switch to other notes.

Seventh, post usage of the notes, students should themselves return to the notes and promote them. If the class topper uses the notes and tells everyone how useful they are, more students are likely to use them.

Having thus highlighted the potential problem areas to check, management could move on to the next problem.

Numeric Issues

The owner of CT has approached the dungeon, complaining that their revenues have dropped. They have asked the dungeon's management to help them work out what might be causing these problems.

Before we proceed, CT is a food joint on the IIM-A campus. Prof. Satish Deodhar has done an excellent job of introducing the café and providing a small brief on it in his medium article.

Dungeon's management takes on the task, breaking up CT's revenue as a simple function of the sum of revenues from each of their food products.

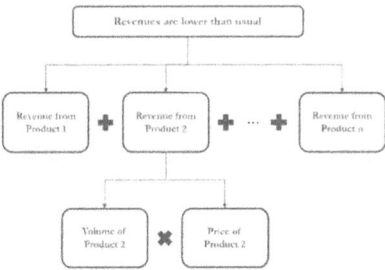

Once the problematic products (drop in revenue) were isolated, they were further analysed. The revenue from a product was once again looked at through the formula of volume of purchase multiplied by the selling price of the product. Beyond this stage, any further analyses required structuring the volume through a customer journey. This is a process issue, which the dungeon's management was already an expert at.

Qualitative Issues

After the first party, the dungeon became a popular tourist attraction at first. However, soon after, the number of visitors began to drop. This of course was a concern for management. They had to first understand what could be leading to the drop in visitors and then reverse the trend.

In this situation, the structure that can be used to analyse the qualitative issue is the same as the one that was used in case 1. As such, we will not waste time going into any further detail right now.

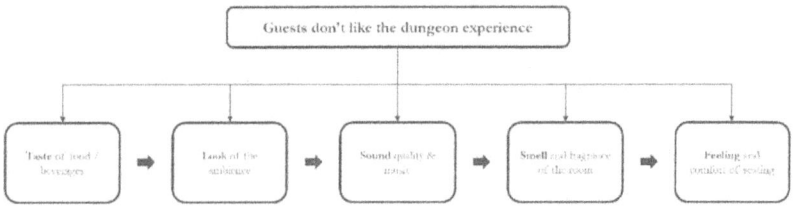

Alternative Selection

At the end of the first year of college, each student usually has the option of applying to have their room changed. With this opportunity in hand, it was important for the dungeon's management to decide which room to apply for (in case they chose to change).

The structure to break down this problem is fairly straightforward. We already know that any room which is to be selected must be in either the old campus or the new campus. If one chooses the new campus, they must also select whether they would apply for a regular dorm, a lotus dorm or a married student hostel.

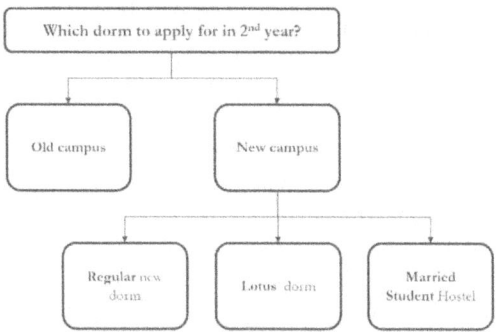

Each of these alternatives would have to be compared based on a fixed set of criteria. For example, weightage could be given to comfort (AC, attached bathroom, room size), proximity to friends, proximity to hangout hubs on campus etc.

Tasks to be Completed

With other food joints like Ram Bhai, Bhavesh Bhai, CT, Tea Post, Radhika's, Café Tomorrow, the Amul shop and Mafa Bhai thriving on campus, dungeon management decided to compete with them. The dungeon became a late-night tea and Maggi shop. To compete, the dungeon differentiated itself with a cooler ambience, nicer music and great conversation. It bundled products such as academic notes along with its tea in order to win over customers. It also provided other services, including screening of matches, late-night xeroxing and innovative new snacks and beverages.

However, right when the dungeon opened up as a part-time café, management was plagued with a tricky question. How much should they charge for each of their products and services?

Tasks to be completed is a particularly interesting structure. This one is distinct from the others in that it has no inherent structure that management can take advantage of. Only the end goal is known, and one needs to creatively come up with possible paths to that end goal. Of course, there is a large spectrum of possible paths to the end goal. So, the structure will try to break down this spectrum into 3 broad types of solutions. What exactly these 3 solutions will be, varies a fair bit with context. To guide one's self in finding the best fit, one can think of one solution which is close to the organisation or situation. One can think of a second solution which is adjacent to the organisation, in the neighbourhood or being used by the competition. And finally, one can think of a third solution which is very distinct from what is currently done, or entirely externally defined.

Does that sound super vague and confusing? I would expect so because we're trying to bring some structure to creative solutions. It's always going to be difficult to put in place hard and fast rules. This idea of 3 parts (inside, neighbourhood and outside) is at best a vague guideline.

Now, returning to the specific context of the dungeon's pricing problem. We know the end requirement, but there is an endless number of ways in which we can come up with an exact price point. We start by looking at 3 broad ideas (inside = based on our costs, neighbourhood = based on competitors' prices and outside = based on how customers value our product).

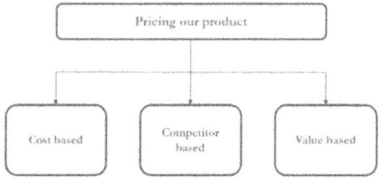

At a later stage, we will explore when each of these approaches can be used. For now, suffice to say that we have structured the problem, and passed on the task of selecting the appropriate method to someone else.

Case Questions
For each of the 5 problems, what would your structure to break down the problem be?

1. Students are not using the dungeon notes.

2. CT's revenue had dropped.
3. Guests are no longer visiting the dungeon.
4. Which room should the dungeon management apply to next year?
5. How should we price our products and services?

Make sure that each of the structures that you put forward is MECE and useful in solving the problem.

Instead of just thinking on your own, I would encourage you to participate in a case discussion on the following Reddit thread. Through case discussion, your ideas may be validated or improved upon. You would also benefit from other people's viewpoints.

Recap
Let's do another recap of everything that I have rambled on about.

- Convergent management thinking is comprised of 4 steps:
    o   Objective Orientation
    o   Structuring
    o   Hypotheses & Efficiencies
    o   Fact-Based Reasoning
- Structuring of complex problems needs to be MECE and useful.
- All business problems fall into 5 classes, each of which has a best structure pattern to use:
    o   Process Issues (draw out the process journey)
    o   Numeric Outcome Issues (write the formula)
    o   Qualitative Outcome Issues (list the properties)
    o   Alternative Selection (list the pre-defined options)
    o   Task to Be Completed (inside, neighbourhood & outside)

But let's keep in mind that all of the above is still just my hypothesis. Hopefully, my reasoning has been compelling enough for you to believe this. But let's keep in mind that we don't yet have facts to back all of this up.

Before you accept my approach to structuring as good enough, here are 2 ways in which you can keep testing it out, improving upon it and forming your own approach to structuring:

- Throughout this book, we will keep applying management thinking to break down problems and arrive at answers. You should think through all of it on your own, instead of trusting me to give you the right answer. In the process, you can work on your own structuring, and decide how useful or otherwise my approach is.
- Consulting case preparation is a setting in which one will repeatedly structure problems. If this is of interest to you, you could try out this approach in cases and see how well it works. The following free resources might be of interest to you:
  - My notes on consulting interview preparation:

  - My notes on structuring (with many examples for each problem class):

  - My notes on consulting frameworks (more structuring examples):

At this stage you should be equipped with the following:

- An understanding of the 4 critical steps involved in management thinking.
- An idea of how to classify and structure any problem. This is in itself a critical step in management thinking.
- A colourful list of curse words that you're ready to hurl at me for the headache that I have caused you.

With this (and a bunch of practice) your convergent thinking should match that of any top-notch manager!

Chapter 6
Divergent Thinking: Outside the Box

You are now a pro at convergent thinking. And since you have moved on to the next chapter, you also seek some sort of masochistic pleasure in reading on. You might be wondering what else could remain for a manager to think about. After all, in the previous 2 chapters, I promised that our approach can be used to solve any problem. Theoretically, and in a scientific sort of way that is correct. But we often say:

> *"Management is a little bit of science and a little bit of art."*

> -Managers concerned about job automation

So, let's bring a little bit of art into play as well. Now and then one comes across a product or service so artistically constructed that you wonder how on Earth someone had this brilliant idea and then executed it perfectly. All of this requires some out-of-the-box, creative thinking. We call this sort of thinking divergent thinking. Essentially, convergent thinking (what we have done so far) helps us converge toward a goal that we have set out. Divergent thinking helps us branch out from the boring and old things that we already do.

Now that we have answered the 'what' of it, we may want to answer the other question words (when, where, why, how and even who?).

Let's now ask ourselves why we might ever want to use divergent thinking? If we don't have a satisfactory answer, that's one less thing we can worry about learning and a chapter that we can discard. I would think that there are only 2 possible reasons one might want to use divergent thinking:

- Convergent thinking might not give us the results we require, so we need to try something different.
- Divergent thinking frees the mind and connects it with the heart and soul.

The average manager doesn't strike me as a very artsy, hippie kind of person, trying to rebel against the system. So, the first line of reasoning might hold more water in our present context. For this to be a good enough reason, there needs to be a range of scenarios in which convergent thinking might fail us. Without being super comprehensive, let me illustrate a few situations in which convergent thinking alone, may fail us:

- Our competition can also use the same convergent thinking and arrive at all of the same answers. They may have better resources available as well. We may therefore need something extra (unthinkable) to win the market.
- Convergent thinking doesn't provide exact answers, only directionally useful ones. We live in a complex world, where we can't predict everything. In highly variable situations, divergent thinking may provide us with an equal probability of success (at a lower cost) than highly calculated (expensive) convergent thinking.
- We work within an imperfect system. Businesses are not perfect in executing the plans that they arrive at through convergent thinking. And consumers are not perfectly rational in their demands. This leaves a lot of room for something random and different to work well in the market, for no clear reason. The entertainment industry is often filled with such examples.

I hope that we can therefore agree that as managers, we sometimes need a little divergent thinking, to break out of one-track, convergent thinking.

Now that we know what divergent thinking is, and given that we have made a case for its use, let's figure out when and where to use it. From our answer to why it's needed, we can implicitly say that whenever and wherever convergent thinking fails us, we can apply divergent thinking. In theory that seems like a great answer, maybe even the 'correct' answer. But in practice, it seems less useful to me. It doesn't seem like an easily actionable answer to me. We have over the course of two chapters seen that convergent thinking can be a long-drawn process, which consumes a lot of time and energy. We know that managers are spending most of their workdays going through convergent thinking processes in some way or form. Therefore, if we have to try out a bunch of convergent thinking processes, observe the results, then learn that it has failed us, and only then begin thinking divergently, it might be a waste of our time.

The alternative at the other extreme is that we constantly use both convergent and divergent thinking. The concern with this approach is that we might spend all of our time thinking, and not enough doing. That defeats the purpose, doesn't it?

And so, now I can say in a sage-like fashion that we must choose the middle path. This means that we need to use divergent thinking now and then, to hedge our bets, and ensure that convergent thinking doesn't lead us to a dead-end, of all done and dusted ideas. This advice is so generic that it must be correct. But I'm sure that it doesn't sound very useful to you. It's the sort of advice that sounds nice but lacks specificity. So, let's shift our answer to something a little less 'correct' and something a little more directionally useful.

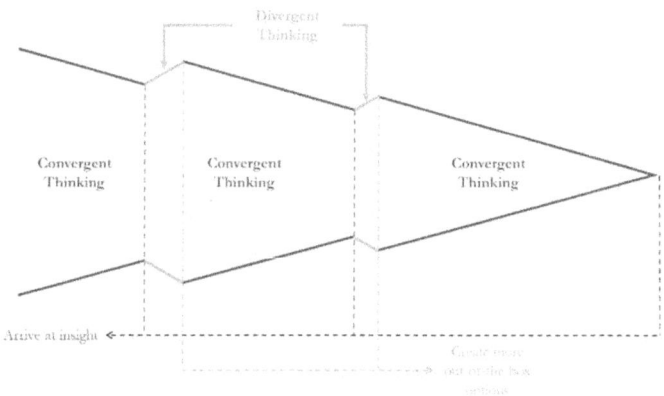

The figure illustrates a suggested solution for when we can employ divergent thinking. The idea here is that as managers we will continue to largely rely on convergent thinking. However, as and when we land on a key insight, it is useful to think creatively and see if there are some interesting options that we might be missing out on.

This general rhythm of alternating convergent and divergent thinking has been borrowed from a few different expert sources (Sreekumar, 2022). I, therefore, believe that it has likely been tried and tested to an extent. The specific idea of using key insights as the inflection point is also probably not a new one. However, as I comb through my notes, I am unable to find a specific prescription on when to switch to divergent thinking. So, what should you do with this vague solution? My recommendation is to take it as a directionally useful prescription.

- Use convergent thinking as thoroughly and effectively as you can.

- As and when you land on key insights, apply just a little bit of divergent thinking to see if you're missing out on anything important.
- Especially when your insights seem less useful or questionable, divergent thinking might provide a helping hand.

The above is just a starting point. As and when you use this process in real life, you might find a rhythm that works best for you.

So far, we have answered all of the really theoretical questions. We know what divergent thinking is. We know why we're talking about it, to begin with. We also know when we plan on applying this abstract concept. Most importantly we've got a cool, arrow-like diagram, which makes us look smart. But how do we think creatively?

This topic in particular has entire books and courses dedicated to it. I am obviously not going to be able to provide you with the same sort of know-how as those resources can. In fact, I will not even attempt to provide a comprehensive answer on how to think creatively. The reason is that it's really hard to provide a structured process to think divergently. Much harder to provide one which you can confidently say works often. But I won't leave you to figure it all out on your own. I will try to provide one framework that I personally like. From here on out you can decide if you like this framework or not. If you hate it, not to worry, a simple google search on divergent thinking will provide you with a range of alternatives that you can read about to find something that works better for you.

A model of divergent thinking that I like is one that I call "constraint release". To be honest, I don't know if there is a more official name for this process. But I like this name, so that's what we'll use for the time being.

In constraint release, we follow 3 simple steps to stimulate more creative ideas:

1. Summarise Insights – Start with the context, and most importantly the key findings that we have so far. Summarise this into just a sentence or two if possible. This is our summarised insight. This summarised insight is what we shall work upon.
2. Identify Keywords – From within our insight, let's identify the keywords. The keywords that we would like to pick out will often specify scope, inputs, actions and outcomes. These aren't the only words which can be

used as keywords. Anything which isn't just a filler word, and is useful in defining our insight can be a keyword.

3. Release Constraints – Each keyword can now be treated as a constraint of sorts. That is, a keyword may specify a specific starting condition, or may specify a specific action to be taken, or may specify an outcome which will occur. We will now take each constraint (keyword) one at a time. For just one constraint at a time, we will now ask ourselves "what if this was not the case?". In doing so, we are able to think beyond just the insight which we have arrived at. This doesn't mean that we can create a world of make-believe, where any random insight works. When we relax constraints, we need to be convinced that any alternate insights that we arrive at are conceivable and likely, even if not proven (yet).

What I like about this framework is that it's super simple. Many divergent thinking frameworks are elaborate and involve several phases that help us change our frame of reference. In constraint release, we can quickly reflect on what we have learnt, draw a box around it, and then easily think outside of that box. This might not be the most effective approach. There may even be many flaws with it. But it's easy, and it works in a lot of situations, so that's directionally useful in my mind.

Case 3

In this case, we're going to take a step back in time. Imagine a time before UPI and mobile payments. A time when one still had to step out of the house with some cash on them. In this historic time, more than 5 years ago, dungeon management decided to start manufacturing mint-based gums. These gums were sold mainly through Ram Bhai. The target customer was the smoker, who would hand in a few notes to pay for cigarettes and receive a few mint-based gums as change, along with the cigarette of their choice. The gums were not only a good complimentary product for the cigarette but an effective replacement for coins for change.

The price of cigarettes, however, went up by a couple of rupees. This meant that the average customer was owed less change on each transaction. This in turn meant that they received fewer mint-based gums on each visit to Ram Bhai. The dungeon's sales volumes thus began to dip. More pertinently, this meant that the dungeon's revenues and profits went down.

This case assumes that everyone reading this has a basic understanding of capitalism. Therefore, it will not spell out any further why we are concerned about dropping profits.

The dungeon's management realises that this drop in profits is a result of something outside of its direct control. Rather than employing convergent thinking, they decide to attempt thinking outside of the box, to solve their problems.

Summarise Insights

The business is less profitable because it receives less share of the revenue from the fixed amounts customers pay for cigarettes and mints if the price of cigarettes increases. I hope that the previous sentence is a satisfactory summarisation of the situation at hand. There may be some better ways of summarising the situation. But this probably isn't horrible, and that's good enough for now.

Identify Keywords

The list of words (groups) identified by management as key phrases is as follows. The specific list identified by any individual may be marginally different, but should largely be in sync with what is below.

- The business
- Less profitable
- Less share of the revenue
- Fixed amounts (customers pay)
- Customers
- Cigarettes and mints
- Price of cigarettes increases

Release Constraints

Management then went through each of the key phrases and came up with some wild ideas, as to how they can be relaxed. This set of ideas is by no means comprehensive. Nor does it necessarily list the best ideas. It's just one set of creative ideas.

- The business – Perhaps this issue is faced by other businesses similar to theirs. If others are in the same situation as them, perhaps there is an industry lobby that could take on the issue instead of just them? If others are facing the same issue, are there any creative ideas that they can copy?

- Less profitable – The volume of mints they sell per customer has gone down. This need not mean that they should be less profitable if they can either reduce the cost per mint or increase the price per mint. In either of these cases, they will still have a lower revenue share of the transaction. But their profitability in that transaction will be increased, which could offset the problem.

- Less share of the revenue – Maybe it's possible to team up with the cigarette companies, or strike some sort of deal with Ram Bhai so that they get some share of the increased prices? Maybe they can focus on bundling their product with a wider range of cigarettes or products? This way they'll still get a lower share but of a larger pie.

- Fixed amounts – Is it possible to create more demand, so that the average amount paid by a customer jumps up? Is it possible to shift customers to digital payments, so that the amounts they pay aren't fixed, round numbers, but are more flexible? This will ensure that they can maintain a fixed revenue per cigarette, independent of the price of the cigarette. Or it may eliminate the need for their product altogether if they're not careful.

- Customers – Maybe they could focus on an entirely different set of end-users? Maybe they can treat the cigarette companies as their customers and focus on co-branding or bundling?

- Cigarettes and mints – Maybe they can bundle their product at a different transaction stage, such as with lighters, or entire boxes? Maybe they can bundle the product with an entirely different category of products, such as a replacement of small change in general? Maybe they should focus somehow on standalone sales?

- Price of cigarettes increase – Is every cigarette getting more expensive? Why are they becoming more expensive? Is there something they can do to lobby and reduce or prevent the effective increase in cigarette prices?

Case Questions

Start with the same core insight, "The business is less profitable because it receives less share of the revenue from the fixed amounts customers pay for cigarettes and mints if the price of cigarettes increases."

1. What are the most creative responses that you can come up with?
2. What is your thought process behind each idea?

Instead of just thinking on your own, I would encourage you to participate in a case discussion on the following Reddit thread. Through case discussion, your ideas may be validated or improved upon. You would also benefit from other people's viewpoints.

Recap

In my mind, at least some of the ideas above would not have come to me if I were just looking at the original problem description. I know that our approach at the end of the day was rather structured, and not exactly what one might call creative. But if we were to juxtapose just the original problem and the laundry list of solutions, it looks pretty creative to me. In any case, this is one possible approach, amongst many others to divergent thinking. It's useful to have your own hack to think creatively when you need to.

And now, we're pretty much done with our first out of 6 sections on business management. For those readers who have not been overly distracted by thoughts of cake, pizza and cigarettes, you might have the following takeaways by now:

- Management thinking involves convergent thinking and divergent thinking. And one needs to know when and how to do both.
- There are 4 critical steps to follow in convergent thinking.
- My structure of structures might help break down any complex problem, and therefore ensure that you can apply convergent thinking to any situation.
- While there are many ways of applying divergent thinking, constraint release is one quick and easy approach to try out.

In a short space of time, I claim to have given you the key to thinking like a manager. Not bad, right? There are of course caveats.

Firstly, the theory of management thinking is easy to cover. But the practice of it takes actual practice; lots of it. Luckily for us, we are going to keep using management thinking throughout this book. All of the ideas that we use in the next 5 sections can be and will be derived through this sort of thinking. I will not explicitly go through each of the steps of management thinking in most situations. However, management thinking will very clearly underly each of the concepts presented. I would strongly encourage you to pause at each new concept, and see if you're able to make sense of it from first principles.

I would claim that all management problems can be solved fundamentally using management thinking. Because we don't want to start from scratch each time, we will learn some results across the next 5 sections, but also get used to deriving them through management thinking for whenever we are in new situations, for which we haven't yet seen templated solutions.

Secondly, just because we have learnt these principles, it doesn't mean that we're fully equipped with them yet. Too often, we forget to apply fundamental principles of thinking to our problems. As soon as we hear about a problem, we are often excited to take a crack at it. It's important to also pause, take a breath and think about what we need to do. This sounds just like the first step of convergent thinking in a sense. The important trick is to always pause, and take a breath. This forces us into our way of management thinking until it has become a habit.

With the above learnings and caveats in mind, you might just have mastered management thinking.

Section II

Strategy, Marketing & Frameworks

Let's treat this section as 'an introduction to business' or 'business 101'. What I would like to cover through these 5 chapters is broadly:

- The major steps in the business process.
- The levers available in each business process.
- The stakeholders involved in each business process.
- How one can be successful in each business process.

The name of the section uses some slightly fancier names than 'business 101'. This is obviously because using business jargon and buzzwords like strategy, marketing & frameworks will capture the reader's interest. More interestingly, there is a reason why each of the words in the section is present:

- Strategy – Rather than separate strategy as a different topic, I believe that it is best to understand strategy as and when one develops an understanding of how businesses work. After all, we develop strategies to make our businesses run better.
- Marketing – In my opinion, marketing is not something which is done just by the marketing department. In any organisation, I believe that marketing is either a profit centre which works alongside all other departments or the role of marketing is itself divided up amongst other departments. More importantly, marketing is very customer-centric as a subject area. This makes it particularly easy to grasp, and intuitive. Since marketing is important to the business and easy to grasp, I, therefore, think that marketing provides an excellent lens to view and learn about the overall business process.
- Frameworks – Both marketing and strategy are subject areas which are not just filled with, but driven by frameworks. This means that most of what we will be discussing in this section will be a long list of frameworks. Keep in mind that memorising these frameworks is not the objective. Each framework is a convenient way to organise our intuition, not a hard and fast rule, dictating how businesses work. It is important to, therefore, study each framework and check if we can derive it from first principles and our intuition. In doing so, we build up a connected system of frameworks through which we can easily understand and analyse any business process.

So, let's use our marketing lens and have a look at what we plan on learning in the next five chapters.

Firstly, we will tackle the fact that I made the grand claim that marketing is a great lens to view the business process. So, in chapter 1 we will have a look at the marketing process, and see how it runs parallel to the overall business process. I will also aim to justify how the other subject areas (covered in sections 1, 3, 4 & 5) fit into and help detail this business process.

Second, we will step into the marketing process, by developing approaches to market research. I will try to convince you that there is some solid science that goes into understanding the marketplace, customer demands and breaking down the customer's psychology. Or I might fail, and you can hold onto the glamourised view of every marketing manager being Don Draper, or some other charismatic ad man.

Third, we will discuss how businesses can identify the right customers and how they successfully go after them. This is the part where a lot of our fancy strategy frameworks fit in.

Fourth, we will get deep into marketing territory. We will talk about the marketing mix and how one can develop marketing programmes. If you ever want to sound smart in a business context, without knowing what you're talking about, flip straight to the fourth chapter of this section.

Fifth, and finally we will look at some of the on-ground sales aspects of the business process. This should be particularly useful to understand how the biggest businesses in the world developed an edge through perfecting last-mile delivery. But it also contains some useful tips on how to sell, which is what most every job comes down to.

Chapter 7
Marketing: A Business Roadmap

Why marketing?

One might wonder why I have chosen marketing as the lens through which I aim to explore the business process. One might speculate that it's because I have a special liking for my marketing professors. I can't deny, that they were quite cool, but that's not the reason. As hinted at the beginning of the section, there are a few reasons why marketing makes an excellent lens to view the business process:

- The overarching structure of marketing, the marketing process seems to align with and almost match exactly most textbook definitions of the business process.
- In real-life companies marketing is often a vital department, the profit centre. Of course, in many companies marketing is not considered that important, as in the context of financial services companies or tech companies. However, even in these cases, a lot of the functions that are a part of the marketing process are of utmost importance. It just so happens that those functions are performed differently, and not necessarily by a marketing team. Thus, the marketing process is still the main business process.
- Marketing as a subject area is largely defined around the customer. Most of us are used to being customers, not managers. This customer obsession makes it easy to grasp the ideas behind marketing.

As such, marketing seems to be a critical subject area, which runs in parallel to the business process and is easy to grasp. That, in a nutshell, is why I believe that we should use the marketing process as our overarching structure to understand how businesses work. All other subject areas can then fit into this framework of how businesses work.

Thus, through marketing, we shall create a skeleton understanding of business. The other subject areas will then be added in as the flesh, muscles and all other vital organs. With that analogy, by the end of the book, you will have an understanding of the anatomy of business. Alternately, we would have created a hideous monster.

The marketing process

Most of the content of this section is in some way or form derived from Philip Kotler's textbook, "the principles of marketing" (Kotler, 2010). This is a sort of bible of marketing, a textbook which is followed in almost every business school. On many occasions, I will fail to know the original creator of certain marketing frameworks. In such cases, I will likely end up attributing it to Kotler, since his textbook is where I have personally derived most of my understanding of marketing from.

Now that blame has been duly assigned for my shortcomings, let's describe the marketing process. This is a process that I have picked up from a combination of Kotler's (Kotler, 2010) and Robert J Dolan's (Dolan, 2014) frameworks. According to them, the marketing process consists of, at the highest level, just 2 steps. First, a business must create some value. Second, the business captures value from customers, by trading in the value that they have created. In such generic terms, one must agree that this is the basic business process for any business. I doubt that one can think of any company which generates money without creating some sort of value for whoever their paying customer is. If a company does manage to make money without adding value, it is likely a scam, which will come to an end sooner or later.

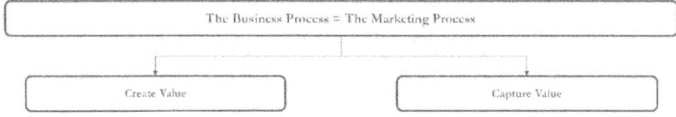

The most accurate and least effective business framework might stop at this level. But the marketing process is broken down into more detail. The process of capturing value is relatively straightforward. One just has to make sure that they collect payments. What this step truly means, however, is sustainably capturing value. Therefore, in this step, a business must also focus on retaining customers, collecting feedback, and ensuring that their business process improves over time. Still, it is the easier part of the process.

Creating value is broken down into 4 smaller steps. The first step involves understanding the market. This includes understanding the marketplace, competition, regulations, technology etc. Most critically it is about understanding the customer, their wants, needs, buying behaviour and everything that could influence the business' success.

The second step involves using the information gathered from the first step to come up with a business strategy. This is a big and wide term, which means many things. But most importantly it includes segmenting the market, targeting only those customer segments who are likely to be profitable for our business and then positioning our brand such that it is attractive to the target customer.

The third step takes the strategy from step 2 and puts it into action. Here we must run marketing programmes. This step is often simplified to the concept of maintaining a 'marketing mix'. In other words, this is where we design the product, set the price, run promotions, and take care of placement (in-store etc). If there's one thing you take away from marketing, it should be these 4Ps.

The fourth and final step ensures that all of the marketing work done so far reaches the customer. To create value for the customer, we need to handle the logistics of getting the product to them. This may involve manufacturing, distribution, retailing and a lot of relationship management. In short, the fourth step is supply chain management and sales.

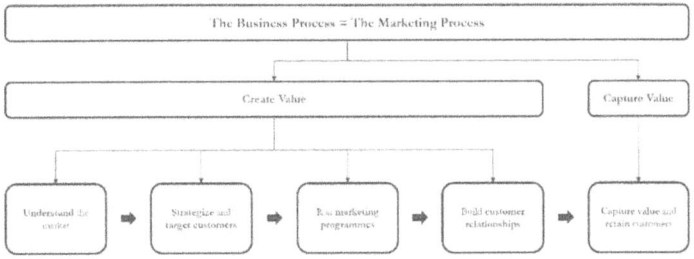

If you notice, these 4 steps of value creation correspond to the next 4 chapters that we will cover in this section. That's not all. Every marketing framework imaginable fits into the 5 steps of the marketing process (Kotler, 2010).

Marketing as a lens for business

The claim that I made earlier on was still taller. I said that the marketing process is not just an overarching structure for every marketing framework. My claim was that every business concept of interest within the organisation fits into the marketing process. Let's verify that claim for a second. If you're not convinced by the end of my argument, that's a little unfortunate. You've now read an awkwardly large amount of text to give up on the book for such a trivial reason. But in any case, here is why I believe that the other business concepts that we will study fit somewhere in the marketing process.

Management thinking, we had said can be applied to any business problem. All of the business problems that we will face should be within the business process. We have already seen that the business process is pretty much the same as the marketing process, from creating value to capturing value. As for where we can see management thinking, the answer is 'every marketing framework'. Each marketing framework can be derived from first principles, using management thinking. There are probably new frameworks which can be derived through management thinking, which would fit snugly somewhere in the marketing process.

Finance is the language of business. Once again, all of the business of interest to us lies in the business process, which is the marketing process. Thus, we will be using finance to keep a track of metrics and get a more objective sense of understanding of each step of the marketing process. Finance is an equally fair lens to look at the entire business process through. I personally find the marketing process to be more intuitive, and financial metrics to be more effective for mathematical analysis.

Operations, technology and math of course are a perfect fit where a business has on-ground or corporate operations which need to be optimised. These tasks are usually present largely in the fourth step of the marketing process. However, as technology improves, the other, more subjective steps are also getting more mathematically influenced. In any case, the marketing process provides the overall view of the business process. And in some of its steps, these subject areas can be used to improve performance.

Finally, the soft skills of human resource management and communication are of use wherever people exist. This of course extends well beyond the organisation. For a manager, the people of interest are likely to only be employees. And the interest that a manager takes in these employees is largely related to the business. I don't mean to take a bleak view of things, I'm sure your manager also cares about you as an individual. Maybe. I don't know what kind of relationship you share. As far as our business understanding of HR and communication is concerned, we are only interested in those concepts which help us improve each of the steps of the marketing/business process.

And so, each of these 4 subject areas fits within the marketing process. Or at least whatever we plan to learn about each of these subject areas is restricted to the steps in the marketing process. Remember, we said we also wanted to study the outside world. That by definition is outside the bounds of the marketing/business process. But it's still important. What we learn about the outside world might influence how we shape our marketing process, since we intend to interact with the outside world too.

Recap

Right now, we have learnt how to think convergently and divergently, like a manager. We have used some of that management thinking to map out the marketing/business process:

- Create value:
1. Understand the marketplace.
2. Strategise and target customers.
3. Run marketing programmes.
4. Build customer relationships.
- Capture value:
5. Capture value and retain customers.

We now intend to learn more about marketing in each of these steps, so that we can successfully create value for our customers as all good managers do.

Chapter 8
What's Going On?: Understanding the Marketplace

In this chapter, as in the next few chapters, we will end up covering a lot of ground. Not just because I enjoy watching you suffer. We planned on using these 4 chapters as an overall framework within which all of business fits. And so, we now need to develop frameworks and a model which covers most of the major business activities.

But, on the bright side, this can all make for very light reading. I will present a pretty long, almost unending series of frameworks. Each of these frameworks is quite intuitive. They basically try to organise very normal activities that you're used to into a standard template so that patterns are easy to recognise. So, rather than getting bogged down by all the new frameworks, you could just read through it like a series of stories. Hopefully, you will easily be able to relate to most of what we will discuss.

Questions to ask

The first step in the marketing process is understanding the marketplace. This implies that there are some questions that we want answers to. Of course, every situation has its own distinct set of questions. To ensure that we don't miss out on asking critical questions, our marketing gurus have provided us with a few different frameworks. There are 2 frameworks in particular that I think are useful here.

The first is the 5Cs framework. The framework is as simple as a list of 5 words, each starting with C. The idea is that we need to make sure that we know all about each of these 5 components, to begin developing an understanding of the marketing process.

Without going into too much detail, the 5Cs that we want to know about are Customers (ours and potential customers), our own Company, Competition, our Collaborators (such as supply partners) and Context (everything else which might be relevant). At first glance, this might not seem perfectly complete. But this framework is largely MECE. It takes a little time to get used to the terminology used. Anything which might seem like it is missed out on can actually be covered under one of the 5Cs. With a little bit of practice, anyone can ask all of the right questions to fill in the 5Cs and develop a solid market understanding (Kinnison, 2019).

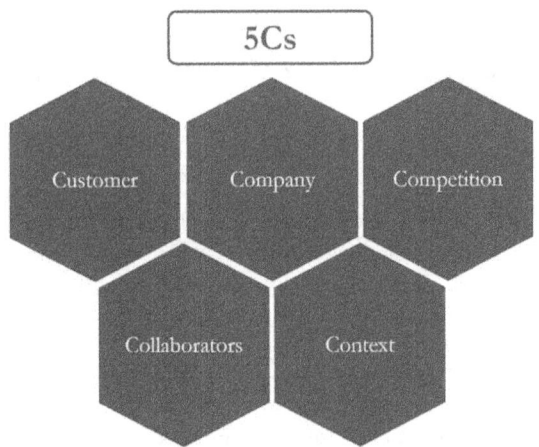

One of the biggest blocks in the 5Cs is Context. It's not as specific as the other 4Cs. Context is perhaps not as close to the manager, and perhaps not always as important. But we know from newspaper headlines that a change in context can change everything. Since it's so important to be thorough while scanning and understanding our context, we have a second framework which gives us another checklist.

The PESTLE framework is used for analysing the macroenvironment. This is once again a list of 6 words, which prompt us to investigate and make sure that we're aware of our context before moving forward with the business process.

PESTLE splits the macroenvironment into 6 factors. It suggests that we should ask whether there is anything of interest/relevance which is happening in our political, economic, social, technological, legal or environmental surroundings. Anything relevant to our business should be noted down, so that we have a better understanding of our context, and can adapt to it (Kotler, 2010).

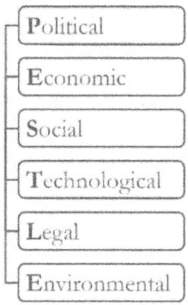

You might have a few questions in terms of the scope of each of the 5 + 6 words mentioned, and how you can use them. As the first line of advice, I would suggest that you google these frameworks. As a general rule of thumb, whatever frameworks I mention, there is probably someone on the internet who has done a much better job of explaining them. The value that I will try to add is organising each of the frameworks such that you know when to use them and how they fit in. Still, I will use most of these frameworks in a case, so that you can develop a rough idea of how they work.

Finding answers

We have come up with a bunch of questions. And we believe that if we answer them, we will have a pretty good general idea of the marketplace. Unfortunately, in the business world, some answers can't just be googled. Sometimes you'll have a colleague that you can ask to help you out, but these school and college tactics are also a little less effective here.

Luckily for us, companies have been dealing with this challenge for decades before we stumbled upon it. And because answering these questions is important, there is often an elaborate system in place to deal with them. At the crux of this system is MIS (marketing information systems). The way it works is that each department has its own MIS resource, who is responsible for doing a lot of data gathering and analysis. Through them, the central MIS team has an idea of what questions need to be answered, and what data is therefore needed. They try to collect as much information directly from customers, so long as it isn't too expensive or invasive. They also rely on other agencies such as Nielsen to gather a lot of information on the market and competition. Wherever possible, publicly available databases are also tapped into. And finally, when no one else seems to have answers ready at hand, marketing research needs to be done from scratch. This research may be done within the company itself, or with the help of organisations which specialise in marketing research. Through one or a combination of these 3 mechanisms, the required data is gathered. Then MIS resources or managers themselves analyse the data to arrive at the answers that they need (Vijayalakshmi, 2021) (Kotler, 2010).

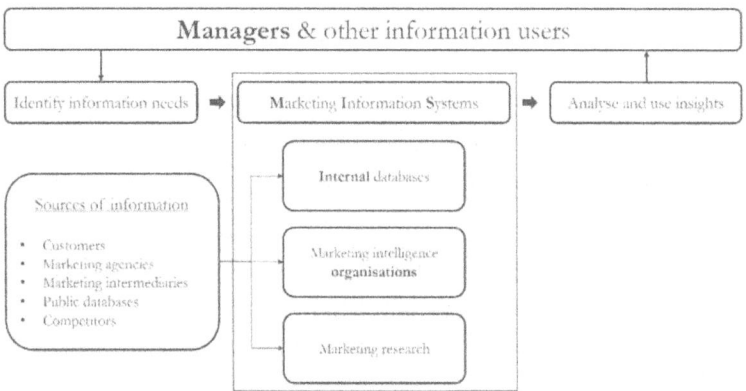

At this stage, you should have a good idea of what kind of questions we seek to ask, and how we attempt to answer them, to understand the marketplace. And you don't need to memorise any of this, because this book, and better yet, Google will always be available. Let's now try and put some of this to practical use.

Case 4.1

It has now been a few months since students arrived on the IIM-A campus. The campus remains a bubble, where no one is going out or getting in. Even before this, most students have chosen to stay safe, and avoided getting a haircut. Long story short, dungeon management believes that there must be a tremendous demand for haircuts on campus. They are planning on opening a dungeon hair salon.

But before launching into this business, management wants to understand a little more about the marketplace. They are not very concerned about coming up with a strategy or running marketing programmes. They're sure to find a marketing expert who can help with that. They do want to collect all of the relevant marketplace information so that their marketing professional is well equipped to help them.

Customer

To begin with, management plans on understanding more about their potential customer. The college administration has made publicly available the list of students across all programmes. A simple search of the college's website also reveals a list of faculty and staff members. Using these publicly available datasets, they have managed to create a superset of all possible customers. Further, using their own database of visitors to the dungeon tea and Maggi shop (from case 2), management can get some more information on some customers. Their database reveals a little bit about the spending patterns of some students and professors. Some frequent customers had also created a 'dungeon account', with an up-to-date photograph. Thus, management also has a smaller list of potential customers who are definitely in need of a haircut.

Company

The dungeon has in its ranks 2 student employees who are capable of giving haircuts. Both of these employees are only confident in giving boys haircuts. As a result, a large chunk of the potential customer base might have to be thinned out. However, these female potential customers could be serviced with manicures, pedicures, facials etc. After a couple of test runs, management is confident that the quality of male haircuts, unisex manicures, pedicures and facials is up to the mark, and can compete with any non-premium salon.

Competition

After reaching out to the campus security team, dungeon management has discovered that some students and professors alike have been booking haircuts via local service apps like Urban Company. Through this third-party service, management has identified their main source of competition. Through a few student surveys, management discovers that most customers are happy with the quality of service. However, they do find the process of waiting for an appointment booking, and a little bit of post-haircut clean-up to be inconvenient. They seem to prefer an on-campus salon, if one existed, provided that there is no waiting time.

Collaborators

The dungeon doesn't have many requirements in terms of collaborators. In terms of communication and a channel of acquiring customers, the internal mailing system should suffice. Dungeon's management decided that it would be prudent to make the college administration a partner and supporter. The administration would have the power to keep competition out of campus and might be needed for operational permissions.

Context

The context in summary is that the campus is currently in a covid bubble. It is unknown for how long it would remain so. As a result of this situation, the demand for haircuts on campus as a service has sprung up. Management attempted to take a more in-depth view of the context. They found that the prevailing political situation in the country suggested that educational institutions would likely be encouraged to maintain this bubble for at least the next few months. The college administration's stance also seemed largely in line with this ideology. The economic situation of the campus residents was strong. They demanded self-care, had missed the opportunity to spend on other luxuries and were likely to spend money on novel haircuts. The social -setting on campus had begun to see a shift. Many students who had now grown their hair for several months were beginning to style it in interesting ways, starting a trend of sorts. Technologically, there were no new developments, but the ease of using local service apps like Urban Company remained a threat. Legal issues were not considered to be a major challenge in this respect. Environmental concerns were also judged to be irrelevant.

Case Questions

Having thus studied the marketplace, management felt confident in moving forward with their hair salon plan.

1. In your opinion, are there any other marketplace factors that the dungeon's management might have overlooked?
2. For each additional factor, specify which of the 5Cs it could have been discovered within.

Instead of just thinking on your own, I would encourage you to participate in a case discussion on the following Reddit thread. Through case discussion, your ideas may be validated or improved upon. You would also benefit from other people's viewpoints.

Researching the market

We have established that our cheat sheet for getting answers to some pertinent marketplace questions consists of using internal databases, marketing intelligence organisations and doing our own marketing research. Two of these are quite easy. Internal databases just need to be queried, and I'm sure someone in the company can do the requisite analysis. Marketing intelligence organisations will also serve up the insights we desire on a platter, for the right price, of course. We call these first 2 approaches secondary research because the answers are already present and buried away. As such we're effectively researching someone else's research work = secondary research. But marketing research seems like work being sent back our way. We call this primary research because we intend to find a brand-new answer for the very first time. So, we're going to have to come up with a simple process for primary market research (Vijayalakshmi, 2021).

Much like any process, we can structure this by imagining our research journey. It might start with us fixing on our problem statement. Once we know what we're trying to research, we can draw out a plan, including where we will search for information, how we plan to analyse it and so on. Third, we would have to act on this research plan, by reaching out to individuals/organisations, collecting data and analysing the data. Finally, we need to interpret the results of our research, to come up with human-understandable insights (Kotler, 2010).

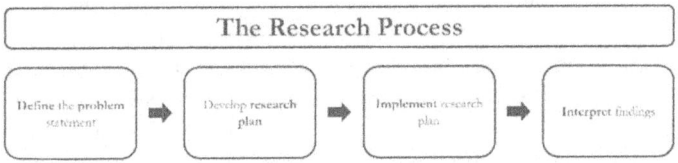

It should be pretty clear what happens in each step, at a broad level. But there are some nuances worth diving into.

While defining the research problem statement one might have a solid understanding of the field, might be clueless, or anywhere in between. While turning in a final project submission, you must have noticed that your level of understanding of the subject has a big impact on how you go about your project. The same is true with marketing research. When we don't know anything at all, we ask exploratory research questions, trying to figure out what trends exist. When we have some understanding of what sort of trends exist, we ask descriptive research questions, trying to get more information on what happens when, how, where and so on. Once we have a good grasp on all of the descriptive details of a trend, we might ask causal research questions, diving into why things work the way they do, and how we can control them (Vijayalakshmi, 2021).

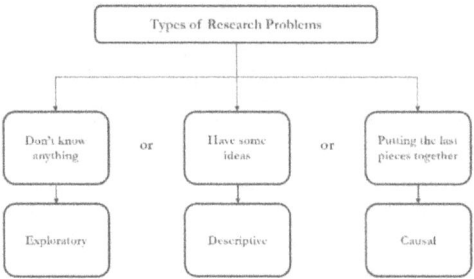

Developing a research plan is a pretty involved field. I will not be able to do justice to it in this short book. But as usual, I will shine a light on some of the key ideas, so that you can dive deeper if this area interests you.

The type of problem statement that we defined initially helps us decide on the most appropriate research approach. In case we are working on an exploratory problem, we want to collect as much open-ended information as possible. This would help us understand what sort of trends may exist. So, we conduct interviews, simply observe users/customers and have discussions about the product with a group of customers/non-customers. In the context of a descriptive problem, we know what trend we want to study in more detail. We also know what other details about the trend we want to learn. Surveys are the most effective instrument in this context. They allow us to target the right set of users and ask pointed questions about the trend in question. There are other studies of user-generated data which may sometimes provide similar information, in case a survey is considered less effective or too intrusive in the context. Finally, causal problems have a very scientific 'why?' question at their heart. Users' answers are not as powerful a source of data as their actual behaviour in this context. Scientific experiments or scientific analysis of past user-generated data are the most useful instrument here (Vijayalakshmi, 2021).

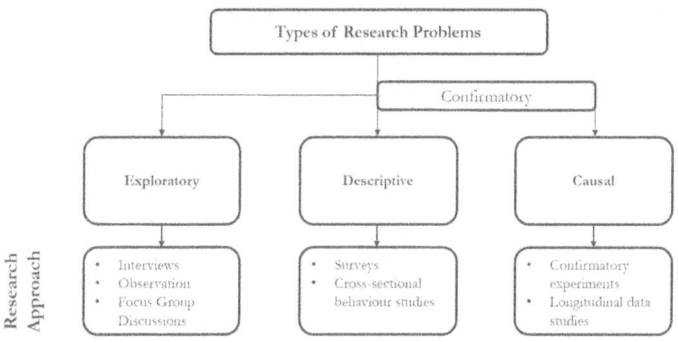

In confirmatory research (descriptive and causal), and especially in causal research, it is useful to begin with a hypothesis, rather than search through all possibilities. 4 traits define a good hypothesis. A hypothesis which doesn't match some of these requirements can usually be improved, to make the research process easier and more effective. A good hypothesis is (Vijayalakshmi, 2021) :

1. Useful – If proven true or false, the implication should be useful to the business.
2. Falsifiable – It should be possible to test the validity of the hypothesis.
3. Predicts a directed relationship between variables – It should tell us how one metric relates to another so that this prediction can be used in the future.
4. Specific – It shouldn't be vague, making its application in a context uncertain.

Before you get lost in the barrage of frameworks that I have thrown your way, let me redirect you back to the research process. We have seen that there are a few different types of research problems that we can solve, depending on how much we already know. We then saw that developing a research plan involves selecting the most appropriate research approach as a function of the type of problem we are solving. We will now move forward to the third step of implementing the research plan. Having done the hard work of planning, this becomes much easier.

Some of the key steps to look out for in the implementation stage are (Kotler, 2010):

- Method of contacting – Respondents for research may be contacted via mail, telephone, in person, online etc. One needs to take a call on what would be the most effective method in their context.

- Sampling plan – There are a large number of probabilistic and non-probabilistic methods to choose from. One needs to decide on sample size, sampling unit and sampling frame as well. Without getting into these technicalities, I have provided you with some useful phrases to google, if you choose to dive deeper into this.

- Research instrument – Each of the research approaches ranging from surveys to experiments to focus groups must be designed with care. Once again, this space is too complex to enter here. However, if you are interested, googling the best techniques to follow in designing these instruments could teach you a lot.

Case 4.2

The dungeon hair salon seems to be a good fit for the current context. But dungeon management has a few more questions on their mind. One of the first questions on management's mind was what sort of hairstyles will customers be looking for. And so, they begin first by doing some secondary research, because that's easy.

Through the college's official student portal, management looks at the photographs submitted by students at the time of their registration. From this database, they develop an idea of the sort of haircuts most students used to traditionally get. They also check the websites of famous hair styling chains across the country. The top choice haircuts here reveal a little bit about the average Indian's haircut preferences.

Management thinks some primary research might be needed here since students' preferences on a range of matters change once they enter college. So, they go on to interview a few students. They also make a note of the hairstyles of students who recently got Urban Company haircuts. They notice a trend of hair colouring, mohawks, a few strands of long hair, and other unconventional haircuts.

Interviewees also expressed a desire to get a haircut different from what they have had before, if at all they get a haircut.

Picking up on the trend of customers desiring novel haircuts, management decided to try and get a little more information. However, IIM-A students are notorious for sending out surveys and failing to respond to surveys themselves. To elicit a high response rate, management decided to create a small online game and send it out. At this stage, it might seem like hair styling isn't the right industry for the dungeon. But not to worry, they'll enter online gaming sooner or later. As a part of the online game, management analysed the sort of avatars students created for themselves and the sort of haircuts they chose. By allowing students to also select the avatars that they thought looked coolest, management got a sense of what hairstyles students preferred.

It appeared that students liked very distinctive haircuts, especially mohawks. There was a preference for coloured hair, but not jarring colours. Hair colours which easily matched with a majority of clothes seemed to be popular.

Dungeon's management was also cognizant of the fact that people's behaviour in games and real-life differ. They, therefore, wanted to build up their confidence in the observed results.

Case Question

In particular, they wanted to understand why students preferred these distinctive hairstyles. Management had a hunch that the next few months of college were considered free time, without interviews or internships to worry about, and this prompted styling experimentation.

1. What types of research problems and research approaches have been employed so far?
2. Help design a 'good hypothesis' to test management's new hunch.
3. What sort of research approach would you use in this context?

Instead of just thinking on your own, I would encourage you to participate in a case discussion on the following Reddit thread. Through case discussion, your ideas may be validated or improved upon. You would also benefit from other people's viewpoints.

Customer Psychology

As promised (or warned) a lot has happened in this chapter.

- We started by asking a few important questions (5Cs & PESTLE).
- We understood how MIS (Marketing Information Systems) uses different secondary and primary research sources to answer these questions.
- We even had a look at the 4 key steps of the research process in some detail.

But we didn't deep-dive into the last step of the research process (interpreting the findings). As long as we're able to successfully interpret our research findings, we should be able to easily develop an understanding of any marketplace, right?

Interpreting research findings seems like a complex and subjective matter. Any finding can be interpreted in many ways unless one is particularly careful. As with most things in marketing (and business) we can simplify our work by using some appropriate frameworks.

Most of what we expect to find when we study the marketplace are insights regarding customer behaviour and user psychology. That's right, even when we ask questions about competition, context etc, what we can learn about the customer's behaviour in the process is often more valuable. We, therefore, have a set of handy frameworks which detail how customers behave in various generic circumstances. This helps because our research findings might be complicated. Having simple templates which we can fit our findings into allows us to quickly spot patterns. Once we have spotted a pattern in our research findings, we can quickly identify which of our frameworks' user behaviour is at play.

I am now once again about to bury you in a set of frameworks. Look beyond the frameworks and see if the story that they tell matches your experience. If it does, you have understood the framework and can easily reuse it as and when you need it.

First up, we understand the decision process that buyers go through. Note that this probably looks similar to one of the structures that we saw in case 2. While this process is broadly applicable to different kinds of buyers, we will focus on consumers as buyers, not businesses as buyers. The first step is recognising that we need something. We then begin searching for information on how we can solve our needs. This may range from online searches to talking to friends to walking into a store. Next, we evaluate alternatives as a function of whatever expectations we have of the product we want to purchase. As long as one product matches what we need and is within our price range, we make our purchase decision. There is then a purchase process, which today can happen in a range of ways including cash, card, mobile, free trial, EMI etc. Finally, we get down to using the product! This is also an important stage in the purchase decision because it can impact repurchase decisions. In the last stage, we have our post-purchase behaviour. This includes activities such as reviewing the product, promoting it amongst friends or even asking for servicing of any sort (Kotler, 2010).

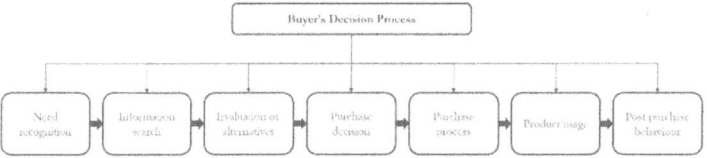

Just like that, we have managed to take a super simple activity that none of us thinks about and break it down into 7 complicated stages. Welcome to the world of business. Truly, this is an important and useful process. Magnifying each of these minute activities is important for us to understand where potential customers may be dropping off. Thus, it is frameworks like this which can make the difference between unheard-of brands and market leaders.

Now that we know the steps that buyers go through, we need to understand what influences the buyer's thinking and decisions through each of these steps. The next framework gives us an idea of the large factors that influence a buyer's decisions. In short, the factors, in decreasing order of influence are the buyer's psychological make-up, their personal details, their social setting and their cultural influences.

Psychological make-up includes factors such as the buyer's motivations, perceptions, learnings and beliefs. Their personal details are simply their age, life stage, gender, occupation, economic situation etc. Their social setting is the role they play in their family and friend groups. Cultural influences are a function of their country, ethnic group, religion and other subcultures to which they may belong. The set of factors which influence one's thought process, as well as the order of the influence they might have, should make sense to you. You may believe that there is some reordering and a little editing required. But once again this should be directionally useful to identify what factors influence buyer decision-making (Kotler, 2010).

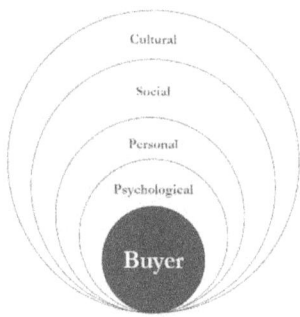

There is another such framework which helps us understand what sort of decisions an individual might make. This happens to be my favourite framework. I find it to be shockingly useful and true. You might not be as attached to it, but I think it's cool nonetheless. Maslow's hierarchy of needs suggests that there are 5 levels of needs that individuals have. This means that once one level of needs has been largely satisfied, we begin to want/need the next level. If, however, a given level of needs has not been taken care of, we find it very difficult to worry about any higher-level need. The first level here is physiological needs. This includes our most basic survival needs, such as air, water, food, shelter etc. Once that has been taken care of, our next set of concerns is safety. This means not just personal security, but also employment, property and some basic amount of wealth. Our third level of needs includes love, belonging and a basic sense of social standing. Once we are able to survive, are safe and belong somewhere, we begin to crave the fourth level of needs, a sense of esteem. This level includes needs such as respect, status, recognition and freedom. At the final level, once all of our other needs have been taken care of, we desire self-actualisation. Self-actualisation is an understanding of our purpose and a sense of being everything that we need to be and can be (Maslow, 1943).

By understanding what level of the hierarchy a customer is at, or which level our product satisfies, we can develop a much better understanding of how they might behave, and thus how we should communicate.

However, a buyer's behaviour isn't purely a function of the influences in their world or of the state of need that they are in. The kind of product makes a big difference to how a buyer behaves. For example, if a customer is purchasing a commodity like wheat or rice, where every brand is similar, and their involvement is low, they won't think much about the purchase. If instead, they're buying chips, where flavours vary a lot, but the stakes are still low, they might look to try new brands and flavours now and then. A customer purchasing an expensive product like insurance, where every provider offers more or less the same service would probably look to minimise their regret. And if the customer is purchasing something like a car, where their involvement is high and there is a big difference between cars, they're likely to get into a lot of the details of the purchase (Kotler, 2010).

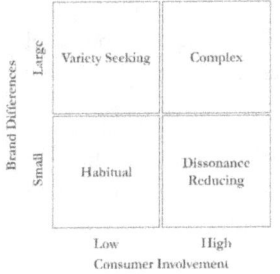

But that's not all. Till now we have assumed that there is just one buyer who is being influenced, has different types of needs and responds differently to different categories. The reality is that there are often a bunch of individuals working together. Let's take the example of an expedition to a shopping mall when we were kids. We might see a toy that we like. Let's say that it's a Beyblade because I miss them. We might initiate the idea of purchase, by asking our parents to buy it. One of our parents might act as the gatekeeper, deciding whether to entertain the request or not. A grandparent or sibling might act as an influencer, asking the parents to buy the Beyblade and keep us happy. One of our parents, you decide which one, will make the decision, on whether to buy it or not, as well as what price range might be okay. Either one of the parents might act as the approver, agreeing to the decision (or not). Whoever brought their wallet along will finally be the buyer. And if all has gone well, we will be the end-user of the new Beyblade. Aside from this specific example, up to these 7 distinct roles can exist in any given buying process. Understanding which person plays which role helps us understand who our real customer is. This sort of thinking is why diapers are targeted at parents, and not babies (which would be less effective, but adorable) (Sharma, 2020) (Kotler, 2010).

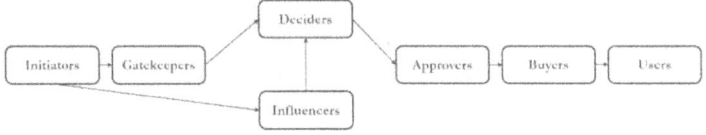

Case 4.3

As of now, the dungeon's management had framed a few vital questions about the hair grooming marketplace in IIM-A. Through a combination of secondary and primary research, they had gathered a large volume of data on the same. To interpret their results, they decided to try and create a customer narrative. The idea is that it would simplify their understanding of how potential customers behave. Thus, they constructed the following customer story.

Shubham is a student at IIM-A. Because Shubham is a pretty common name. And I like the idea of each of the Shubhams in my batch wondering whether this is about them. It is not. Over the last 8 months, Shubham has not got a haircut. During this time, he has enjoyed the novelty of his long hair. At first, he enjoyed the newfound activity of brushing it aside now and then. He spent time shampooing and conditioning it, and even straightening his hair now and then.

When his hair started covering his eyes during zoom classes, it was still fun. But when strands of hair began to block his view while gaming or playing football, it began to bother him. He didn't like the idea of wearing a rubber band, so he began to consider getting a haircut. Still, he had his reservations.

There was a range of cultural to psychological factors influencing his thought process. While growing up, he never had distinctive hair or a distinctive look. He looked like all of the other boys in school, with a simple crew cut. His parents simply wouldn't allow him to grow his hair out like Dhoni. They said he would look like a girl. When other guys in school or college started spiking their hair, he also briefly tried to emulate it. But once again, his mother threw out his hair gel and suggested he use hair oil instead. Right now, he neither has placement interviews, nor his internship around the corner. His parents can't control what he looks like either. If he doesn't take advantage of this and maintain a distinctive style now, when will he ever have the freedom to again? Moreover, people in college knew him by his distinctive long, flowy hair. He didn't want to lose his identity because of a small hindrance.

There were a couple of conflicting levels of needs in Shubham's mind. On the one hand, there was the minor physiological inconvenience of hair getting in his eyes. This interrupted activities that he usually enjoyed. He needed to find a way around this. On the other hand, there was the more newly discovered need for social belonging and acceptance. This was centred around the identity that he had built for himself. As other people also began to grow out their hair, he didn't want to step out of a campus trend. One need would probably outweigh the other.

Shubham might respond in one of two ways to this decision. He might remain highly attached to his hair. If so, being highly involved in this decision, he is likely to pick the salon where he trusts that the barber will not cut his hair too short. But only maintain a length, where his hair is easy to brush out of his eyes. Alternately, he may realise that this phase is short-lived, and revert to his low involvement mindset. Still, given that he has more freedom at this time, he is likely to seek another novel haircut, such as a mohawk.

Surely, at some point in time, as the summer internship comes around the corner, each of the Shubhams of the batch is likely to get back to their habitual behaviour of adopting a safe and acceptable haircut.

We have all made an outrageous styling choice at some point in time or the other.

1. What's the story behind your strange styling choice?
2. Use the customer behaviour frameworks to try and put each step of your choice in context.

Instead of just thinking on your own, I would encourage you to participate in a case discussion on the following Reddit thread. Through case discussion, your ideas may be validated or improved upon. You would also benefit from other people's viewpoints.

Recap

You have now made some commendable progress on your way to becoming a top-notch manager.

- You know how to think like a manager, converging on your goals and spicing things up with a little creative thinking.
- You understand that businesses create value for customers and trade that in for value that they derive back.
- You know that 4 steps are involved in creating value:
  - Understanding the marketplace.
  - Strategising and targeting the right customers.
  - Running marketing programmes.
  - Maintaining profitable relationships.
- You even have an in-depth knowledge of how to garner marketplace understanding:
  - Ask the relevant questions 5Cs + PESTLE.

o   Use MIS to get answers through secondary research or the primary research process.
o   Fit the uncovered data into our models of customer behaviour.

Chapter 9
STP: Aim, Fire, Strategise

Welcome to chapter 9. I have good news. Well, it's good news for me. You have made it this far, through the hurdle of frameworks that I put you through. That must mean that you are truly interested in this approach to learning about management. It could also mean that you exclusively use this book to pretend like you're studying, while you're scrolling away on your phone. The good news is that either way, I don't need to worry about wearing you down with frameworks anymore. Frameworks are our friends, and every chapter will be filled with them. Hopefully, the cases and examples in between make it easier to understand each framework and forget about them until they are needed again.

In this chapter, we are going to build on the understanding of the marketplace that we developed in the last chapter. As a business that understands the marketplace, my next goal would be to pick a chunk of that market and target it. Once I have decided whom to target, I would hope to have a strategy that ensures that I am successful. So, that's what we will discuss in this chapter. How to segment, target and position. And how to develop a strategy to succeed.

What's the plan

In this second step of the marketing process, we achieve quite a lot. We start with an understanding of the marketplace, and we end up with a strategy for success. Some rather impressive plans must be hatched up in this step. There are 2 big questions that we try to answer in this step. They are "whom do we target?" and "how do we win them over?".

As a part of the first question, we need to identify who all exist in the market (segmentation). And then we need to identify which of these customer groups are the best for us to target (targeting).

Similarly, the act of identifying how to win the customer over is akin to asking what we need the customer to think of our product so that they do all the work required to purchase it. What the customer thinks of our product, or the mind space that it will occupy is what we call positioning. Our strategy includes everything that we need to do as a business to achieve this ideal positioning.

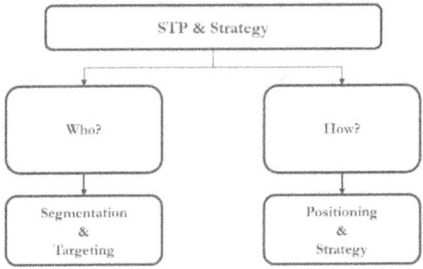

Segmentation

As a first step to targeting the right people, we need to know which people exist. Imagine, for example, that it's the first day of college. You need to decide which group to get in with early on so that you have a good social life. Immediately you might divide your batch into boys and girls. That's an easy way of segmenting the batch because it requires very little prior knowledge of social dynamics. But it's not very useful unless you plan on just being friends with all of the boys or all of the girls. Instead, you could break up the batch based on people's hobbies of choice. This is largely how groups naturally form in a college setting. People in the music club hang out together, as do people in sports teams, and people in various organising committees and so on. Of course, college social dynamics are much more complex than this and go beyond just hobbies of choice. But for my sake, let's ignore that for a moment. This is a much more useful way of segmenting your batch, because people are already organised this way, and you can easily find a group that you will get along with well.

For a business looking to target the right customers, how can they segment and group the market? To an extent, people do naturally organise as a function of their interests and hobbies. But they also organise as a function of their gender, geography, religion, and a whole lot of other preferences. Further, it depends on what sort of people the business is looking for. Since there is no one right answer to this question, we rely on a guiding framework.

A good segmentation can be based on any discriminator, including geography, demographics, psychographics, behaviour, usage of a product, the type of customer that they are, or a bunch of other discriminators. But a good segmentation must necessarily fulfil the following criteria (Sharma, 2020) (Kotler, 2010):

85

- Measurable – The size (number of people in) each segment must be measurable. If it isn't, it would be hard to decide which segment to target. The entire segmentation would then become redundant.
- Substantial – Ideally the number of segments should be limited, and the percentage of the universe in each segment should be substantial. If not, the segmentation isn't much better than a list of each individual in the market. This ensures that some segments are large, yet cohesive.
- Accessible – Each segment has to be one which the business can reach via their communication and with their product. If not, independent of how attractive the segment is to the business, they're not of any value.
- Differentiable – One segment should be clearly distinct from another. When segments aren't differentiable, all of our business actions are still targeted at the entire market. This, of course, defeats the purpose.
- Actionable – Whatever is common across all members of a segment, should be an actionable trait for the business or product in question. For example, the knowledge that a segment consists of art students doesn't help a packaged foods company identify how to target them. On the other hand, knowledge of their geographic location provides useful information about the kind of food they like.

Thus, any segmentation approach which is used must result in measurable, substantial, accessible, differentiable and actionable segments. It would be cool if it spelt out a word, but it doesn't. So, you might have to flip this book open every time you forget how to segment.

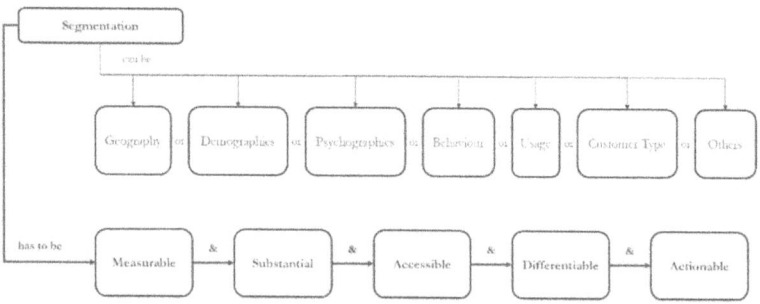

Targeting

Targeting is theoretically easy. Most of the hard work has been done in segmenting the market. From your marketplace analysis, you should have a rough idea of which segments are attractive and which segments you can win. The intersection of attractive and winnable segments should be what we target. Unless you enjoy a challenge or deliberate failure. But in business, we usually focus on where our return on investment is higher.

Still, there are different ideologies behind targeting. As a function of our understanding of the marketplace (from step 1 of the marketing process), and of the most useful segmentation that we have arrived at, we may choose one of 4 types of targeting approaches.

In an undifferentiated targeting approach, we target the entire market. Here we may believe that every customer could purchase our product, and only advertising efforts or distribution will make the difference. This is often true in the case of commodities. Alternately, we might believe that the factors which help us determine who will purchase our product are very hard to identify ahead of time. Therefore, it makes sense to just target everyone, and allow the customer to decide, instead of us trying to find the right customer. This is the case for packaged water brands, where the effort of targeting isn't usually worth the reward (Kotler, 2010).

Differentiated targeting takes broad cuts of the market. Brands which offer different products by gender, age, usage etc need to only split the market into a handful of segments. They may also not cater to each segment, but importantly, segmentation is simplistic in these cases. This is the case for many cosmetics, which cater to men, women and a few specific skin types (Kotler, 2010).

Concentrated targeting takes the idea of segmentation and differentiation a step further. The number of targeted segments increases. The differentiation and attention paid to any given segment increases. Sports gear is one such example. We have different shoes by gender, sport, terrain and then further differentiation for functionality (Kotler, 2010).

Micro-marketing must be very familiar to everyone on the internet. Here customised products and communication are targeted either at the individual or at a very niche and small group. Most effective online advertising follows this sort of model (Kotler, 2010).

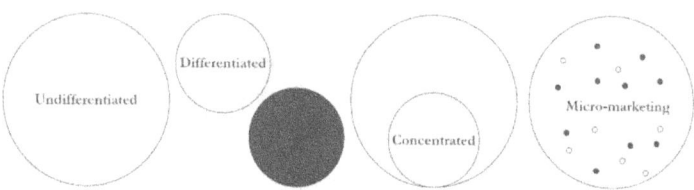

Positioning

We now know what the marketplace looks like. We have identified who is in the market and segmented them into groups. We have even identified which segments we're interested in targeting. Our positioning is the mental real estate that we would like to occupy in the target customer's mind. For example, if we are a beer brand. Our target customer might be a male in the age range of 20-something (depending on the legal drinking age) to 50-something. We might want to position ourselves as the drink that they always have with them when they kick back at the end of a long day to watch the match. As such the mental real estate that we would occupy is that as soon as they lay back on the couch and turn on the TV, they would think to open a bottle of our beer.

Positioning is a beautifully complex space. When positioning is done right, a brand's position is incredibly intuitive and easy to explain. The process of developing a positioning statement (or more complex structures) is however usually very involved. Once a brand's positioning has been fixed, it may not change for a decade or more.

Because of how difficult this task is, there are a whole lot of frameworks that are focused on the positioning. But this time, I will be sharing only one of them with you. I think that the brand key model is absolutely brilliant as an exercise. There are different variants of the brand key, which have slightly different numbers of components, and shapes. But most of them have the same basic structure (Griffiths, 2010).

You start by outlining the competitive environment in which your brand is present. Next, you identify within this who your target customer is. Third, we outline what our key customer insight is. This could be an insight into how the customer uses the product, why they feel a need for it, what they find lacking and so on. But the key insight, which you think the rest of the market has been ignoring, but you intend to play on should be used here. So far, in the first 3 steps we have drawn on what we have learnt when we understood the marketplace, and then from our segmentation and targeting process (Miecznikowski, 2016).

In step 4, we list out the benefits that our target customer sees in our product in particular. In step 5, we try to personify our brand. Looking at the product, its packaging, communication and any other tangible aspect of it, if it were a person, what sort of personality would it have. What are the values that it stands for and is born out of? This can be a little tricky at first. I would encourage you to find some brand key examples online and practice some on your own to get the hang of it. In step 6, we list out the reasons that a customer has to believe in our product and its stated benefits. This could include scientific facts, such as its contents, the promoters of the product, or anything else which truly convinces users of its benefits. In step 7, we list out the discriminators or the unique selling point of our product. It is easy to end up using the USP as the answer for a lot of the previous steps as well. Now would be a good time to backtrack and make sure that you haven't done that (Miecznikowski, 2016).

Finally, in step 8, we put down in a single sentence or phrase, what the essence of the brand is. This should not be a selling statement. The essence of the brand is closest to how it makes the target customer feel. In the context of our beer brand, we would want to distil that feeling of being on one's couch, watching the game with a cold one in hand, into the essence of the brand (Miecznikowski, 2016).

Case 5

We are now bang in the middle of the winter. As much, as the pleasant cold weather is appreciated, taking a shower becomes impossible in the old campus. Moved by this predicament, the dungeon's management decides that it might be a good idea to enter the bathroom accessory/fitting business. More specifically, they intend to manufacture a range of shower heads and other relevant fittings.

Having completed a market study, they find that there is a range of different needs that users have. Common complaints are that the water pressure is too low, and the stream of water out of the shower is also too thin. Users' preferences in terms of water temperature, consistency and texture of flow, area of waterfall etc seem to vary to a great degree. There are of course other brands which address many of these concerns. The market offerings seem to be fairly pricey. Moreover, the effort required to get a plumber to install a new shower head is excessive. A big takeaway from the marketplace study is that most users find something lacking in their shower, and would love an easy fix.

Segmentation

Management knows that they need to begin by identifying the different users in the market that they could cater to. They started by analysing the data on water temperature preferences. They found a strong correlation to gender. But they decided that this wasn't a good segmentation. Showers are often shared by more than one person in the family, so a gender split might not be useful. Furthermore, temperature settings are not the biggest challenge. But they were inspired to build fittings which easily remembered temperature preferences.

Next, they realised that water pressure preferences were strongly correlated to age. They thought this might be a better segmentation. Even within the same household, parents and children often use different bathrooms. So, this is possibly a more actionable segmentation. Still, this didn't seem in and of itself a deep enough segmentation. Preferences for water texture seemed to be correlated to activities that the user was involved in, such as sports, employment, housework etc. Segmenting the market based on age as well as predominant activity of choice seemed promising.

And then, they stumbled upon the biggest differentiating factor of all. Wealth was the biggest discriminator in responses. In lower-income families, the complaint was relatively similar. Users just wanted higher pressure and better water flow. Whereas in higher-income families, there was a great degree of customisation demanded. Where each user wanted a certain kind of water texture/flow, a different waterfall area and so on.

This combination of segmentation based on wealth, and then further discrimination in the high wealth bracket based on age and activity seemed to be the way to go.

All of the segments drawn up seemed attractive to management. Further, all of them seemed winnable as well. Often it is prudent to pick a single segment, to begin with, rather than attempting to win the entire market. So, as a starting point, they chose to target just the lower-income bracket, with a simple and singular product. The reasoning was that this was the largest segment in size, and it would be the easiest to begin catering to.

The dungeon began manufacturing a plug-and-play showerhead fitting. Without calling a plumber, one could simply attach it over the existing shower head. Magically, the water pressure and volume would be fixed. When management was questioned about the physics that went behind this miracle product, they asked us to focus on targeting in this case, and not worry about how such a product could exist.

The dungeon, therefore, started with a differentiated targeting strategy. In the future, they would aim to launch a wider range of higher-end products. In doing so, they would shift towards a concentrated model of targeting.

Positioning

Before launching the product into the market, management was aware that they had to be clear on what their positioning was. They believed that they were rather clear on what the competitive environment was like, who the target audience was and what the key customer insight was as well. They began to brainstorm some ideas to complete their brand key. It was suggested that the key benefits offered were higher water pressure and a greater volume of water flow. Another key benefit was the low price point and the ease of installation. The personality of the brand was thought to be that of an energetic, refreshed and youthful teenager. The values that the brand held were simplicity and excitement over just cleanliness. A key reason to believe in the brand was the strong customer-driven social media promotion. The virality of videos showing demonstrations of the improvement in shower pressure made for a convincing argument. The biggest USP that the brand had was the convenience in price and installation. The essence of the brand was thought to be "freshness of body and mind".

Still, management wasn't sure if they had got their targeting or positioning completely right. After all, it was a crowded market, and they weren't sure if consumers were willing to try purchasing a product online to try on their own.

1. Which segment would you target and why?
2. Construct a brand key from scratch and think through each of the 8 components.

Instead of just thinking on your own, I would encourage you to participate in a case discussion on the following Reddit thread. Through case discussion, your ideas may be validated or improved upon. You would also benefit from other people's viewpoints.

Strategy

We seem to have already come up with our entire plan to make the business successful. And we aren't even 2 full steps into our 4-step marketing process to create value. We have studied the marketplace. We have segmented the market, picked out our target segment, and we know what position our brand should occupy in the target customer's mind. All that remains now is to run some marketing programmes. Surely, with some straightforward implementation, we can communicate to and convince the target customer of the positioning that we have envisioned. We then need to manage some relationships, handle supply and allow the customers to purchase our product. So, why isn't the book over yet?

The steps that we have completed so far are quite theoretical. A lot of it can be done with a good internet connection and some thinking time. Of course, there are large investments that go into high-quality market studies. But this is also small change compared to the expenses that we will incur in steps 3 and 4 of the marketing process. We, therefore, need to ask ourselves how confident we are of our answers from step 1 and step 2 before we incur the large expenses of the following steps. In college, it's alright to get a few steps in a problem wrong. You'll still get partial marks. But in the business world, you'll be millions of dollars in the red, with a broken brand image.

Okay, you're aware of the stakes, but what are we going to do about it? Strategy as a field offers a bunch of great frameworks and templates, which allow us to short-circuit large parts of the 4-step marketing process. Thousands of successful businesses have been studied, and patterns have been recognised. Those patterns have then been consolidated into frameworks. The benefit of using these strategy frameworks, in addition to the marketing process frameworks is that they help highlight red flags. Instead of just looking at a small part of one step, strategy frameworks often help us get a bird's eye view of our business plan. If small errors across our first 2 steps are derailing us, using some of these strategy frameworks right now will come in handy to figure out if we're on the right track or not.

Alas, having hyped up strategy so much, the field is just way too big for me to offer you anything useful. There are thousands of expert books on business strategy. There are hundreds of books which have studied these thousands of books and attempted to consolidate their insights. I cannot do justice in a portion of a chapter. What I will do is name some frameworks that I urge you to google. These are popular frameworks, which you must know as a manager. The list that I will provide is neither MECE nor comprehensive. But it's a starting point nonetheless.

Business Portfolio
There are a few frameworks which help you take a glance at your business portfolio. They might put into context which of your businesses/brands is sinking and which is swimming. They may even provide useful direction in terms of what to do with your current and potential businesses.

The BCG matrix is a classic 2x2 framework which helps you identify which businesses to milk and which ones to let go of (Zakon & Henderson, 1970). What's more, each of the quadrants has a pretty colourful name. And now google away.

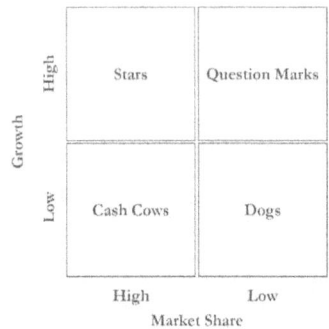

	High	Low
High (Growth)	Stars	Question Marks
Low	Cash Cows	Dogs

Market Share

The Ansoff matrix provides some direction in terms of what sort of expansion is appropriate for a brand. It looks at what markets and products a brand can play in, to provide a course of action (Ansoff, 1957). Once again, people on the internet will guide you from here.

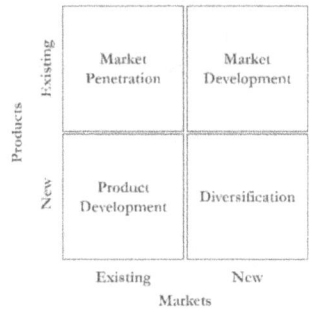

	Existing	New
Existing (Products)	Market Penetration	Market Development
New	Product Development	Diversification

Markets

Positioning

While looking at how our product is positioned in the market, or more specifically against competition, there are a few frameworks which can give us quick clues as to where we stand.

The SWOT analysis is in fact even more generic than that. This universal framework can always be thrown in to get a quick sense of where our business stands. It's the pros vs cons list of the business world. Here we list out our business' strengths, weaknesses, opportunities that we have and threats that we face. When each of these 4 is pitted against each other, we have a solid idea of what to look out for (Humphrey, 1960).

94

Strengths	Weaknesses
Opportunities	Threats

Rather than coming up with a detailed positioning plan after months of research, one can start by picking one out of 3 of Porter's generic strategies. This framework is so easy to use, and yet so visible in the real world, that it hardly requires any explanation (Porter, 1980).

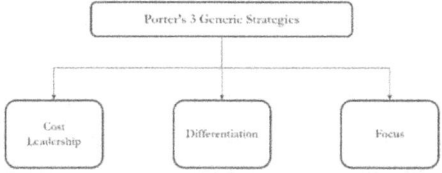

Overview

As promised, strategy frameworks can give a powerful bird's eye view. One of the first things that top-level executives might want to understand about a new business is how it's fairing in the business environment and the forces that it is up against. Porter's 5 forces summarise this like no other framework. It is once again as clear and obvious as any framework can be. We look at the 5 major forces which have the greatest impact on a business. In doing so we scan for which of these forces is the biggest threat. And we then plan for how that force can be adequately tackled (Porter M. E., 1979).

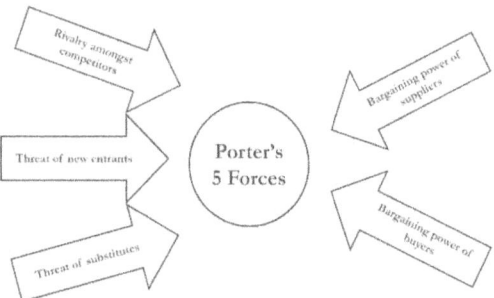

McKinsey's 7s framework is a sort of checklist for any and every business. It lists 7 factors which together make or break the business. By studying just these 7 factors, one gets as quick an overview of everything you need to know about the business and how it will do (Peters & Waterman, 1970s).

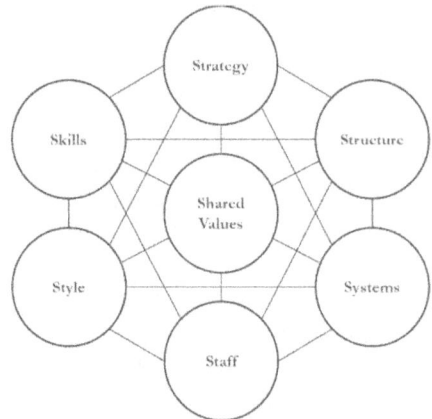

Recap

We are now done planning out all of our business success. All that we have left to do is implement our plans and make it happen. Here's how we got this far:

- You became a boss at management thinking. You can think convergently and divergently in your sleep.
- You decided to create business value to get value back from customers.
- In order to create that value, you decided to:

- o   Understand the marketplace.
- o   Segment, target & position. And then strategise for safety.
- o   Run marketing programmes.
- o   Maintain profitable relationships.
- You already completed step 1 out of 4. You built up an in-depth knowledge of the marketplace:
  - o   Asking the relevant questions 5Cs + PESTLE.
  - o   Using MIS to get answers through secondary research or the primary research process.
- You then went on to step 2 out of 4. You came up with a plan for success, built on:
  - o   A segmentation of the market.
  - o   A choice of customers to target.
  - o   A mental positioning that we plan to occupy.
  - o   And some strategies to double-check our plan.

Presumably, we will now go through steps 3 & 4 together. And then you'll have an enviable top-level understanding of the business process.

Chapter 10
4Ps: And Other Frameworks Worth Tattooing

We've done most of our planning. That doesn't mean that all of the thinking work is over. But we do know what the marketplace looks like. We also know to whom we want to sell our product. We even know how we need to make them feel, to succeed. To this end, we have even compared our plan with some templated strategies, so that we know we're on the right track. Now, we get down to the implementation. This is the part that most people would most strongly link to marketing. This is the part which comes to mind when we think about what any business does. This is perhaps the most critical of the steps in the business process. But that doesn't give us any leeway to mess up any of the other steps either.

To better understand the role of running marketing programmes in the business process, let's take an analogy. Let's say that you were single, when you entered college, and you were looking to find someone special. After all, love and placements are the 2 driving forces that might have got you to join business school. You started by scoping the marketplace. You understood your potential 'customers' needs, you know where you stand, who your competition is, who your wing people are and the general dating context on campus. Then, you got super structured and segmented the marketplace. You picked up a target (or a few). And with the help of your team of wing people, you know exactly what they're into. So, you know how you need to position yourself in their mind. You've also borrowed a few moves from friends, and compared your strategy with tried and tested strategies. It's all looking good.

Some of the things that you're going to have to do to actually court this special someone are as follows:

- Product – You need to be the kind of person that they like. Perhaps ensure that you're living an interesting life (just generally good advice). And without completely changing your personality, make some adjustments that even you believe make you a better person.
- Price – You might want to come off as more or less within their league. Maybe a bit out of their league, but not so far out that they don't even think about you. You definitely don't want to seem well below their league. And you definitely don't want to come off as high maintenance.

- Place – Being the right kind of person isn't enough. You need to be at the right places at the right times. So, you find common activities and excuses to hang out. You make sure that you text them reasonably often so that you're also on their mind. Of course, you don't want to be that stalker who is always around and is texting incessantly. There is a middle ground.

- Promotion – How you talk and present yourself matters immensely. It helps tremendously if other people are also impressed and talking about you. Some good word of mouth and an insider who pushes them to take the plunge with you can help seal the deal.

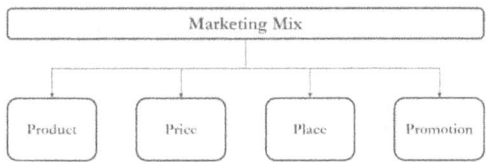

The question on your mind right now is why I'm not writing a book on how to find your soulmate and win them over. Not to worry, I'll write that book too, in good time. But right now, we have 4Ps to worry about. Much like in love, in marketing too, there are sometimes a few more than 4 levers that you could look at. Often Ps like packaging, process, people and planning are added to the mix. So, you may see frameworks with more than 4Ps in some combination. But, the 4Ps framework (often called the marketing mix) is the cornerstone of marketing. Most of the things that matter (even in the other Ps) can usually fit into these 4Ps. You just need to get used to what factors you look at within each of the Ps (Kotler, 2010).

In this chapter, we will now go through each of the Ps one by one. For each of them, we will have a look at how the lever can be used to take us one step closer to achieving our dream positioning and therefore becoming wildly successful. And as usual, we will study each P with the help of a ton of frameworks.

Product

This might come as a bit of a surprise, but one of the things that a business needs to do is develop and manufacture a product. As it turns out it's pretty hard to make money without a product. What exactly the product is, is actually a little harder to outline than might appear. Take the laptop on which I'm typing this book for example. At its core, the product is a tool for personal productivity, work, entertainment and a way to stay connected. But, searching for that on Amazon might provide disappointing results. The actual product is a Microsoft Surface Book 2 with 8GB RAM, the Intel Core i5 processor, running Windows 10 Pro. Much better results on Amazon with this search phrase. On the other hand, this is as good as Greek and Latin to your grandparents. Unless of course, your grandparents are fluent in Greek, Latin or computer technology. We could even take this a step further. The augmented product is one which can be connected to a variety of accessories, such as speakers or the surface pen. It's a product which can be used for taking notes in class or designing your portfolio, while also acting as your singular academic and professional resource. This description might make sense to someone who has looked forward to this purchase for a while. To someone else, it may seem like unnecessary hype.

Understanding the different levels at which the same product exists is useful because different customers have different levels of investment. Each of them will view your product at one of these levels, but not necessarily the others (Kotler, 2010).

That being said managers need to do more than think about the core, actual and augmented product. They need to make several difficult decisions in designing and developing the product. Those decisions begin with designing a product mix. Take Nike for example. The width of their product mix includes shoes, jerseys, shorts, bats, footballs and so on. Each of those items is a product line. The length of a product line like shoes includes running shoes, football studs, basketball shoes and so on. And the depth of a product line includes running shoes for concrete, mud, grass and so on. The first decision is what this mix looks like, which products to introduce, remove and so on. Next, one will have to fix on product attributes. Managers will decide what sort of features the product will have, what quality it should be of, the sort of design that it has etc. Branding is often an optional decision because strong brands try to retain the same sort of branding, rather than tinkering with it for each new product. Packaging and labelling of course are decisions which can help catch the customer's attention in-store. To maintain loyal customers, managers may often have to introduce some support services (Borah, 2020) (Kotler, 2010).

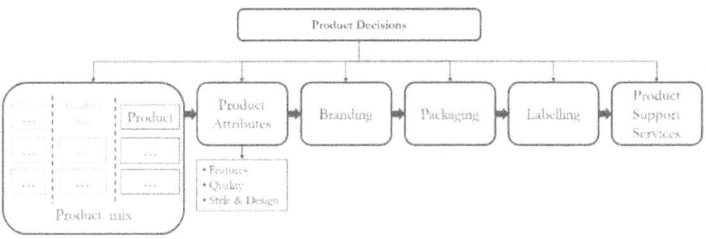

We've skimmed through each of these steps, but most of them are difficult and important decisions to make. That being said, any manager who can navigate each of these decisions successfully should have a deadly product on their hands.

Before we get too happy, thinking that we have conquered the product, as always, there are some caveats. First and foremost, when we say 'product' we mean to include services as well, not just physical products. Because we like frameworks so much, let's not just rely on intuition, but let's detail what makes a service. For one thing, services are intangible, unlike products. This is pretty obvious. Notice also that with most products we can manufacture them at one time, and the customer can buy it months later. But with services, the time of production and consumption of the service are inseparable. We have come to expect products to be super standardised, what with the efficiency of factories. But with services, I'm sure each of us has a lot of complaints about variation in quality. Products can also usually be stored and served up later. But services can't be stored, they perish immediately. None of this should come as a surprise. But keeping these 4 key differences in mind might ensure that our design of services vs products is a little more thoughtful (Amblee, 2021).

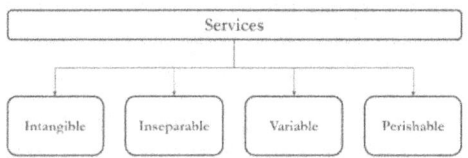

Now that we understand how to manage a mix of products or services, let's have a look at one of the biggest decisions we have to make. Sometimes products need to be taken out of the mix, and sometimes new products need to be brought in. This decision too will often match your intuition. Products have a lifecycle, much like humans do. Product development is the stage that customers don't see. Then we have introduction, where the product just begins to pick up through customer trials. Good products then begin to grow. At a certain point, most of the market knows about the product. The product has reached maturity and will sell as much as it ever will. From there on out, the world and the market will change at some point or the other, and it will be time for the product to slowly decline and then retire (Kotler, 2010).

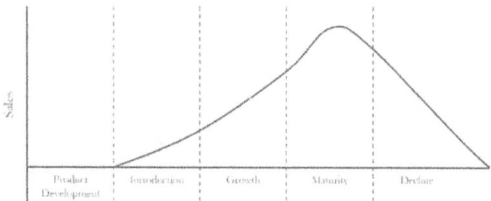

Aside from the management decisions involved with existing products, there are a few extra steps that we follow with a new product. The new product development process, of course, starts with coming up with ideas and then filtering out the crazy ones. The concepts behind selected ideas need to be further developed, to the point of coming up with a marketing strategy. This, along with the business analysis is similar to what we have seen in the first 2 steps of the marketing process. Now that we're satisfied with our plans, we need to get started with implementation, meaning developing and manufacturing the product. As a bit of a trial run, we might want to test the market. Of course, test marketing only makes sense if the cost of failure is high and the likelihood of the product being copied is low (amongst other such factors). And if we're satisfied with the results of test marketing, nothing is preventing us from launching at scale and profiting (Borah, 2020).

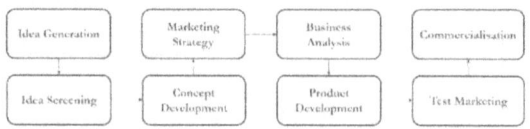

The dungeon has now entered the online gaming industry. Sure, market analysis and the STP suggested it would be a good idea. But mainly because I had promised we would in case 4.2, the dungeon had to enter the industry at some point in time or the other. They started by launching a few simple mobile games like 'angry bats', based on the bats that hide between the stairs and the walls in dorm 12. They then expanded into a range of first-person shooter games, to compete with the likes of counter strike. Their biggest success however came from their online version of dungeons and dragons. Management tried to expand the role-playing game into a very open-ended fantasy world-building game. Packed with many smaller in-game games, communities, forums and other features, dungeons and dragons has become almost a gaming platform of its own.

Unfortunately, picking up on the success of this format, various competitors, with much deeper pockets have started launching similar games and platforms, seeking to wipe the dungeon out of the market.

What's the Product?

As the first point of action, management decided to get a better sense of what their product is, what it can be, and most importantly what the core value to the customer is.

The actual product in this case seemed to be an open-ended fantasy world-building game. That was a simple enough question to answer. They speculated that the core customer value was a break from the mundane world in which users live. It was an opportunity to break free momentarily and create a more interesting world, where they had the power and capabilities that they dreamt of. It was also a community that they felt more connected to than the immediate neighbourhood in which they lived. When management analysed the augmented product, they found it to be a complex platform, loaded with features for character and persona development and customisation. It contained a range of smaller games catering to different types of gamers, all buried within a larger fantasy world-building game. Importantly, it also had a set of forums to facilitate user interaction through text, voice and video chat, discussion threads, meme pages and more.

Product Decisions

After spelling out what their product is, the dungeon's management realised that they were falling short on a few fronts. While their core customer value, still stands, they may no longer be the best at providing this value. They seemed to be falling short because other products in the market matched the same actual product. Furthermore, because newer platforms offered a wider range of games and more engagement features, dungeons and dragons was no longer the most immersive augmented product. This of course meant that dungeons and dragons was relatively falling short on their core customer value delivery.

With this in mind, management decided that it was time to relaunch dungeons and dragons. They planned to launch a new version of the game. They had a list of new ideas aimed at improving the user's experience and mimicking the best-in-class competing games. To signal the big step up in quality, they didn't refer to dungeons and dragons 2 as a game. Rather, they launched a brand-new gaming platform. As a part of the platform, the revamped game experience was better on almost every front. There was even a portion of the world map where users could revisit the old dungeons and dragons game for a nostalgic experience.

The user interface of the website was inviting and showed off the best-in-class graphics that the platform had to offer. Videos on the home page showed glimpses of hidden parts of the fantasy world that users could aim to discover through game-play, thus drawing users in. To ensure that existing subscribers didn't feel alienated, anyone with an existing dungeons and dragons account was given a heavily subsidised update. Subscribers of the new platform were also promised discounted updates if ever newer versions would be released.

Case Questions
Analyse the new product launched by the dungeon.

1. In your opinion, for such a game what is the core customer value?
2. Is this a product or a service?
3. Draw out the product decision map and categorise each of the decisions taken into the appropriate heading.

Instead of just thinking on your own, I would encourage you to participate in a case discussion on the following Reddit thread. Through case discussion, your ideas may be validated or improved upon. You would also benefit from other people's viewpoints.

Price

The problem of pricing might seem familiar. Even in case 2, we had a brief encounter with the problem. We had figured out then that there are broadly 3 approaches to pricing. We can look at our costs and set a price which gives us enough of a margin, without being unfair to the customer. We can look at what the competition is doing, and set a price in the same ballpark. Or we could identify how much customers value our product, and price it within the range that they would be willing to pay for the product. Of course, cost-based pricing provides a floor, below which prices would be unprofitable, and value-based pricing provides a ceiling, above which no one would be buying our product.

So, how do we decide which of these pricing approaches to use? In a commoditised market, where there is very little differentiation between one product and another, no market player can charge much more for their product than the costs that they incur. This is the case because no business is adding much value beyond the costs that they incur. If they tried charging more, competitors would undercut their prices. And a price war would bring the prices back down to a cost-based system. Think about the cost of money exchange. Some businesses charge a bit more for convenience. But by and large, the price that you pay is a function of the cost of exchange. Markets which are very competitive and have low switching costs are driven by competitor-based pricing. The ride-hailing market and the pre-paid telephone package market are prime examples. The margin that each player can make is a function of the margin that competition is making. If anyone is charging more than the competition, all customers will switch. This locks all businesses in the same price range. Markets which aren't either of the above tend to be freer. The belief is that businesses are adding a good amount of value to the raw materials, and producing a great product. Thus, they can charge as much as the customers value the product. Electronics are a good example of the same (Borah, 2020) (Kotler, 2010).

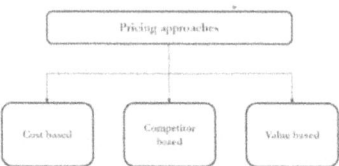

There's a very simple law that governs how value-based pricing works, and it's at the heart of microeconomics. That's right, you seemed to already know a lot about pricing and I had to sound impressive somehow. The demand curve demonstrates how price elasticity works. This fancy sentence just means that as we increase the price, fewer people are interested in buying the product. But some products are not that price elastic (price inelastic). Necessities, like water or electricity, will still have largely the same amount of demand, even when the price moves up or down. One might change the amount of frivolous usage of these utilities as a function of the price, but for the most part, it won't change. Products which are considered more of a luxury will have a big change in demand if the prices change. Theatres in Chennai, for example, are often fuller than theatres in other parts of the country. The government's price control of tickets ensures that there is a great amount of demand, and seats rarely go empty. Presumably aside from the factor of price, Chennai's theatre ticket demand shouldn't be any different from other metro cities (Chatterjee, 2020) (Kenton, Demand Curve, 2021).

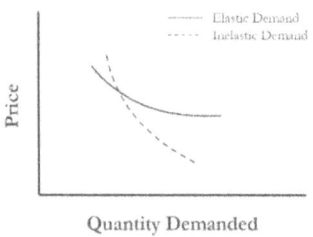

Quantity Demanded

Pricing so far seems like a pretty straightforward marketing mix dimension, right? There's just one simple framework which explains almost everything. Of course, I'm not going to let you off that easy. Pricing is actually a very complicated field, with layers upon layers of nuance. It's also constantly changing. We live in a world where payments themselves are changing. Business competition often relies on the dimension of price, and innovations come in every year. The point that I'm trying to drive home is that over and above the 3 broad approaches that we discussed, there are hundreds of different more nuanced pricing strategies.

This is once again a field to which entire categories of books are dedicated. I will not delve very deep into it. But I will provide you with a few cues which you can take to start googling. New products often use either a market skimming strategy or a market penetration strategy. Market skimming means keeping the price as high as possible to just pick up the highest-end customers. The price is then slowly brought down until the business captures just the volume of customers they desire. This strategy allows us to maximise our profits by slowly finding the point where volume multiplied by profit margin is maximum. Market penetration is a strategy where we focus on maximising volume. So, we start with as low a price as possible to attract as many customers as we can (Borah, 2020).

Pricing isn't done for each product as a standalone but is done for all products in the mix. While there are many considerations to look at, let's just look at bundling. Bundling is the process of offering multiple products together at a single price. This can be done while also offering the individual products at separate prices, or the individual products can be taken off the market. The key idea of bundling is to set prices such that customers who would purchase only one product find it meaningful to purchase a couple of them together. The price should still ensure that the business isn't making a loss on these bundles, but is in fact increasing their profit per customer (Chatterjee, 2020) (Borah, 2020).

Pricing is of course rarely a one-time affair. Prices are constantly changing. One way in which prices change is through discounts, which hope to promote purchasing. Some, more agile brands keep changing their prices up every day, or more frequently, to smartly maximise volumes and profits. Very creatively, we call this sort of dynamic pricing, 'dynamic pricing' (Kotler, 2010).

One of the toughest things to navigate as a manager is a clever competitor, who is playing around with their prices. They might drop their prices, forcing you into a corner. They might increase their prices, indicating that they have the upper hand over you. So, what should one do in the face of price cuts, or worse yet, a price war? Some common wisdom suggests, not to fight price wars, but to try to compete on quality instead. Rather than dropping prices, one could offer to match any lower price, if brought up by a customer. This ensures that you can capture higher profits whenever possible, without losing price-sensitive customers. Importantly, it signals to competition that you can take them on in a price war, and you also believe that customers see the superior value in your product. Other strategies include complex pricing which makes price comparison difficult, and the launching of new products to have different offerings in different price ranges (Borah, 2020).

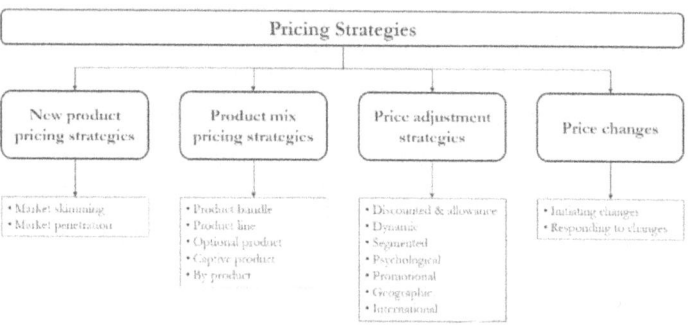

If pricing is starting to seem complicated, let's complicate it further. What if prices weren't fixed, but were different for different people. Yeah, welcome to our world of capitalism. 1st-degree price discrimination is when each individual could pay a different price. Insurance and credit often come this way. There are a bunch of different factors used to calculate your customised rate or fee. This is also the case in those fancy pay-as-you-like cafes. 2nd-degree price discrimination groups customers together, and then charges each group differently. Customers decide which segment they belong to. This is the case for a lot of products which have basic, average and premium versions. 3rd-degree price differentiation also groups customers, but the business decides which group each customer falls into. One might notice that at tourist attractions in India, Indians pay a lower price than foreigners (Borah, 2020) (Chatterjee, 2020).

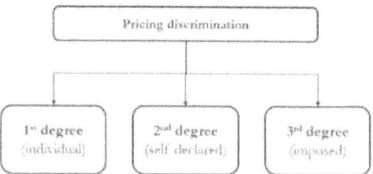

As if all of this wasn't enough of a complication, we haven't yet come up with any approach which tells us exactly what our price should be. So, let's introduce one method which gives us at least a clear numeric range for our price. The Van Westendorp pricing method suggests asking potential customers what price they think might be too cheap, too expensive, no longer a bargain and no longer expensive. Using collated responses to these 4 questions, we can graphically plot a range of prices within which we can maximise our volumes and profits. Once again, I will leave the task of explaining this in greater detail to a good samaritan on the internet (Vijayalakshmi, 2021) (Sadwick, 2020).

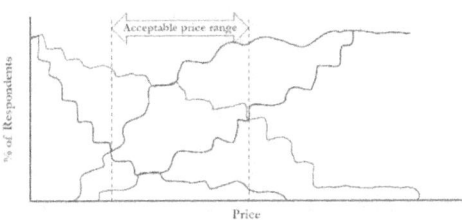

Case 6.2

As management launched the new version of dungeons and dragons, they were faced with the opportunity and task of reviewing pricing. In the original launch, they did not expect to be as successful as they were. They had originally launched the game on a CD at a fixed price, matching the price of the average PC game. Once they saw a little bit of success, they began offering a yearly subscription for a marginally more feature-rich version of the game. However, management always believed that they were charging less for this product than they needed to. With the relaunch, they wanted to put more thought behind a good pricing strategy.

Pricing Approach

Online gaming consisted of a few different tiers. Mobile gaming was largely commoditised, with new games coming out every couple of weeks, trying to grab gamers' attention. Online PC gaming, however, was a much more premium market. That being said, there was still a good amount of competition. In each genre, a handful of giants existed. Dungeons and dragons too had to compete with 2 other gaming platforms from industry giants. The average gamer couldn't afford subscriptions for each platform. Most of them selected one and remained loyal, until online reviews and twitch streamers managed to convince them to switch. Because dungeons and dragons couldn't claim to be head and shoulders above the competition, they had to use a competitor pricing approach for the yearly subscription.

On the other hand, the dungeon did benefit by having a strong portfolio of mobile games, and a stronger set of community forums. Management, therefore, decided to start charging users for each of these smaller games at a nominal price. Each of these components, in truth, suffered a small loss in users because of this. While they had loyal audiences, they were to date largely free. However, by now charging the user instead of relying on ad revenue, the net profitability of the small games and forums in the dungeon's portfolio went up. Most importantly, management was now able to start offering bundled packages to subscribers of the new dungeons and dragons platform. Because gamers across their different games (including dungeons and dragons) overlapped, many users believed they were getting a good deal. At the same time, the dungeon was now earning a higher profit margin from players who used to pay a lower amount for dungeons and dragons and used to be able to play their mobile games for free. This small price hike was thus disguised as a good bundle offer, simply because standalone prices seemed higher.

The bulk of revenues however was not generated through yearly subscriptions. The long tail of subscribers paid nothing over the yearly subscription amount. However, the most loyal and valuable customers paid large amounts for in-game purchases. Many of these purchases were limited-time offers for rare in-game artefacts. By introducing NFTs as unique in-game collectables, the dungeon was able to drive this revenue from valuable users up.

To ensure that the top, valuable players kept spending, dungeon management also invested in making sure that there was an active audience for dungeons and dragons on twitch. When top players had active audiences, they were themselves able to earn good money. Some of their collectables were then sold on a secondary market (on the dungeons and dragons platform itself) for a profit. Thus, by enabling the top 10% of players to make money from viewers, the dungeon was able to maximise its revenue from the top 10%.

Case Questions
Analyse the pricing approaches used by management.

    1.   What different pricing strategies and models have been applied here?

2. What other pricing strategies do you think might have worked in this context?

Instead of just thinking on your own, I would encourage you to participate in a case discussion on the following Reddit thread. Through case discussion, your ideas may be validated or improved upon. You would also benefit from other people's viewpoints.

Place

I would say that we're doing well on our marketing mix. We have carefully designed a product that customers are bound to love. And we have painstakingly set a price which will attract just the right set of customers. We also know how to keep adapting our product and pricing as a function of what is happening in the market. But for any of this to result in cash money, we need to reach the customer. So, we're going to ask ourselves two questions. At what place can our product meet the customer? Within this place, where do we place our product? In case you missed it, we're going to be talking about placement.

As a starting point, what sort of places (stores) can we put our product in. There are a lot of ways in which this problem can be structured. But because the retailers of the world didn't read the first section of my book, they have gone ahead and structured this problem in a whole lot of ways simultaneously. Assuming that you are a person who has money, you have probably been to a few of these store formats. So, what we're about to discuss should be quite clear. There are 5 different dimensions along which retailers try to differentiate themselves.

Based on the level of service at one end we have stores like Amazon Go, which are the extreme of self-service. On the other hand, we have a lot of grocery stores and supermarkets where we expect to be assisted by store workers in the aisles (Kotler, 2010).

One of the most visible ways of differentiating between stores is on the basis of the width, length and depth of their product line. Some supermarkets and hypermarkets try to have all of the categories, brands, products and variants, becoming the one-stop destination. Other category killers try to specialise in just one category, with a greater length and depth of assortment than you can hope to get anywhere. Others still minimise assortment across the board, but try to be conveniently available in as many locations as possible, for routine purchases (Kotler, 2010).

Shopping is a fairly frequent expense. And so, the cost matters. Thus, a bunch of stores have stood out by differentiating themselves on the basis of lower prices. And because pricing is in itself complex, multiple store formats prop up with different pricing propositions (Kotler, 2010).

From your friendly mom-and-pop store to Walmart, there are a bunch of different organisational and ownership structures which exist. On the whole, this industry is moving towards consolidation. But still, the organisational structure makes a difference to the style of shopping and the in-store culture (Kotler, 2010).

This book being written in 2022, I can't ignore the elephant in the room. A lot of our shopping is non-store based. The first thing that comes to mind is e-commerce, of course. But in the early days of the internet, we also had email-based shopping. Even before the internet, we had direct selling, telemarketing (which refuses to die) and vending machines around each corner (Kotler, 2010).

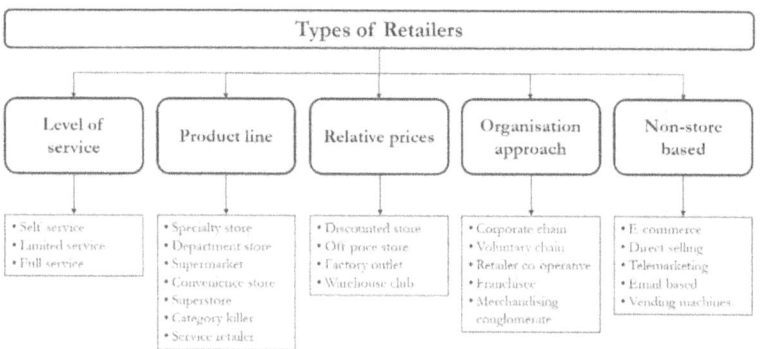

While we discussed a wide range of retail formats, these vary tremendously from one part of the world to another. Advanced economies have more centralised chains and

112

large retail spaces. Upcoming economies are skewed towards unorganised, small retail spaces in much larger numbers. Even within one country retail formats vary a great deal between urban and rural parts of the country.

As a function of whom we're trying to target and the cost of reaching this market segment, we decide on which formats of retailing make sense for us. Once we have got our foot in the door, we can't leave the retailers to put our products wherever they please. They too have a vested interest in selling as much as possible. But they can sell our competitor's product and make just as much (or more) money. So, salespeople and merchandisers from competing companies meet in-store and have a good old-fashioned shoot-out, to decide whose product goes where. I am joking of course, but the competition for the best spots can get quite heated. In theory, and in more advanced economies the retailer (or central chain) agrees on a planogram with all brands in the category. A planogram is a diagram of the shelves for the category. It details which brands get which shelves. It also specifies how many spaces will be allocated for each product and variant. Eye-level shelves, close to the counter and in other high-traffic spaces are in the highest demand. Sometimes listing fees and placement fees need to be paid to get your product into the store and into the right spots.

In the digital world too, many placement decisions need to be made. We need to take a call on whether we expect customers to find us on a website or a mobile app (or both). We need to decide whether to be present exclusively on our own site/app or other online marketplaces as well. We must choose whether we hope to be found exclusively on shopping platforms, or whether we will use intermediaries like google ads for discovery. We must choose whether we will pay to promote ourselves through ads, or whether we favour being found through organic search traffic. Once we have listed ourselves and/or promoted ourselves, we must also decide where on the site/app our product should be visible. This too is like designing a supremely more complex planogram.

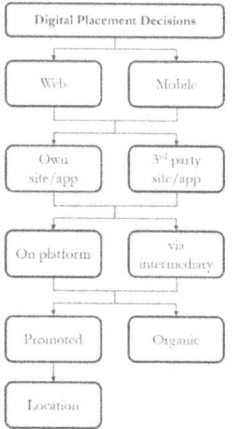

Case 6.3

With the previous release of their dungeons and dragons video game, management had followed a simple strategy. They tried to place their CD in video game stores and electronics stores, as far as possible. While updating the game and offering an annual subscription, they hoped that most users would discover this option by visiting their website or social media handles. Beyond this simple approach, management had not tried anything more deliberate the last time around.

Now that there is much more competition to worry about, management is hoping for a more thorough placement plan to be in place. Given that the relaunch of the game as a platform requires no physical or tangible purchase, to begin with, it would be difficult to use any store-based retail formats. Nevertheless, management intends to release "dungeons and dragons 2" boxes in retail outlets such as video game stores, electronics stores, book shops, music shops and children's toy stores as well. These boxes would come with a limited-edition user's guide to the fantasy world in which the game is set. The inside would also contain a QR code, which the user could scan to create an account. Management has been considering charging a little more than the annual subscription for this sort of collector's edition account and providing these users with some valuable in-game items, to begin with.

The traditional placement for the game will however be predominantly on their own website. Each of the already popular mobile game apps released by the dungeon would also feature new menus through which users could integrate their mobile

114

gaming profile with a new dungeons and dragons account. Thus, they would be able to use all of their own gaming assets to maximise the placement of the new launch.

Additionally, management believes that it would be important to also sell the same collector's edition boxes being sold in game stores online, through their website, and also through channels like Amazon.

Case Questions

Basis your understanding of the gaming industry and the dungeon's plans.

1. Which of their placement strategies do you think will drive maximum traffic?
2. What would your placement strategy be?

Instead of just thinking on your own, I would encourage you to participate in a case discussion on the following Reddit thread. Through case discussion, your ideas may be validated or improved upon. You would also benefit from other people's viewpoints.

Promotion

At long last, we have implemented so many of our plans. We have a solid product, the price is right and we've even placed it such that our target customers can easily find it. Now, all that remains is to promote our product. Finally, we can see that a small little part of marketing is the glamorous world in which Don Draper and other characters from Mad Men live. But, promotion itself is also a bit bigger than just advertising.

To put it simply, promotion is all about moving potential customers forward in their stages of readiness and prompting purchase. For this, we have to understand the stages that buyers go through. This is distinct from the stages in the purchase process that we looked at in our consumer behaviour model in chapter 8. That process related to customers who were going to purchase our product (or competitions). Here we're looking at a larger pool of potential customers, with a different objective at hand. There will of course be significant overlap between the 2 processes. But here we prefer to look at some different stages. Our potential customer is more passive. They don't yet have a big problem or an intent to buy. The first stage is awareness of our brand. From there on out maybe they pick up some knowledge of the product, from ads or friends. Still, none of this is solicited. If we succeed in building up the right brand knowledge, they might like the product. If they like it strongly enough, it might even become their preferred product in the category. Remember, they still haven't felt the need to buy such a product. But if this preference is strong enough, it might grow into a conviction that they need such a product (and they prefer our product). This should then flow to the point of purchase (Kotler, 2010).

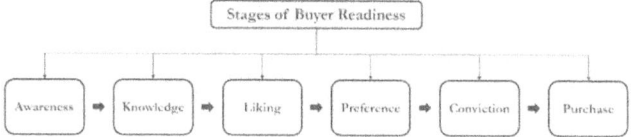

While it's nice to keep drawing out these process flowcharts, now and then managers need to also deliver results. So, how do we move customers forward to the next stage of buyer readiness? At last, we can talk about advertising.

Advertising in the real world comes down to more than creative copywriters, eureka moments and gorgeous actors. Much like most things, it fits into boring frameworks. This one uses 6Ms. First of all, we need to fix our mission and market. The choice of the market is often taken care of in step 2 of the marketing process. But it's always possible that one target customer segment is already hooked, and we only want to focus on a part of our overall target segment. So, we need to decide which market we want to focus on for this specific promotion campaign. The mission is our goal in terms of what we want to communicate, and what we hope the end result of the promotion campaign will be. Sometimes our mission is just awareness, sometimes it's an increase in sales, and it could be any other stage of buyer readiness. The amount of money that we're willing to put in determines the scale, duration and other such factors for the promotion campaign. It can tell us whether or not we can afford to get a celebrity, although that decision should ideally be taken based on our style of messaging and our intent. While designing the message, there is a range of strategies that one can use. Once again, I am not equipped to shine a light on this topic. The style of messaging execution can also vary. Some ads present scientific superiority, some use brand ambassadors, some use jingles and some paint a fantasy image. This is hardly a comprehensive list of the messaging styles that can be used (Borah, 2020) (Richard, 2006).

Unlike messaging, the choice of media is much more scientific. One can choose the ideal media vehicle, the reach that they aim to have and the frequency and timing of ads based on their mission, market and money.

Finally, all of the previous Ms would be in vain if we did not measure the outcome. We look for impact against the stated mission. And independent of whether it was a goal or not (it usually is a goal), we tend to look at the effect on sales, profits and our return on investment (Borah, 2020) (Richard, 2006).

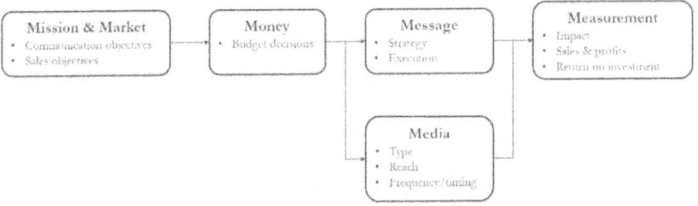

I haven't given you a simplified framework this time of the types of promotions that can be run. I have of course assumed that there isn't much value in me listing out examples such as print ads, billboards, TV, online, radio etc. But I will present you with a framework within which you can fit any and every promotion (not just advertisements). In fact, you can fit each promotion into this framework twice.

Some promotion campaigns are above the line. This means that it's a blanket promotion campaign. This is similar to the idea of undifferentiated targeting from chapter 9. Radio, TV and print ads fall under this category. Others are below the line, where they are hyper-customised for each target. This is similar to micro-marketing again, from chapter 9. Targeted emails, customised online ads, and special coupons all fall under this category. Through the line is of course a middle ground. A lot of social media marketing and events which target small groups of people in one go fall under this category (Kotler, 2010).

Aside from these 3 buckets, all promotions can also be classified as either push or pull promotions. In push-based promotion, we try to push the product toward the potential customer. This includes trade promotions (bulk discounts) and telemarketing. Pull-based promotions create demand amongst target customers so that they attempt to pull the product towards themselves. Most traditional advertising campaigns are pull-based, where customers then go to a store, asking for the product (Kotler, 2010).

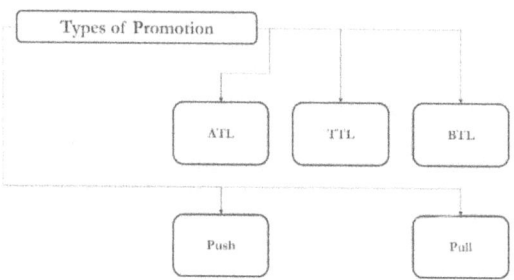

Case 6.4

Dungeon's management is fairly pleased with the new dungeons and dragons platform that they have developed. They are convinced that the price point is perfect to maximise profits and that their placement could not be any better. They now intend to spend heavily on promotion to try and win over the majority of users in their target market. Their focus market, to begin with, includes all PC gamers in the age range of 12 to 25. Management is convinced that this market not only knows about the new dungeons and dragons platform but also likes the same. They aim to shift buyers to a stage of strong preference, from where they expect that buyers will automatically shift towards purchase. Management's main objective is to drive a 1 million increase in subscribers over 3 months.

The dungeon has sufficient funds to pay for the requisite promotional campaigns. The focus media vehicles are advertisements on video streaming platforms and video ads on mobile games. Each of these redirects to limited-time free trial versions of the game.

The video advertisements produced by management are of 2 kinds. The first one shows a small portion of gameplay, with a focus on displaying the realistic graphics, the expanse of the fantasy world and how the larger game feels. This ad is targeted at any user who seems to be in the appropriate age range or is watching videos related to gaming keywords. The second advertisement is a longer ad that shows top gamers broadcasting segments of their gameplay. This ad focuses on the active community, the wide range of new cutting-edge features, and highlights the celebrity-like top players. This ad is targeted at a smaller section of users whose cookies suggest an interest in a platform like dungeons and dragons.

Case Questions

On the basis of the dungeon's promotion plan.

1. Use the 6Ms promotion framework to organise the activities planned by management.
2. Do you think this is a good plan? How would you improve upon it?
3. Classify the activities being undertaken as ATL, TTL, BTL, push and pull.

Instead of just thinking on your own, I would encourage you to participate in a case discussion on the following Reddit thread. Through case discussion, your ideas may be validated or improved upon. You would also benefit from other people's viewpoints.

Recap

We have completed the lion's share of our marketing effort. Here's how we got this far:

- We learnt about management thinking. We have extensively been using convergent thinking, structuring in particular and divergent thinking along the way.
- We got started with 4 steps of business value creation so that we can capture value from customers in return. As such, we have:
  - Understood the marketplace.

119

- Segmented and targeted the market & positioned our brand. And then we strategised for safety.
  - Run marketing programmes.
  - Planned to maintain profitable relationships.
- You already completed step 1 out of 4. You built up an in-depth knowledge of the marketplace:
  - Asking the relevant questions 5Cs + PESTLE.
  - Using MIS to get answers through secondary research or the primary research process.
- You then went on to step 2 out of 4. You came up with a plan for success, built on:
  - A segmentation of the market.
  - A choice of customers to target.
  - A mental positioning that we plan to occupy.
  - And some strategies to double-check our plan.
- Most recently you completed step 3 out of 4. You ran marketing programmes, building your marketing mix by:
  - Introducing new products and services in the product mix. You even went through a range of tough product decisions, to develop the core value, actual product and augmented product.
  - Setting the price, by carefully selecting the appropriate approach. You further worked your way through a huge number of potential pricing strategies and models and figured out which ones make sense for your product today.
  - Placing the product in the right retail formats. You then bargained with each of the retailers to get your preferred placement within their store, website and app.
  - Promoting the product well enough to move buyers through the required stages of readiness. You used 6 different Ms to ensure that your promotions would be on point, across ATL, BTL, TTL, push and pull promotions.

Now, if we can just work our way through step 4, we would have set up a sustainable and profitable business. And the money is sure to pour in.

Chapter 11
Profitable Relationships: Every Job is Sales

We've gone through almost the entire business process. First, we understood the marketplace. Then we divided up the market, decided whom to target and came up with our positioning and strategy to target them. Recently, we designed a marketing mix and implemented it. Through those 3 steps, our business should be running. After all, most recently, we developed a product, priced it, placed it in stores and promoted it to customers. They should therefore be able to start going and buying it.

Step 4 isn't going to change any of the first 3 steps. It's just going to ensure that the marketing mix that we have implemented, remains implemented, and smoothly so. There are several people and variables involved in executing the marketing mix, and therefore running a business. Anyone who has worked on a group project realises that people are unreliable, and are just the worst. Anyone who has had a bit of a social life realises that people can be pretty amazing too. Step 4 of our business process is about managing relationships with people, to make sure that everyone involved is helping our cause, not harming it.

But isn't section 5 supposed to be about soft skills, communication and managing human resources? It absolutely is. Since you seem to clearly remember our diagram from chapter 2, sections 1, 3, 4 and 5 all fit into the business process that we are going through in this section. Much like management thinking, even financial administration, operations management and human resource management are required across each of the steps of the business process. Step 4 in particular requires a lot of people skills and management of people outside of our organisation. We will go into much more depth on how to manage different groups of people in section 5.

For now, we shall aim to understand who outside the organisation we need to manage. We shall also look at how these collaborators are organised. Clearly, our focus in this chapter is largely on our collaborators and our customers, not so much on the people within our own company.

We need these collaborators for many tasks. Let's imagine for a minute that we're contesting an election for some secretary position on campus. In terms of building profitable relationships, this is uncannily similar to running a business. Now, what sort of tasks might we need collaborators for? We would need some people to help promote our name, and spread the word. We would need people to help get us the right information and put us in touch with useful contacts. Maybe we would need help with financing as well. And of course, we need someone right by our side to help with all sorts of negotiations that we can't handle on our own. Finally, we need a lot of help with day-to-day operations, the printing of flyers and distribution of pamphlets and whatever else wins elections. I hope that analogy wasn't too veiled. But businesses usually have collaborators who help with things such as promotion, information, contacts, financing, negotiation, operations and distribution. There are probably a bunch of other things that collaborators help with as well, but this is a list to get us started.

Rather than looking at each of these complex spaces one by one, we shall focus on just one space, which should give us a rough idea of how to manage these relationships. We shall look at a generic supply chain, with a focus on the sales and distribution side. The organisation structures involved here will be used in different permutations and combinations in any of the other spaces. Thus, this should be a useful illustration.

Supply Chain

The supply chain is in many ways the circulatory system of a business. It's what keeps resources pouring into the organisation, and finished goods coming out of it. Without this, we wouldn't be in business. There's an innumerable set of theories, formulae and well-thought-out ideas on how to optimise one's supply chain. But we shall leave that for another section. For the time being, let's just have a look at what the basic parts of a supply chain are.

We start with suppliers, to stay true to the supply chain name. These are third parties from whom we get the raw materials that go into our manufactured products. These supplies need to be transported towards our factories. Because that sounds straightforward, let's give it a fancy name like inbound logistics. At the factory, if all goes according to plan, some manufacturing will happen. Try as we might, it's difficult to get supply to match demand perfectly every day. So, it helps to have warehouses to store produced goods until we can ship them to customers. From the warehouses, more often than not, we first transport our goods to resellers (distributors, wholesalers, retailers etc), rather than straight to the consumer. This entire process of getting the manufactured goods from our factories to resellers is called outbound logistics. And then finally the resellers are usually the ones who sell our products to the end customer. That simple 5 step process, with hundreds of other layers and nuances buried in it, is the supply chain.

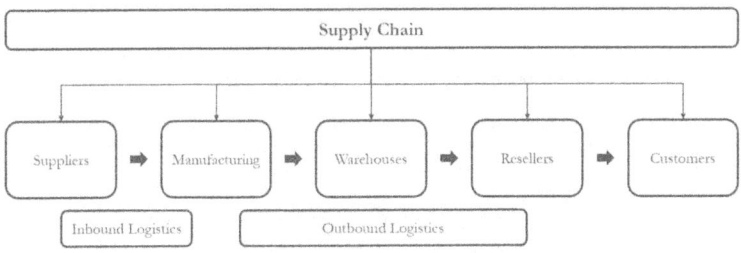

Sales

All of the steps in the supply chain warrant a deeper look. But for the time being, let's take a deeper look at sales, the portion between warehouses, resellers and customers. You might think that I'm choosing to dive deeper into sales because of the 2 years of experience that I have had in sales-related roles. You would not be entirely wrong. But there are a couple of other good reasons why too:

- We will take a deeper look at operations management in section 4. That will help us understand parts of the steps before sales.
- Understanding how to manage distribution and sales is useful for understanding how to manage any team of people (there are a lot of them). So, this is a good starting point in any case.
- Understanding how to sell is useful independent of what you think your job is. Every job at the end of the day is sales. At the very least you're trying to sell to someone above you what a good job you have done.
- A lot of what we have looked at in terms of promotion (the last part of our first 3 steps) was pull-driven. Push-based promotion is also an integral part of business and is best seen through sales. Thus, sales is a natural closing point for our marketing lens of the business process.

Hopefully, you are convinced that taking a deeper look at sales is useful for us. If not, my book, my rules, let's move on. Let's start by structuring sales. This structure might look familiar. Sales can be to other businesses. It might be directly to end consumers. Or it might be somewhat in between, to end consumers, but through other businesses.

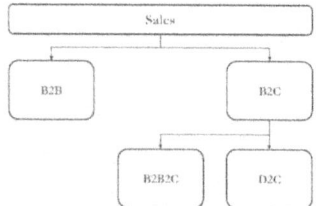

There are of course differences between each of these styles of sales. And each of them comes with a host of implications for the sales team, the business model and the business on the whole. But once again, I'm going to leave the task of detailing these sales models to the gurus of the internet. While you google this, you might also be interested in looking at sales models like multi-level marketing. It's another type of B2C selling model, which we won't have time to cover here. But it's always useful to be able to differentiate between an innocent multi-level marketing model and a pyramid scheme. Spoiler alert, one of them will get you sent to jail.

What is worth taking a deeper look at is how sales teams may be organised in any of the above sales approaches. Independent of whom we're selling to, it's common to organise sales teams based on at least 1 of 4 dimensions. Geography is an obvious approach since teams in different regions are going to have to work a little independently and differently. A lot of companies have so many products, that the approach used to sell some are very different from the others. Even if the selling approach is the same, you just may need to pay enough attention to each product. In either case, it makes sense to have different sets of salespeople for each set of products. Sales itself can be broken into smaller tasks, such as approaching new clients, collecting orders from existing clients and servicing other needs of existing clients. Thus, salespeople could also be organised based on the sales function that they work on. Importantly, some customers are big and others are small. Some are in very different industries from others. Whatever the differences may be, it often makes sense to give one salesperson clients of a similar kind and thus organises salespeople on the basis of the types of customers that they cater to. Most sales organisation structures are a complex combination of the above 4 types of sales organisation structures (Chandwani, 2022) (Kotler, 2010).

124

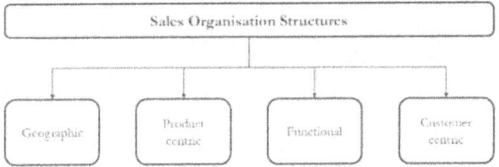

With that, we have a basic understanding of 3 different sales models and 4 organisational structures (which can be used in combination). This just gives us an idea of how to arrange our salespeople and whom they need to sell to. After having completed 10 chapters, you should have guessed, I'm going to add a few more steps in between. There is a whole process of sales management that we have to go through, what with us being managers and everything. The first step is designing our sales organisational structure and strategy. We have already seen how we can go about doing that. Next, we will need to recruit some salespeople, otherwise, our structure is pretty pointless. Those recruits will probably have to be trained both initially and every now and then. Because no one wants to work voluntarily, we will need to have some supervision in place, either by bosses or through automation. We won't get into recruitment, training and supervision in too much detail just now. Those are topics that we will leave for section 5 and human resource management. But our sales management process isn't done just yet. We also need to evaluate whether the sales performance has been up to the mark or not. And based on the evaluation, we ought to compensate the salespeople accordingly (Chandwani, 2022) (Kotler, 2010).

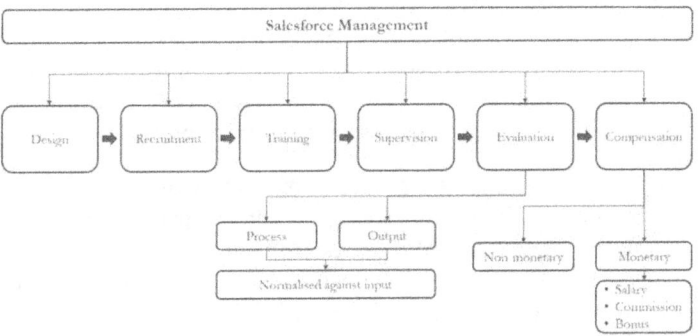

While evaluation and compensation can also be dealt with in section 5, let's have a small look at it right now. Evaluation and compensation are what drive sales in a lot of ways. Without the right compensation, it's not a job that a lot of people would take up. But with the right compensation, it's a gold mine for the right salespeople. When we evaluate salespeople, we want to look at not just their output (sales and revenues), but also the process. This is important because we don't want salespeople to just make money from one large client, but to pay attention to the whole range of customers, and sustainably grow their portfolio over time. When we look at just output metrics and not sales process metrics, salespeople will begin to take shortcuts for short-term growth, which comes at the cost of sustainable long-term performance. Just this alone might upset a lot of salespeople. Each salesperson has a different territory and different customers. It's important to normalise sales goals as a function of the kind of customers catered to, the amount of sales promotion available and so on. This ensures that the goals that each salesperson is evaluated against are truly fair and achievable (Chandwani, 2022).

Once our salespeople have been evaluated, they would fairly expect compensation. Compensation comes in many forms. There is of course a salary, which anyone with a job could expect. Salespeople often earn a commission based on how much they sell. This is a powerful tool to get them to sell more. This must be used carefully so that salespeople with smaller clients aren't at a disadvantage. Salespeople also look forward to bonuses upon achieving daily, weekly, monthly, quarterly and annual targets set for them by the company. But that's not all. Much like any employee who is performing well, salespeople will often expect to be compensated non-monetarily, in the form of promotions, recognition and awards. This can be just as big, or even more powerful a motivator when used effectively (Chandwani, 2022).

With those few ideas, we have a decent sense of how sales management works. Which is great, if all we ever had to do was manage salespeople. Like I said earlier, every job is a sales job in some sense or the other. Let's, therefore, look at a traditional salesperson's role, and understand their selling process.

The details of the selling process vary tremendously from one industry to another. It even varies from one sales channel to another. For that matter, 2 great salespeople could also follow fairly distinct sales processes. What we shall try to highlight here are some of the broad steps that could be used by any salesperson. To begin with, someone or the other must prospect new customers. This may be a different function, carried out by a different salesperson, or might be done by the same salesperson who will carry out other tasks. Next, one must prepare for a day of sales meetings. This includes having an idea of which clients one will meet, what their challenges, wants and needs are, and what you hope to get out of the sales meeting and how. With that plan in hand, you approach the client. This doesn't just mean walking into their office. It could include a specific way in which you should greet them. Often, it includes activities such as checking the stock of your product that they have available before you begin a conversation. Once the conversation has begun, there is usually some sort of a script that the company has provided the salespeople. This script might not contain all of the words to be used. But it does provide keywords which are more effective and guardrails which prevent the conversation from going in directions which are hard to recover from. To this end, an important part of the script is objection handling. This requires the salesperson to be able to listen to common complaints or concerns and assure the customer of success using whatever tools the business may have provided them with. This could range from stories of the product's effectiveness to guarantees that the company will buy the product back if it doesn't work as expected. At the end of the sales pitch, it is also important to summarise the sale, end on a positive note, and remember to follow up on any loose ends, to maintain a strong customer relationship (Kotler, 2010).

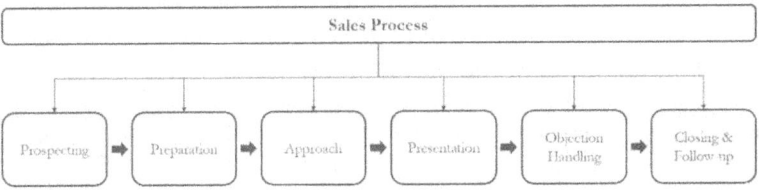

Once again, I would like to reiterate that we have gone through the steps of the supply chain, sales management and the sales process very quickly. Each of these has a few dozen frameworks and nuances which fit into each step. These are all spaces which also have tons of expert books written on them. This is of course just an overview of how they work.

Case 7

Dungeon's management has decided to get into the sanitiser business because pretty much everyone was entering it once the pandemic began. There are already a few established brands in the business, and so management knows that they need a tremendous marketing effort to make a dent in this market. But because we've done such a great job of going through the first 3 steps of the business process, let's imagine that customers are lining up to get some of that dungeon sanitiser.

Management now needs to ensure that their distribution is as extensive as possible to make the most of the marketing efforts. To this end, they decide to sell B2B, D2C and B2B2C. Management has created a special online portal where corporate houses including hotel chains, hospitals and any other business can place orders directly with the company. On the dungeon's website, customers can place orders for ultra-premium sanitisers. Because of the high price point and limited demand for this variant, management has decided to offer D2C fast shipping for these valuable customers.

The bulk of the business comes from the B2B2C model. Management has set up a complete sales team with regional headquarters in Delhi, Kolkata, Bangalore and Mumbai. Each of the 4 regional offices has a large team working out of it. Each regional team consists of smaller e-commerce, modern trade and traditional trade teams. The e-commerce team usually consisted of a handful of account managers, who would coordinate stock levels, new product listings and the like with regional warehouse managers of large e-commerce companies. The modern trade teams were marginally larger. They too consisted of key account managers. Each account manager handled a few modern trade accounts such as big bazaars, D-marts etc. These account managers had marginally more control over promotional pricing, planogram negotiations and new product listings. The traditional trade team was by far the largest. Each state in the region had an area sales manager. Each area sales manager had a few territory sales managers reporting to them. The territory sales managers were each responsible for handling a few distributors. The distributors, however, were not owned and operated by the dungeon. They were third parties on a contract. These distributors usually also ran operations for other companies, but none in the same industry.

Each distributor employed an accounts manager, delivery personnel and a few salespeople and merchandisers. As per the contract with each distributor, a fixed number of salespeople were allotted to the dungeon's sanitiser. These salespeople would visit retail outlets allotted to them as per a fixed schedule daily. At each retail outlet, they would check stock levels and start a conversation with the shopkeeper. Throughout the conversation, the salespeople would punch in the shop's sales order for the dungeon's sanitiser on their hand-held tablets. Salespeople were incentivised to drive orders across different variants of the sanitiser and different pack sizes while trying to maximise the sales order. Salespeople were also evaluated on the basis of the frequency of outlet visits, the frequency of successful orders from each outlet and the number of outlets visited in a day.

Often territory sales managers would accompany a salesperson on their market visit. In this process, they would monitor performance, and provide guidance and coaching on how they could improve. At each distributor, the accounts manager constantly received orders from all salespeople. Every morning, a list of the previous day's orders was printed and given to the delivery personnel. The delivery personnel loaded their trucks with the correspondingly required stock and visited outlets to deliver the same, with a 1-day turnaround time. As and when stock levels at the distributor began to dip, it was the territory sales manager's responsibility to place a replenishment order, which would arrive from the dungeon's closest warehouse within 3 days.

In addition to this, on a different schedule, merchandisers employed by the distributor would visit the larger outlets on their fixed schedule. In each outlet, the merchandiser's role was to rearrange products (with the shopkeeper's permission) so that they were visible and easy for customers to spot.

Salespeople, delivery personnel and merchandisers received their fixed salaries from the distributor. Territory sales managers and upwards received their fixed salaries from the dungeon. In addition to this, all sales-related employees (and salespeople) received bonuses for achieving centrally allotted goals each month. There were multiple goals and bonuses based on overall sales volumes, the spread of products being sold, the number of outlets being reached and the frequency of orders being placed. Each sales employee received unique targets, which were generated by a machine learning algorithm. This algorithm factored in the outlets that the employee was responsible for, the historic sales and seasonality factors, to provide goals which would steadily improve performance, without being out of reach.

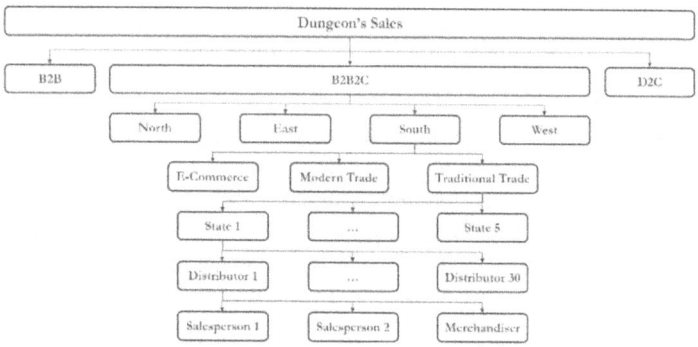

Case Questions

From your analysis of the dungeon's sales structure.

1. Which types of sales organisation structures have been employed at each level of the hierarchy?
2. What types of compensation have been used?
3. How can the compensation system be further improved?

Instead of just thinking on your own, I would encourage you to participate in a case discussion on the following Reddit thread. Through case discussion, your ideas may be validated or improved upon. You would also benefit from other people's viewpoints.

Recap

That's all there is to it. You now not only think like a manager, but you're also well versed with the entire business process.

- You learnt about management thinking. We have extensively been using convergent thinking, structuring in particular and divergent thinking along the way.
- We got started with 4 steps of business value creation so that we can capture value from customers in return. As such, we have:
  - Understood the marketplace.
  - Segmented and targeted the market & positioned our brand. And then we strategised for safety.
  - Run marketing programmes.
  - Maintained profitable relationships.
- You already completed step 1 out of 4. You built up an in-depth knowledge of the marketplace:
  - Asking the relevant questions 5Cs + PESTLE.
  - Using MIS to get answers through secondary research or the primary research process.
- You then went on to step 2 out of 4. You came up with a plan for success, built on:
  - A segmentation of the market.
  - A choice of customer to target.
  - A mental positioning that we plan to occupy.
  - And some strategies to double-check our plan.
- You ran marketing programmes, building your marketing mix by:
  - Introducing new products and making tough product decisions.
  - Setting the price, using a wide range of pricing strategies and models.
  - Placing the product in the right shops and the right places in the right shops.
  - Promoting the product with the 6Ms and moving buyers through the required stages of readiness.
- You finally completed the last step of the business process by:
  - Setting up a smooth supply chain.
  - Organising your sales team well, and ensuring that the selling process runs perfectly.

In case you are interested in learning more about marketing, I don't know of any starting point better than Philip Kotler's textbook on the principles of marketing. I have made my own personal notes on the textbook and made it available on the internet, in case it is of use to anyone else.

With that sort of an overview, you are ready to be the CEO of any business. But as it turns out, they don't offer CEO positions as a starting role. So, we might have to take a deeper look at each of these steps, so that we're capable of running smaller operations as well. Next, we will try to understand the language of business, so that we can diagnose any business and understand how each of the business steps that we just learnt about is performing. We will get our hands dirty by picking up some hard skills and some soft skills so that we can manage both operations and people, in any department. And before we're ready to join or start a business of our own, we'll learn a little about studying the outside world, to use it to our advantage.

Section III

Finance

Welcome to the section on Finance. Amongst the people who have made it this far, I can imagine that we might have two types of outlooks. One set of people might be wondering whether we really have to get into finance and numbers and all of that. The other might be wondering why we took so long to nicely frame things with some math and money. The second question should have been addressed in section 2. While finance is a great lens to look at a business through, I chose marketing as the primary business lens, because it seems rather intuitive and people-friendly to me.

Now, to answer the first question, even within a marketing lens, a basic financial frame of reference is indispensable. The entire business process that we have looked at so far has been built on subjective frameworks. These are easy to understand, but as a standalone are not perfectly reliable to act on. To make difficult decisions as a manager we often need clear decision criteria. Our end goals relate to money, and a lot of what we can measure at any point in a business is related to money. Thus, our decision criteria in most management situations are financial metrics.

This is often why investment bankers can analyse financial statements and take a call on how businesses are likely to perform. This is also why the finance team in a company usually works closely with all other departments. Especially on large projects, major investments and big decisions. That being said, a manager can't decide to be financially illiterate just because they don't intend to work in finance themselves. They too need to understand for themselves what the company's financial reports communicate. They too need to be able to identify the most useful financial metrics for their contexts and use them for decision-making, without expecting assistance from finance teams. More advanced financial analysis beyond that is always a bonus, but might not always be necessary.

So, just those basics of financial literacy are what we're hoping to cover. To this end, we will try to develop an understanding of the 3 key financial reports, how they're made, what they contain and how to read them. Over and above this, we shall look at some common and useful financial metrics, understand how to calculate them, and what they tell us.

In the first chapter, we shall have a look at the basic financial reporting process. We will develop an understanding of what the 3 key financial reports are and get used to some basic terminology that we will be using. Along with this, there are a few critical accounting principles that we shall get comfortable with as well.

In the second chapter, we shall deal with balance sheets and understand how to construct them. In the third chapter, we shall similarly look at income statements, also known as P&Ls (Profit and Loss statements). In the fourth chapter, we shall deal with cash flow statements.

In chapter five, we will deal with a range of more complicated business scenarios. From payments not happening at the time of purchase to requiring support financing our business to paying tax to the government, running a business can get complicated. To make sure that our financial reports remain correct and reflect the actual state of the business through these complexities, we shall understand how each of the 3 financial reports detail these complexities.

In chapter six, we shall take a pause and use a detailed case to illustrate everything that we have seen in the last few chapters. A picture's worth a thousand words, so 3 financial reports should be worth a few million.

In chapter seven, we will look beyond the basic process, and figure out what to make out of each of the reports. We will detail out the most common financial metrics and understand how to calculate them, as well as what to make of the calculated results.

In chapter eight, we'll take a small peek at the rest of the world of finance. We are only touching the tip of the accounting iceberg in this section. Therefore, I will provide some clues as to what else financial experts know, so that the readers who are so inclined can pick up more advanced books on those topics.

Chapter 12
Ground Rules: Accounting Dictionary

At this stage, we already have an understanding of the business process. We are also equipped with the brilliance of management thinking. However, financial reports still baffle us. As such, we might not have a great read on how our business is performing. Of course, we all know that more profits are better. But as managers, I think we can hold ourselves to higher standards.

So, in this chapter, let's try to understand the basic process underlying financial reporting. We shall get used to some concepts, terminology and key principles. With all of that knowledge, we still won't be able to make heads or tails of any financial reports. But we would at least have a decent idea of what we don't know in the world of financial reporting. And that's a pretty good start.

Financial reporting process

We're introducing a new concept. This far into the book, I'm sure you know the drill. We're going to ask some of the big question words. First, let's understand why we have a financial reporting process. If we don't get past this question, you can skip ahead to the next section of the book. As a part of the overall business process, we had to make decisions at many points in time. The objective of those decisions was usually the business's profitability. Other constraints or factors to consider would usually have revolved around the amount of money (resources) available. And if we have information about similar past decisions that would certainly be useful in making these decisions. All of this information, and even more guiding information is available in financial reports. This is the primary reason why managers, even those outside the finance department expect the company to produce timely and accurate financial reports. These reports are so useful that while deciding whether to invest in a company or even join a company (the ultimate investment) most people review the company's financials first. Also, the government kind of mandates that legitimate companies publish their accounts annually. So, avoiding jail time or your business being shut down is a pretty good reason to go through the financial reporting process.

Now that you have decided that you don't want to fight the government on this, let's understand what the financial reporting process is. The financial reporting process goes along each and every step of the business process. It doesn't just fit into a certain step but runs in parallel the entire time. Each of our decisions in the business process results in some sort(s) of company transactions. A lot of these transactions may involve operational activities. Others may involve investments in infrastructure, equipment or other financial holdings. And some may involve financing the business. As soon as any of these transactions happen, we must record them. For this purpose, we have two systems, one is called the journal, and the other is called the ledger. But more on that later. Now and then, we transfer the cumulative effect of transactions in the journal and ledger towards our financial reports. You can think of the journal and ledger as a rough notebook and the financial reports as the clean outcome that we submit in the end. The 3 key financial reports are a balance sheet, an income statement (P&L) and a cash flow statement. We'll discuss what each of them is later. For now, they're smart, rich people's words which you can throw around while reading a newspaper in your suit, in the morning. The contents of these financial reports are used in some permutations and combinations by managers to make even more decisions as a part of the business process. Of course, this isn't the only information that managers use (remember MIS from chapter 8), but it's a part of it.

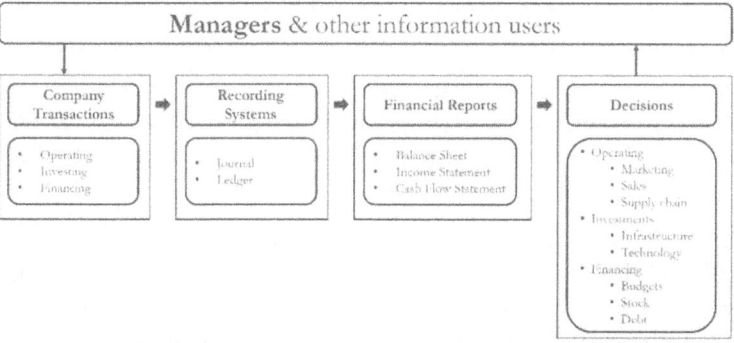

Now that we know why we go through the financial reporting process, and what it is, let's get into when and where it happens, as well as who manages it. The accounting team, often consisting of a set of expert auditors is largely responsible for tracking all of the company's transactions, ensuring everything is in order and preparing the financial reports. The finance team around this accounting team is responsible for ensuring that the financial reports are not only correct but also look good (for the business). To this end, they can't fudge the financials but have to nudge all other departments to make the sort of decisions which will keep the company's financial reports on track. They're sort of like google maps, giving you directions and also beeping if you begin to cross speed limits, go down one-ways and so on. While google maps doesn't know how to drive (ignore self-driving cars), it understands the maps and is able to provide this direction. So, that's who makes financial reports, and where they come from to influence us as managers (Gandhi, 2020) (Anthony, Hawkins, & Merchant, 2017).

As for when the financial reporting process happens, the only fair answer is always. As soon as any company transaction happens, you can imagine that one transaction going through the reporting process, at least up to the journal and ledger. In companies of scale, thousands of transactions, if not millions, happen on a daily basis. Because we need someone to be willing to take on the job of an auditor, we can't update our financial reports daily. Every company may have its own process. But you can imagine that most financial reports are produced at the end of each month.

How financial reports are produced is the bulk of this section, so we shall get into that slowly.

Useful concepts

Now that we understand the flow of the financial reporting process, let's quickly equip ourselves with some fun facts. With these few tidbits of information, it'll be much easier for us to understand each part of the process without breaking the flow.

Balance Sheet

The balance sheet gives us an idea of the company's financial situation at a specific point in time. It details the company's assets on the left side. On the right, it details the company's liabilities and the owner's equity. It's called a balance sheet because it provides the balances of these 3 categories. But it's interesting to note that the left side and right side always balance, that is the sum of amounts must always be equal on each side of the balance sheet.

Income Statement

The income statement is a snapshot of the company's operating performance for a given period of time. The period of time chosen is called the accounting period. The income statement starts with the company's revenue (the top line) for the accounting period. The next few lines detail various expenses, including operating expenses, taxes, interest etc. After subtracting the relevant expenses, we see the net profit (the bottom line) for the accounting period.

Cash Flow Statement

The cash flow statement details the sources and the uses of cash throughout a given period of time called the accounting period. This statement gives us an idea of how the company is running its operations, rather than just the end result. The cash flow statement is organised into the 3 different types of transactions, operating, investing and financing.

Basics

There are a few basic concepts which explain each of the rules that we will follow while accounting. Most of these concepts should seem obvious. In some way or form, we have either been using these ideas already or have taken them for granted (Gandhi, 2020) (Anthony, Hawkins, & Merchant, 2017).

- Entity – The business must be treated as an entity of its own. When we maintain these accounts, they are accounts of the business, not of any of the people involved in the business.

- Money Measurement – In financial accounting, we will deal only with those things which can be expressed in monetary terms. If it cannot be expressed in such a fashion, it will not be included.

- Going Concern – We expect that our business entity will continue existing in the future unless we are explicitly aware of any information to the contrary.

- Consistency – The accounting practices that we use in one period should be carried forward into the next. The same sort of situation must be treated uniformly. Unless there is a good reason to make a change, such as error correction or a government-mandated change.

- Materiality – We must include everything significant in the context of the financial statements. This allows us the benefit of not having to count and track the most insignificant of transactions. However, this principle should be used carefully, it should not be an excuse to cut corners.

- Dual Aspect – There are two aspects to every transaction. For example, we spend money and buy some asset. In doing this, we must record the money that we have reduced, but also the amount of this asset that we have increased.

- Historical Cost – Some of the things the business owns will have a changing market price. This may go up or down. The value at which we must record these items is their historical cost, that is the cost at which the business acquired them.

- Realisation – While recording how much money we have, we must be conservative. While selling goods/services, we must first manufacture the goods/services and deliver them to the customer. We must then either collect the payment or an agreement that the customer will pay us. Only after all this is done will we 'realise' this earning in our books.

- Matching – When expenses are incurred to earn revenue, we must recognise this expense in the same period that we realise the associated revenue. However, if the expense is not related directly to the product earning the revenue, it should be recognised in the period when the expense is incurred.

- Conservatism – We should be conservative about our earnings and expenditure. Thus, we record earnings only once we are very confident that the money will be in hand. However, we should record expenses as soon as there is a decent likelihood that the expense will be incurred. The threshold for recording expenses is lower than that for recording earnings.

Accounting principles

So far, this chapter should be a walk in the park. We have understood the overall financial reporting process. We have understood at a top level what the 3 key financial reports are, and we have also listed some obvious, but important concepts to keep in mind. In furtherance to those basic concepts, we must now outline a few more significant accounting principles (Anthony, Hawkins, & Merchant, 2017).

- Relevance – Any information used in the reporting process must be relevant to the reports being made and the users of the reports. The criteria for relevance are how useful the information is, and the timeliness of the information. All relevant information must be used.

- Reliability – Any information used in the reporting process must be objective and verifiable. If it doesn't fit either of these criteria, the correctness and therefore usefulness of all of our reports come into question. Any information which is not reliable should not be used. When there is a trade-off between relevance and reliability, reliability matters more than relevance.

At this stage, this pile-up of concepts and principles might be starting to get a bit vague. They probably individually seem like ideas with some merit. But you might be wondering how you're supposed to remember all of this, and how any of these translate into clear and definite accounting rules. Not to worry, these are simply the principles which underly very specific accounting rules. Whenever an accounting rule confuses you, one or a combination of these principles will probably provide a justification and an explanation. You definitely don't need to worry about memorising any of these, because there are innumerable resources which detail accounting rules for any situation that you might find yourself in. You might want to look up the generally accepted accounting principles (GAAP) and the international financial reporting standards (IFRS).

With that assurance in hand, let's touch upon the most important principle of accounting that we will be using (Gandhi, 2020).

- Accrual accounting – The style of accounting that we will be using is concerned with the economic impacts of the given accounting period. This means that when a transaction has some sort of impact on our business within the accounting period, but cash doesn't change hands in the accounting period, we will still record this transaction in our financial reports. If in the current accounting period the cash changes hands, but the economic impact was in a prior (or later) accounting period, we will only record that transaction in our financial reports in the accounting period when the economic impact was felt, not in this accounting period when cash changed hands.

Recap

We've made great strides towards managing a business. Some of the highlights of our journey so far have been:

- Management thinking. We have extensively been using convergent thinking, structuring in particular and divergent thinking along the way.
- We got started with 4 steps of business value creation so that we can capture value from customers in return. We are capable of understanding

the marketplace, positioning our brand to target the right customers, designing an effective market mix and managing relevant relationships along the way.

- Just now, we decided to understand the language of finance, in order to empower our decision making. To this end, we have understood:
    - o The financial reporting process.
    - o What the 3 key financial reports are.
    - o Basic concepts and accounting principles.

With this basic understanding in hand, we're ready to get our hands dirty with some financial reports. The hope is that over the course of the next few chapters, we will be able to get a read on any business situation. In combination with our existing understanding of the business process and ability to think like a manager, no situation will be able to stump us.

Chapter 13
The Financial Situation: Balancing the Business

After having understood that some objective math needs to be brought into the business process, I have vaguely described a long list of terms, ideas, reports and principles. It is therefore time for me to put my money where my mouth is, and bring some objectivity into our business management. There is no better way to take an objective view of a business than by looking at the balance sheet. We have already noted that it captures the company's financial situation at a point in time.

In this chapter, we shall deconstruct that idea of a financial situation. We shall have a look at the different elements that one needs to look at to understand the financial situation. We shall through practice understand how to read and construct a balance sheet.

Accounting equation

At the centre of financial reporting is the idea that money can't appear out of nowhere. This is a good principle to ensure that money laundering doesn't happen. While some of us as managers would like to make the impossible happen, the accounting equation helps keep us grounded.

On the one hand, it says that it's important to list out all of the assets that we have. This is all of the money that we have and the other things that the company has ownership over, which are in some way or another like money (in that they have value).

Now we need to prove, that none of this appeared out of nowhere. So, on the other hand, we list out liabilities. Liabilities are debts that we need to pay, bills that we need to pay and so on. This attributes the value of some of our assets to these sources from which we have derived value. But the liabilities alone don't cover all of the assets that we own. If they did, our entire company would belong to banks and suppliers. Owner's equity captures the money put in by the shareholders and the profits generated (and retained).

Thus, the accounting equation simply states that the sum of everything on the left side of the balance sheet (assets) is equal to the sum of everything on the right side of the balance sheet (liabilities and owner's equity) (Gandhi, 2020) (Anthony, Hawkins, & Merchant, 2017).

$$\text{Assets} = \text{Liabilities} + \text{Owner's Equity}$$

Assets

Assets are half of the balance sheet. So, as a starting point, let's make sure that we know exactly what counts as an asset. Broadly an asset is something that the company owns which has some value. But there are a few conditions which they usually fulfil (Anthony, Hawkins, & Merchant, 2017).

- Assets must have arisen from some transaction or event. In this transaction, the asset must have been acquired at some sort of measurable cost.
- Assets must be owned and controlled by the business.
- Assets should produce (or be expected to produce) some future benefit to the business.

The above rules probably don't come as a surprise, but they help us filter out some fringe cases, which we can't treat as assets.

Assets are a pretty large class of items. After all, they take up half of the balance sheet. It, therefore, makes sense to break them down into smaller classes of assets. On the balance sheet, assets are usually divided into (Gandhi, 2020):

- Current Assets – These are assets which are either cash or will be converted into cash or consumed within the next year or so. The time frame of a year is taken from the date of preparing the balance sheet and is usually a rough guideline.
- Non-Current Assets – These assets are all the other assets. Those which will not be consumed or converted into cash for at least a year. Essentially, they're assets with a longer life.

The current assets are at the top of the balance sheet, with the non-current assets below them. Another divide exists, which is less visible. Some assets are tangible. Most of them are. But some assets may also be intangible, such as fees which have been paid. These fees also have some value which may be derived over some time, and so match the definition of an asset, but are intangible (Gandhi, 2020).

Liabilities

Equipped with an understanding of what an asset is, we should now understand the flipside, a liability. A liability in a financial sense is pretty similar to our understanding of the word in a more general sense. It's something that weighs our business down because it needs to be taken care of in some way or another. More properly, a liability must fulfil the following criteria (Anthony, Hawkins, & Merchant, 2017):

- They arise from past transactions.
- In the present, they take the form of an obligation or debt to an external party.
- They involve future economic payment or sacrifice of some sort.

Just like assets, liabilities too can be classified as current or non-current. The same distinction applies, where current liabilities are those which must be resolved (paid off) within 12 months. Whereas non-current liabilities may remain liabilities for more than a year (Gandhi, 2020).

Understandably the distinction of tangible vs intangible is moot in the case of a liability since all liabilities are essentially intangible.

Owner's Equity

To understand the flipside of our assets completely, we need to understand what all owner's equity is comprised of. Unlike assets and liabilities, this header doesn't contain a long list of possible items.

One way of mapping out what remains on the right side of the balance sheet is by looking at how any of our assets might have come into existence. To begin with, the owners put some capital in. This must have been traded in for some assets. The business might have then taken on some debt, and purchased supplies, with bills which are due. All of this also must have led to the creation of some assets. In addition to this, the company probably created some value and sold goods or services at a profit. The net profit from this activity must have been added to the assets available. We already know that liabilities are captured within the debt and bills which are due. Owner's equity is therefore made up predominantly of common stock and retained earnings.

Recap

In our attempt to understand how to manage a business, we have thus far learnt:

- Management thinking. We have extensively been using convergent thinking, structuring in particular and divergent thinking along the way.
- We got started with 4 steps of business value creation so that we can capture value from customers in return. We are capable of understanding the marketplace, positioning our brand to target the right customers, designing an effective market mix and managing relevant relationships along the way.
- To understand the language of finance, we have understood:
  - The financial reporting process.
  - What the 3 key financial reports are.
  - Basic concepts and accounting principles.
- Next, we understood the components of the balance sheet (assets, liabilities and owner's equity). We also understood how they relate to each other.

With this start, we shall now aim to understand the remaining financial reports.

Chapter 14
Profits & Losses: The Bottom Line

Hopefully, after the last chapter, you are a little more convinced that financial reports can provide some objective information about where a business stands. Still, just a balance sheet can be fairly misleading. Surely, the volume of assets held by a company is also a reflection of the industry, the age of the company and a range of other factors. It doesn't necessarily give us a great idea of how it's performing.

When we want to find out how a business has been performing, what are some of the first questions that come to mind? If we quickly browse through some of the vocabulary that we picked up by watching shark tank, we might wonder what a company's revenue was, and what its profits were. These 2 questions alone contain the key to a lot of questions about a business' performance.

In this chapter, we will have a look at how we can use the income statement (P&L) to understand how any business is performing. From the top line to the bottom line, we will have a look at all the useful performance indicators this financial statement has to offer.

Reading an income statement

A balance sheet can be looked at as a financial statement with some stuff on the left and some on the right, without a fixed direction that you have to read it in. An income statement, on the other hand, reads rather sensibly from top to bottom. Of course, more seasoned financial experts may have their reasons for jumping between specific line items of interest to them. But I am not such an expert, so I shall go through it from top to bottom.

Right at the top, we start with the revenue that the company has made in the accounting period. This may be called out as revenue, sales or earnings. All of them mean the cumulative amount that any sort of customer has paid the business. It is important to keep in mind that even if we have made a sale, and haven't yet received the money, but are owed, this would be counted under the revenue amount mentioned here. This is understandably called the top line (Anthony, Hawkins, & Merchant, 2017).

We have already presented all of the money which has come into our business. Almost everything else in the income statement will now represent various expenses, the money which is going out of the business. Immediately below the top line, we show the cost of goods sold (COGS). This usually includes the cost of manufacturing, shipping and promoting the goods. The rule to remember is that if the cost can be directly attributed to and apportioned amongst each product, then it can be included in the cost of goods sold. This is a useful rule to use because COGS can be thought of as the cost involved in selling 1 item, multiplied by the number of items which were sold. In more complex cases, where the company produces more than one type of product, you can imagine doing this for one product at a time, and then adding it up (Gandhi, 2020).

The most sensible thing to do on the next line is to subtract the COGS from the sales amount. The sales amount minus the cost of sales is what we call the gross margin. This number on its own is a good indicator of the profitability of the product or service that we are selling. Keep in mind that this isn't the business' profitability, because the business incurs a lot of other expenses. Gross margin is a simple and clear name, so we decide to complicate things a bit by creating another number called EBITDA. Aside from being a heavy-sounding word that can be used in menacing questions, EBITDA is a very informative name for this intermediate profit margin. It stands for earnings before interest, taxes, depreciation and amortisation. The EBITDA is the gross margin minus operating expenses (not depreciation and amortisation). That gives us a pretty good idea of what all expenses we have not yet subtracted from our earnings (Anthony, Hawkins, & Merchant, 2017).

The next bucket of expenses that we subtract from the gross margin is called the operating expenses. As the name suggests, these are the expenses involved in operating the business. To be clear, these are not the costs which can be directly apportioned to each product, but all of the other expenses involved in running the entire business. This usually includes things like salaries, utility bills and rent payments. Most obviously this must include the cost of depreciation of any equipment and the amortised cost of licenses. This means that when we buy machinery of any kind, we never include that entire cost in a given year's income statement. Rather, we estimate how long the machinery will last, and use some method of apportioning the cost of the machine across each of these years. Each of these operating costs is usually listed as separate line items under a larger header of operating expenses (Anthony, Hawkins, & Merchant, 2017).

Once again, it makes sense to then sum up what earnings remain. So, we subtract the operating expenses from the gross margin. What remains is the operating income. This name also makes sense because this is the income that is left with the business once they are done with their business operations. This is also called EBIT. The origin of this name should be rather obvious at this point. We have subtracted depreciation and amortisation from the business' earnings. But the operating income is still the earnings before interest and tax expenses are subtracted (Anthony, Hawkins, & Merchant, 2017).

Understandably then, we will have lines where we show the expenses paid as interest, debt repayment and tax payment. We may even have a line in between to show the income before taxes. But we will necessarily have the last few lines of the income statement showing the expenses for interest and taxes.

Finally, after subtracting these last expenses from the operating income, what we are left with is the net income. This may be the profit or the loss that the company has made. And appropriately, it is called the bottom line. However, there may even be lines below this, declaring how much dividend will be paid out to shareholders, and then what the retained earnings are after that. But more on that later (Gandhi, 2020).

Recap

In our attempt to understand how to manage a business, we have thus far learnt:

- Management thinking. We have extensively been using convergent thinking, structuring in particular and divergent thinking along the way.
- We got started with 4 steps of business value creation so that we can capture value from customers in return. We are capable of understanding the marketplace, positioning our brand to target the right customers, designing an effective market mix and managing relevant relationships along the way.
- To understand the language of finance, we have understood:
  - The financial reporting process.
  - What the 3 key financial reports are.
  - Basic concepts and accounting principles.

149

- Next, we understood the components of the balance sheet (assets, liabilities and owner's equity). We also understood how they relate to each other.
- Then, we understood how to read an income statement, with an emphasis on what intermediate numbers are of significance, and what some of the important line items are.

Now, there is one more major financial report for us to understand, to begin piecing the puzzle together.

Chapter 15
Cash Flow: Follow the Money

We have now not only understood the general financial reporting process but also how to read and use 2 of the important financial reports. The remaining report is the cash flow statement. Having read the business' balance sheet and income statement, the hope is that we have an understanding of the business' financial situation and operational performance. Despite this, there are 2 good reasons to read through a cash flow statement as well:

1. The cash flow statement helps develop a clearer understanding of what the business is trying to do today. The balance sheet may provide a picture of a financial situation which is more impacted by the past few years than it is by recent activities. The income statement does provide a picture of business performance in recent times, but not necessarily an idea of what the company is investing in, where they're making their money and where they're trying to put it today.

2. Accrual accounting is a double-edged sword. One of the key principles that we have built our accounting practices on ensures that we don't discount transactions just because we don't have the money in hand today. This is good because it means that we can remain forward-looking, and not be too focused on just cash in hand. On the other hand, what if all the big bets the business is taking are just about to fall apart. The income statement would still look brilliant. The balance sheet might tell us that we are expecting more from the future than we have today. But only the cash flow statement will raise a clear red flag that we are not bringing any liquid cash into the company.

And so, hopefully, I have made a case for understanding how the cash flow statement is constructed and how we can read it.

Direct vs indirect

In each of the 2 previous financial statements, we saw what the key components were, and we had a good idea of where to get the information. But it wouldn't be fun if all 3 reports were as straightforward. So, there are 2 ways in which we can construct a cash flow statement.

The direct method of making a cash flow statement is as the name suggests, direct. We look at each of the operating, investing and financing activities, and we tally them up.

The indirect method is more convoluted but actually simpler, much like this statement. In the indirect method, we borrow all values from the income statement and the balance sheet. In a fixed order we go through the financial statements that have already been prepared, to arrive at the same values for operating, investing and financing activities.

The direct and indirect methods will both arrive at the same overall values for each of the 3 buckets. However, in the indirect method, we can easily rely on the other 2 financial reports. The specific line items that we will see in cash flow statements from each of the methods are distinct, but provide similar information in totality.

It is important to note that the income statement that we use should be of the exact same accounting period as the cash flow statement. We will use 2 balance sheets, one each as on the starting and ending dates of the relevant accounting period. We will usually look at changes between these 2 balance sheets, rather than any item in just one of them.

Operating activities

The first section of the cash flow statement aims to show how much cash the company has generated (or lost) through its operations. This section, like each of the other 2 will list out some positive and some negative cash flows, and add them up to arrive at a total operating cash flow.

As a starting point, we pick up the profit before tax from the income statement. This is after all the earnings that the company has left, after all of the operating expenses have been paid for. Thus, this should definitely feature in our operating cash flow.

However, it is important to keep in mind that in this financial report we are focused on actual cash in hand, and not just earnings accrued in the accounting period. This number is different from the net income. So, we shall now go about complicating the whole matter by adding and subtracting various amounts.

First, we shall add back the operating expenses (from the income statement) which are associated with either depreciation or amortisation. This is done because these amounts were reduced from the accounting period's earnings (not present in net

152

income). However, these expenses were not paid for in cash (in this accounting period). And so, by adding this amount back, we are one step closer to the actual cash amount the company has from operations in this accounting period (Anthony, Hawkins, & Merchant, 2017).

Using similar logic, we shall subtract the change in accounts receivable. Note that any increase in accounts receivable would have already been factored in as earnings (within the net income), without the business having received this cash. Similarly, any drop in accounts receivable means cash which has been received, without having been factored into the net income. Similarly, any increase in accounts payable must be added, and any decrease in accounts payable must be subtracted. This is because this change in accounts payable would have already been factored in as an expense, but cash has not yet left the business (Anthony, Hawkins, & Merchant, 2017).

It would probably be useful to pause at this point and review an income statement. Look at each of the expenses and ask yourself which of the expenses used up cash in the current accounting period. Similarly, look at the earnings, and ask how much of the earnings resulted in actual cash in this accounting period. This is the fundamental question from which each of the line items in the operating cash flow arise.

Before we conclude, there are a few more similar additions and subtractions to the operating cash flow. Changes in inventory and changes in prepaid expenses must be subtracted. Changes in other payables must be added. The logic for all of these changes is the same. In case it is not clear from the examples of accounts receivable and accounts payable, perhaps the case later in this section will help detail the same out (Anthony, Hawkins, & Merchant, 2017).

Investing activities

Whether one uses the direct or the indirect method the cash flow from investing activities is almost identical. As the name might suggest, within this section, we aim to capture the cash generated from or spent on investments. Most of these investments are expected to be those which are related to the business, such as machinery, land etc. However, these investments may also include diversifications such as investments in stocks and bonds.

The cash flow from investing activities is straightforward. Any non-current assets which have been purchased are considered an investment. The amount spent on these non-current assets in cash is to be reduced from the investing cash flow. If instead a liability (debt or payable) is created to purchase such non-current assets, only the portion of such liabilities which is paid off in that accounting period should be subtracted from the investing cash flow (Gandhi, 2020).

Similarly, when any non-current assets are sold, the amount received for these assets in cash should be added to the investing cash flow. If assets such as receivables are created on the sale, only the amount of cash received for such receivables in the current accounting period should be added (Anthony, Hawkins, & Merchant, 2017).

Both of the above types of investing cash flows can easily be discovered by looking at the 2 relevant balance sheets. However, there are a few more items of interest in the indirect method. Certain income lines from the top line of the income statement may be relevant to investing activities. In case any of the sources of earning are sales of machinery, sales of stock (of other companies), interest or dividend paid (from stocks of other companies) these are investment returns. These items would then be subtracted from the operating cash flow, as they were included in the net income, and they should be added to the investing cash flow. As such the cash from these investments would be counted only once, but under the investing cash flow, not under operating cash flow (Anthony, Hawkins, & Merchant, 2017).

Financing activities

From the point of view of making the cash flow statement, the financing activities section is just about as simple as the investing activities section. There are of course a different set of line items. These have to do with how the business gets cash from investors and lenders, as well as how it returns that cash.

Therefore, we add the amount of cash which was raised by issuing debt or stock. We of course must also subtract the amount of cash that was used to pay back debt or retire stock. In addition to these items which are visible in the balance sheets, we can also see the amount of dividend which was paid out, in the income statement. This cash amount must also be subtracted.

After having gone through each of the 3 sections of the cash flow statement, it may at first seem like a long list of cash-generating or sinking activities which have been classified. That can seem confusing at first. But that's also exactly what it is, and it is useful to read through. It tells the reader exactly where the business' money is going and coming from. As a standalone, it seems complicated, because of all of the added rules. But in combination with the balance sheet and income statement, it helps highlight any red flags. If operating, investing or financing cash flows don't seem as strong as the income statement and balance sheets make them look, there might be an issue. If this trend continues for multiple accounting periods, most likely the business isn't living up to its promise.

Recap

In our attempt to understand how to manage a business, we have thus far learnt:

- Management thinking. We have extensively been using convergent thinking, structuring in particular and divergent thinking along the way.
- We got started with 4 steps of business value creation so that we can capture value from customers in return. We are capable of understanding the marketplace, positioning our brand to target the right customers, designing an effective market mix and managing relevant relationships along the way.
- To understand the language of finance, we have understood:
    - o The financial reporting process.
    - o What the 3 key financial reports are.
    - o Basic concepts and accounting principles.
- Next, we understood the components of the balance sheet (assets, liabilities and owner's equity). We also understood how they relate to each other.
- Then, we understood how to read an income statement, with an emphasis on what intermediate numbers are of significance, and what some of the important line items are.
- Finally, we learnt how to construct and read a cash flow statement, to supplement our understanding of the business' performance. We understood each of the 3 types of transactions and how to map out the specific cash flows within each bucket, through the direct or indirect method.

Now that we have understood the overall financial reporting process and each of the key financial reports, we must learn about some more nuances that make financial reporting so challenging, and also important.

Chapter 16
Reporting Caveats: Living in a Complex World

We are now a good few chapters into the finance section. What we have to show for it is an understanding of the overall financial reporting process. We should be confident of reading the financial situation from a balance sheet, understanding company performance from an income statement and deducing how cash is being generated and used through the cash flow statement.

But because accountants keep themselves awfully busy, there are a bunch of other caveats involved in the reporting process, as well as in reading these reports. As promised, I will not take you through all of the nitty-gritty of accounting. But, let's have a look at a few important caveats to get a flavour of the complexity involved.

Accounting records

While discussing the financial reporting process, we had said that there are intermediate accounting records. The purpose that they serve is to make it easy to keep track of the thousands of transactions which take place. From these intermediate records, we will later build up the three financial reports that matter.

As a starting point, we need to make at least one entry for each transaction which takes place. As it turns out, we make 2 entries for each transaction which takes place. These entries go straight into an accounting device called the journal. And each transaction gets noted down as one debit entry and one credit entry, each of the same amount as the transaction.

There are 5 classes of financial elements which can be credited or debited in each of these entries. These should seem familiar. They are assets, liabilities, owner's equity, sales and expenses. These are of course the classes of elements which exist across the balance sheet and income statement. Thus, each of the line items in each of these 2 financial statements may get credited or debited in each transaction. Further, the meaning of credit and debit varies from one class of financial item to the other (Anthony, Hawkins, & Merchant, 2017).

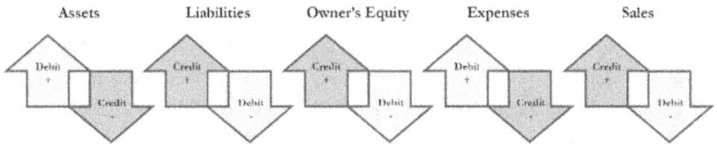

	Assets	Liabilities	Owner's Equity	Expenses	Sales
	Debit +	Credit +	Credit +	Debit +	Credit +
	Credit −	Debit −	Debit −	Credit −	Debit −

The journal is a long and difficult device to use. And so, each accounting transaction is transferred from the journal to a ledger. The ledger is made up of a series of t-accounts. Each financial statement item (across the balance sheet and income statement) has its own t-account. A t-account is so called, because it looks like a 'T', with a line dividing the left and right. The left side is the debit side, with all of the debiting entries and the right side is the credit side. The benefit of maintaining t-accounts is that a long list of journal entries gets reduced to a smaller, fixed number of t-accounts, where the debit and credit sides are totalled. Depending on the type of financial item, either the debit - credit value or the credit - debit value is then taken as the value to be entered into the balance sheet or income statement. That's pretty much how the journal and ledger help translate thousands of transactions into 3 financial reports (Gandhi, 2020).

Revenues vs receivables

One of the side effects of living in a complex world is that our revenue isn't always what we expect it to be, even after all of the sales are done and the bills are counted. There are a large number of intertwined factors to be blamed for this complexity. Accrual accounting is one of the culprits. Remember we said that we would start recording revenue when we have earned it, even if we don't have cash in hand. More precisely, we recognise revenue when revenue has been earned and realised. As you can imagine, this sort of a convoluted definition creates a bunch of headaches. Nonetheless, each of these convolutions has been inserted for good reason, so, let's understand them.

Revenue is said to be earned if the customer agreed to buy the goods/services, the company delivered the goods/services and pretty much did everything that they're obligated to. Revenue is said to be realised if either the money is in hand, or if the business reasonably expects to be paid. As you can guess, having a reasonable idea of whether or not we will get paid is a big part of the problem. Let's, therefore, understand just how big a gap lies between our revenues and receivables, as a business.

One such gap is a situation where cash is received in hand first, but the revenue is earned only at a later stage. This may be the case if a customer makes a down-payment or purchases a voucher and hasn't yet redeemed it. In this case, the revenue has been realised, but it hasn't yet been earned. Therefore, despite having the cash in hand, we can't yet recognise this as a sale. In this fringe case, the received cash is recorded in the balance sheet, and a liability called deferred revenue is also recorded on the balance sheet. However, the income statement won't reflect the transaction yet. Once the service has been delivered, or the voucher has been redeemed, the deferred revenue liability will be reduced and the income statement can now reflect this as a sale (Gandhi, 2020).

On the other hand, sometimes we don't receive cash on completion of a transaction. In those situations, we update our accounts receivables, rather than cash, on the balance sheet. However, we usually treat accounts receivable as sales, because we reasonably expect to receive the corresponding cash. Of course, sometimes we don't receive that cash, for a number of reasons. If you have ever lent cash to a friend, I'm sure you can come up with a few reasons why accounts receivable might not be received. And so, we create a provision for not receiving some amount of our accounts receivable. This is usually called bad debt. We create a 'contra account' on the balance sheet called allowance for bad debt. This means that we have negative values here, which effectively helps us reduce the amount in accounts receivable. As for the amount that we put under allowance for bad debt, several methods can be used here, but for the most part, we rely on past experience. Because each transaction needs to have 2 entries, we also make a corresponding entry on the owner's equity side, called bad debt expense. As and when the accounts are received, or written off, we square off these amounts appropriately. This may seem unnecessarily complex, but this is the cost of accrual accounting. And accrual accounting helps ensure that the financial reports are truly reflective of the business, and not just technically correct (Gandhi, 2020).

Alright, now we understand what happens if we get cash before delivering the service and what happens when we deliver service before receiving cash. But what happens if a good is sold, the cash is received and then the customer wants to return the product? Yeah, maybe you'll think about the accountant the next time you ask to return your product to Amazon. This case too is treated similarly to the case of bad debts. Rather than creating a contra account, we record an allowance for sales returns on the liabilities side. Once again, as and when refunds are actually realised (or not) these numbers are adjusted as is the cash amount on the balance sheet (Gandhi, 2020).

In case you haven't yet accepted that what happens with sales and marketing creates havoc in accounting, let's take another example. Sometimes we run promotions where customers stand a chance to get a discount on their bills. In the context of trade-related businesses, customers keep placing orders throughout the month. At the end of the month, they settle their bill. In these contexts, the business would like to incentivise customers to pay earlier, rather than later. So, customers are often offered a small discount for clearing their bills before a certain date. In these contexts, we don't know how much cash to expect exactly. This too is fairly similar to the case of returned goods. We record the accounts receivable, to begin with, but also create an allowance for cash discounts (liability) along with corresponding estimated cash discounts (owner's equity). Of course, when we realise the actual cash discount, these numbers are adjusted, as are the accounts receivable and cash on the balance sheet (Gandhi, 2020).

Inventories

Clearly, in this chapter, I'm trying to convince you that however straightforward we had made financial reporting look, it's not. Before you ask why I need to go into this much detail to convince you of these complexities, the answer is that these complexities are important, not just daunting, but useful. Now that I have claimed that these nuances are important, I'll have to justify why inventories are important to keep track of. Obviously, we don't want to lose track of our inventory. But more to the point, keeping strict accounting records of our inventory helps us understand the cost of manufacturing the goods that we sell. This is a much more important number, because it informs us of our profitability, and therefore impacts a range of decisions.

So, how could something as simple as keeping track of inventory get complicated? For one, there are a lot of different types of inventory, for just one type of product. Aside from the multiple components that might be a part of it, inventory goes through many different stages, from raw materials to work-in-progress to finished goods to the all-important cost of goods sold. Each of the first 3 stages of inventory must be included on the balance sheet, at any point in time. Further, while inventory moves forward from one stage to another there are other costs which need to be added to their value, such as the cost of labour and the depreciation cost of machines used in their production. The final value of the finished goods which have been sold will be used as the cost of goods sold.

Alright, so there are a few more steps involved than expected, but tracking inventory is still pretty straightforward, right? Now, what if the cost of our raw materials or some other intermediate manufacturing step changes halfway through. Then we would have a mix of inventory at each step, which has a different cost associated with it. The all-important question is what cost should we record for the goods being sold? There are generally a few simple approaches which can be taken to solve this question. Usually, we track our inventory using either the first-in-first-out (FIFO) or last-in-first-out (LIFO) method. Even if neither of these approaches reflects the exact approach we use to manage our inventory, we must pick one which reflects our approach in principle. This is then the approach that we use while maintaining our financial records. The finished goods which are used to map the cost of goods sold will also follow the LIFO or FIFO or any other method that the business selects (Gandhi, 2020).

Now that we have realised that different items of the same inventory can have different values, let's complicate matters further. What if some inventory gets damaged. If you run a business long enough, this is bound to happen. Independent of whether damaged inventory is sold for a lower price or must be completely thrown away, we start by calculating the overall cost that we will end up with as a result of the reduced revenue, cost of disposal etc. We then identify all the items of the inventory across which we plan on distributing this added cost. As and when these items are sold, this overall cost is added as a part of the cost of goods sold for these items. Further, the overall value of that inventory is reduced by the same amount. Thus, both our balance sheet and income statement will reflect this lost value.

Assets

Having already brought complexity to our accounting process, revenue and inventory, perhaps the next step should be our assets. Let's look at how the value of assets are set and how they change.

To begin with, the value of an asset is set as the cost involved in acquiring the asset. This idea is further extended to include the costs of making the asset useful for us. So, if a machine is purchased, transported to a facility and then installed, the costs involved in all three of these activities contribute to the value of the asset.

At some stage, we might find that our assets need to be improved in some way or form. The machine might need to be repaired, or maybe new appendages are added to bring in new functionality. Each of these is usually treated differently. In the case of a routine repair or maintenance, the cost of repair is treated as an expense. However, in the case of an improvement of the asset, we treat the money spent as an increase in the asset's value. The key distinction is that one is an expense to ensure normal functioning, whereas the other is money spent to improve the asset in some way (Gandhi, 2020).

Of course, we have the concept of depreciation of assets. The non-current assets that a company invests in ideally ought to last the company a few years. And because it's hard to digest that a ton of money was spent on any such expensive asset in one year, we choose to spread out these costs over a couple of years. Usually, we use the straight-line method of depreciation, where we identify how long the asset will last us, and how much it'll be worth when we sell it. Each year we deduct a corresponding amount of its asset value from the balance sheet and add it to the depreciation expense on the income statement.

And finally, we have the situation where we're done with an asset. This doesn't necessarily mean that the asset itself is useless and needs to be scrapped. Sometimes these assets are still sold to someone else. Whatever money we make from this of course is added to our income statement as another source of sales.

Liabilities

Once we have complicated assets, it makes sense to complicate liabilities. The standard liability is pretty straightforward. There is some amount of value that we expect to owe in the future, and so it is recorded as a liability.

As opposed to a standard debt, where the interest rate increases the amount which is due each period, businesses sometimes have the option of taking a zero-coupon loan. This is one where the payment amount and the fixed period for payment are pre-decided. In this case, the effective interest rate is calculated. This effective interest rate is used to increase the liability amount each year.

Let's now take a big step forward and look at the term liability in the most common sense of the word. We think of a liability as something which may weigh us down or cause problems. With most of these figurative liabilities, we don't know for a fact whether they will impair our performance. Just that there is a chance. In business, and especially in financial reporting, it is difficult to work with these probabilities. For example, what if a water shortage is predicted for the next year, and it may impact our business' ability to carry out operations? How do we register the financial impact of such a prediction? There are a couple of guiding principles in this context. The first principle is that we record a liability or reduce the value of an asset when there is a reasonable probability associated with whatever predicted event of concern. The second principle is that we do any of this only when we can calculate with some confidence the effect and the impact of said event. When both of these conditions are met, it makes sense to record a liability and be prepared for the worst-case scenario (Gandhi, 2020).

All of the details

What on earth was the point of this chapter, you might ask. After all, in the first 4 chapters of this section, we had a look at a relatively simple model of financial reporting. At this stage, there are so many added caveats and nuances that one might not be sure of whether they understand financial reporting anymore. What's more, this chapter isn't anywhere close to touching the tip of the iceberg.

The point was to sensitise one to the fact that the overall guiding principles of financial reporting are in fact fairly sensible. But there are a lot of nuances involved. Luckily, some accountants have trained to be experts in dealing with these nuances. Our role as managers is to develop a strong enough understanding of the reports to be able to use them, even if we don't prepare them ourselves. To this end, it is always helpful to understand in more and more detail what goes on in the background.

You could look at my more intricate notes on financial reporting rules on my website, in case you are interested in getting better equipped with the dirty details.

Recap

In our attempt to understand how to manage a business, we have thus far learnt:

- Management thinking. We have extensively been using convergent thinking, structuring in particular and divergent thinking along the way.

- We got started with 4 steps of business value creation so that we can capture value from customers in return. We are capable of understanding the marketplace, positioning our brand to target the right customers, designing an effective market mix and managing relevant relationships along the way.

- To understand the language of finance, we have understood:
  - o The financial reporting process.
  - o What the 3 key financial reports are.
  - o Basic concepts and accounting principles.

- Next, we understood the components of the balance sheet (assets, liabilities and owner's equity). We also understood how they relate to each other.

- Then, we understood how to read an income statement, with an emphasis on what intermediate numbers are of significance, and what some of the important line items are.

- Finally, we learnt how to construct and read a cash flow statement, to supplement our understanding of the business' performance. We understood each of the 3 types of transactions and how to map out the specific cash flows within each bucket, through the direct or indirect method.

- Over and above that we learnt about a few nuances which make financial reporting more complicated, powerful and useful.

Next up, we'll have a look at an example, to make sure that we practically understand everything that we have covered.

Chapter 17
Case Example: A Picture's Worth a Thousand Words

In the previous section on strategy, marketing and frameworks, we had a case in just about every chapter. I hope that that helped make each concept easier to grasp. It might have even helped slow things down so that you have time to get a grip on the large volume of content. In this section so far, we have had 5 content-rich chapters, and I haven't given you a single case to illustrate and explain the jargon that I have thrown at you.

So, now I'll fix that. We'll go through one mega case, to illustrate everything that we have covered so far in the finance section. The reason that we have had to hold out till now, is that it is difficult, and not as useful to look at smaller cases in isolation. It is of course possible. And during your MBA you will likely solve cases targeted at just one financial report in isolation. But keep in mind that these obscure details. In the real world, anything which is happening to the business impacts all 3 important financial reports all at once.

Now that we have an understanding of how each of the reports works, let's put pen to paper and try to create all of them in one shot. The case provided below is inspired by my financial reporting and analysis end term case at IIM-A. A lot of the twists and turns have been borrowed and appropriately changed. I have chosen to adapt and simplify this case, rather than write a case from scratch, because I believe that it was a wonderful illustration of all the accounting principles that we learnt put together. Before proceeding, I think it only fair to express my gratitude to Prof. Shailesh Gandhi and the other faculty involved in designing the course, and this case in particular.

Case 8 (Gandhi, 2020)

Within a few months of entering campus, most students search for laundry services for some reason or the other. Some students would rather have their formals ironed professionally. Others find it easier to outsource the entire process from washing to ironing. A few laundromats and the dhobis that represent them are reliable. Some are less so. It's the less reliable services which have a way of spending more time on reaching students, taking their money and then slacking off on the service. In this setting, the dungeon's management decided that they should launch a service to improve this market. Further, they reasoned that they're well equipped enough to launch not only within the IIM-A campus but across several campuses across the country.

While analysing what would go into the business, it was identified that a lot of detergents and other advanced cleaning chemicals would be a large part of their operating purchases. They were hoping to also leverage a few tax rebates and subsidies since the government was offering such schemes to further new businesses. These schemes and subsidies would come in handy because the dungeon's new venture was likely to require a large amount of capital. This capital might be employed for industrial equipment like washing machines, ironing machines and the setup of large spaces for the same. Over and above this a large number of employees and transport vehicles would be required to make this a realistic venture.

Given the complexities involved, only 2 members of the dungeon were particularly interested in being a part of this sensible but less than glamorous business. Let's call the individuals involved dungeon master A and dungeon master B.

While there are a lot of things that need to be paid attention to while starting a new business, our focus here is financial reporting, so that we can study how the business is doing. To this end, the dungeon's management has decided to prepare a balance sheet for the financial year 2020-21, when they were completing the initial setup of their laundry service. They have decided to then prepare all 3 major financial reports for the financial year 2021-22 when they began operations.

Initial Setup

Getting a company started can be a little tricky. It involves registration, financing, locating a space to work, designing and building it, recruiting talent, purchasing machines, putting in place supplier relationships, attracting customers and much more. But because both dungeon masters are experts in running and operating businesses, they have a grasp on what to do. They began by registering their new company under the name "Dungeon Laundry Private Limited". They expected that this name might be misleading and attract the wrong sort of clientele and possibly government raids. But what is a business without a little bit of whimsy?

No revenue was generated before 31st March 2021. However, there were other important pre-commencement transactions which were completed:

- They issued 5,00,000 shares of the company, to denote its entire ownership. Each share was sold at a face value of INR 10. Dungeon master A bought 3,00,000 shares, while dungeon master B bought 2,00,000 shares.

Financial Element Class	Journal Entry	Credit/Debit	Amount
Equity	A's Equity increases by 300,000 shares	Credit	₹ 30,00,000
Equity	B's Equity increases by 200,000 shares	Credit	₹ 20,00,000
Assets	Cash raised through issue of shares = 50,00,000	Debit	₹ 50,00,000

- Before launching services, the dungeon spent INR 1,00,000 on a combination of company registration, some financial advice and a lawyer. They decided to treat these as "preliminary expenses". Because these expenses were incurred before beginning but would be useful going forward, they have decided to write them off over 10 years.

Financial Element Class	Journal Entry	Credit/Debit	Amount
Assets	1,00,000 cash spent on preliminary expenses	Credit	₹ 1,00,000
Assets	Preliminary expenses of 1,00,000 stored up	Debit	₹ 1,00,000

- Next, management decided to rent a few building spaces to use as their central laundry plants. Within any city, these are the spaces where they would install washing and ironing machines and would transport clothes to clean. Cumulatively, the security deposit that they had to pay amounted to INR 4,00,000. The monthly rent amount that they paid totalled to INR 50,000 per month. Further, they rented out each of these facilities starting from 1st October 2020. Within the first 6 months, before the start of operations, they planned on setting up the facilities. These 6 months' worth of rent were treated as capital costs, added to the asset of furniture.

Financial Element Class	Journal Entry	Credit/Debit	Amount
Assets	7,00,000 cash spent on deposit + rent	Credit	₹ 7,00,000
Assets	Security deposit of 4,00,000 paid up	Debit	₹ 4,00,000
Assets	Furniture worth 3,00,000 paid for	Debit	₹ 3,00,000

- Given that the company would require large industrial machines, they thought it best to take on a loan to finance these purchases, rather than buy them with the limited capital that they had of their own. They thus took a loan for INR 50,00,000 at a 10% interest rate, with a 5-year moratorium period. Post the moratorium period, the loan is expected to be paid back in

5 equal instalments. The loan was taken out on the 31st of March 2021, so no interest is due yet.

Financial Element Class	Journal Entry	Credit/Debit	Amount
Liabilities	50,00,000 loan @ 10% taken on	Credit	₹ 50,00,000
Assets	50,00,000 of cash available from loan	Debit	₹ 50,00,000

- With this added cash in hand, management decided to purchase some non-current assets. They purchased machines (washing and ironing) for INR 50,00,000 with an estimated life of 5 years. They furnished the plants for INR 15,00,000, with an expected lifetime of the furniture at 10 years. And they purchased transport vehicles for INR 20,00,000 with an expected lifetime of 4 years. These costs are all-inclusive. The salvage value for all these assets is INR 0.

Financial Element Class	Journal Entry	Credit/Debit	Amount
Assets	85,00,000 cash spent on machines + furniture + veh	Credit	₹ 85,00,000
Assets	Machines worth 50,00,000 purchased	Debit	₹ 50,00,000
Assets	Furniture worth 15,00,000 purchased	Debit	₹ 15,00,000
Assets	Vehicles worth 20,00,000 purchased	Debit	₹ 20,00,000

- The government offered a capital subsidy grant to new ventures, amounting to INR 5,00,000. Management decided to write this subsidy off against the furniture account.

Financial Element Class	Journal Entry	Credit/Debit	Amount
Assets	5,00,000 cash received through subsidy	Debit	₹ 5,00,000
Assets	Furniture subsidised by 5,00,000	Credit	₹ 5,00,000

Opening Balance Sheet
The opening balance sheet thus looks like this:

Dungeon Laundry Private Limited	
Balance sheet as on: 31st March 2021	
Particulars	Amount
ASSETS	
Current assets	
Cash/Bank	12,00,000
Non-current assets	
Preliminary Expenses	1,00,000
Security Deposit	4,00,000
Furniture	13,00,000
Machines	50,00,000
Vehicles	20,00,000
Total	1,00,00,000
IABILITIES AND EQUITY	
Current liabilities	
Non-current liabilities	
10% Loan for 50,00,000	50,00,000
Equity	
A's Equity	30,00,000
B's Equity	20,00,000
Total	1,00,00,000

First Year of Operations

Within the first year of operations, the dungeon's laundry service went from simply paying to accumulate assets, to actually earning revenue and incurring expenses. To begin with, let's have a look at some of the expenses that they incurred during the financial year.

- For the first 12 months, management was of course expected to pay rent. The rent for a year, as seen earlier, amounted to INR 6,00,000.

Financial Element Class	Journal Entry	Credit/Debit	Amount
Assets	6,00,000 cash spent on rent	Credit	₹ 6,00,000
Expenses	Rent amounting to 6,00,000 paid	Debit	₹ 6,00,000

- The various managers involved in the laundry operation are paid a total of INR 4,00,000 per month. Because their salaries are paid on the 5th of the next month, manager salaries for March 2022 are still due to be paid. Laundry line workers, drivers and other labour are paid a total of INR 15,00,000 per month. These workers are paid before the 1st of each month. Thus, worker salaries for even the month of April 2022 have already been paid.

Financial Element Class	Journal Entry	Credit/Debit	Amount
Assets	2,39,00,000 cash spent on salaries	Credit	₹2,39,00,000
Liabilities	4,00,000 managers salaries payable for Mar '21	Credit	₹ 4,00,000
Assets	Pre-paid workers salaries worth 15,00,000 paid	Debit	₹ 15,00,000
Expenses	Manager salaries worth 48,00,000 incurred	Debit	₹ 48,00,000
Expenses	Worker salaries worth 1,80,00,000 incurred	Debit	₹1,80,00,000

- Various machines broke down now and then. Some important pieces of furniture also required some sort of repair and maintenance. Rather than recording this under either the machines or furniture assets, the expense of INR 4,00,000 for repair and maintenance was recorded against cash payments. Similarly, fuel used by both vehicles and backup generators totalled to an expense of INR 5,00,000.

Financial Element Class	Journal Entry	Credit/Debit	Amount
Assets	9,00,000 cash spent on rent	Credit	₹ 9,00,000
Expenses	Repair and maintenance of 4,00,000 paid for	Debit	₹ 4,00,000
Expenses	Fuel amounting to 5,00,000 paid for	Debit	₹ 5,00,000

- The total electricity bill (for the full year) across all of the laundry plants was INR 20,00,000.

Financial Element Class	Journal Entry	Credit/Debit	Amount
Assets	20,00,000 cash spent on electricity bill	Credit	₹ 20,00,000
Expenses	Electricity amounting to 20,00,000 paid for	Debit	₹ 20,00,000

- The dungeon's laundry service began ordering a proprietary detergent which gave all the clothes that they washed a special aromatic smell. They ordered this detergent from an exclusive supplier of theirs. For the year they had paid for INR 50,00,000 worth of detergent and still had to pay for INR 5,00,000 worth of detergent which they had already received. At the end of the financial year, they were holding INR 5,00,000 worth of detergent.

Financial Element Class	Journal Entry	Credit/Debit	Amount
Assets	50,00,000 cash spent on detergent	Credit	₹ 50,00,000
Liabilities	5,00,000 detergents payable remained	Credit	₹ 5,00,000
Assets	Detergents inventory worth 5,00,000 remained	Debit	₹ 5,00,000
Expenses	Detergents consumed worth 50,00,000	Debit	₹ 50,00,000

- The dungeon directly paid an advanced tax amount of INR 10,00,000 for the financial year 2021-22. In addition to this, a tax amount of INR 1,00,00,000 was deducted at source from the revenue received by the company.

Financial Element Class	Journal Entry	Credit/Debit	Amount
Assets	1,10,00,000 cash spent on advanced tax + TDS	Credit	₹1,10,00,000
Assets	Advanced tax of 10,00,000 paid for	Debit	₹ 10,00,000
Assets	TDS of 1,00,00,000 deducted	Debit	₹1,00,00,000

- Since the business was performing well, the dungeon decided to purchase a few new machines. They spent an additional INR 20,00,000 on machines on the 1st of October 2021.

Financial Element Class	Journal Entry	Credit/Debit	Amount
Assets	20,00,000 cash spent on machines	Credit	₹ 20,00,000
Assets	Machines worth 20,00,000 purchased	Debit	₹ 20,00,000

- A new vehicle, worth INR 5,00,000 was purchased on the 1st of January 2022. Only INR 1,00,000 was paid for this vehicle. The remaining INR 4,00,000 was fronted by the vehicle manufacturer, through a loan at 10%. The loaned amount, along with interest has to be paid through annual instalments, due on 31st December each year.

Financial Element Class	Journal Entry	Credit/Debit	Amount
Assets	1,00,000 cash spent on vehicle	Credit	₹ 1,00,000
Liabilities	4,00,000 vehicle loan @ 10% received	Credit	₹ 4,00,000
Assets	Vehicle worth 5,00,000 purchased	Debit	₹ 5,00,000

- An old vehicle, originally worth INR 4,00,000 was sold for INR 2,50,000 on the 30th of September 2021. By this point in time, because of depreciation, the fair value of the vehicle had reduced to INR 3,50,000.

Financial Element Class	Journal Entry	Credit/Debit	Amount
Assets	4,00,000 worth vehicle sold	Credit	₹ 4,00,000
Expenses	Vehicle depreciation of 50,000 incurred in 0.5 year	Debit	₹50,000
Assets	2,50,000 cash received for sale	Debit	₹ 2,50,000
Expenses	Loss on sale of 1,00,000 incurred on sale	Debit	₹ 1,00,000

- A dividend of INR 1,00,00,000 was declared at the end of the first financial year.

Financial Element Class	Journal Entry	Credit/Debit	Amount
Assets	1,00,00,000 cash was paid as dividend	Credit	₹1,00,00,000
Expenses	Dividend of 1,00,00,000 was declared	Debit	₹1,00,00,000

- A variety of short-term investments in the stock market were made. This was done as a means to diversify the business, to reduce risk, as well as a mechanism to raise some funds. In the process, INR 20,00,000 was made as a short-term profit.

Financial Element Class	Journal Entry	Credit/Debit	Amount
Sales	20,00,000 sales was earned through investments	Credit	₹ 20,00,000
Assets	Cash of 20,00,000 was earned through investements	Debit	₹ 20,00,000

- A total of INR 11,00,00,000 was earned through sales revenue. Of this, only INR 10,00,00,000 was received in cash, from which INR 1,00,00,000 was already deducted as TDS. Of the receivable amount, INR 10,00,000 has already proven to be bad debt. Of the remaining receivable amount, 5% has been maintained as a provision for doubtful debts.

Financial Element Class	Journal Entry	Credit/Debit	Amount
Sales	11,00,00,000 sales was earned	Credit	₹11,00,00,000
Assets	Cash of 10,00,00,000 was earned through sales	Debit	₹10,00,00,000
Expenses	10,00,000 bad debt expenses were incurred	Debit	₹ 10,00,000
Assets	Accounts receivable of 90,00,000 remain	Debit	₹ 90,00,000
Assets	4,50,000 of doubtful debts was registered	Credit	₹ 4,50,000
Expenses	4,50,000 doubtful debts were provisioned for	Debit	₹ 4,50,000

- Another 1,00,000 shares were issued (to other buyers). These shares were issued at a premium of INR 20.

Financial Element Class	Journal Entry	Credit/Debit	Amount
Equity	Other Owner's Equity increases by 100,000 shares	Credit	₹ 10,00,000
Equity	Share premium increases by 20 x 100,000 shares	Credit	₹ 20,00,000
Assets	Cash raised through issue of shares = 30,00,000	Debit	₹ 30,00,000

- Despite the large amounts that have already been paid in the form of advanced tax and TDS, the accountant estimated that the tax amount that would be due for the year would only be INR 60,00,000.

Financial Element Class	Journal Entry	Credit/Debit	Amount
Liabilities	Provision for tax of 60,00,000	Credit	₹ 60,00,000
Expenses	Tax expense of 60,00,000 incurred	Debit	₹ 60,00,000

- Two loans had already been taken out by the dungeon. On the 10% loan for INR 50,00,000, an interest amount of INR 5,00,000 had been accrued but wasn't due yet. Similarly, on the 10% vehicle loan, an interest amount of INR 10,000 had been accrued but wasn't due yet.

Financial Element Class	Journal Entry	Credit/Debit	Amount
Liabilities	Vehicle loan interest accrued of 10,000	Credit	₹10,000
Expenses	Vehicle loan interest of 10,000 incurred	Debit	₹10,000
Liabilities	10% loan interest accrued of 5,00,000	Credit	₹ 5,00,000
Expenses	10% loan interest of 5,00,000 incurred	Debit	₹ 5,00,000

- The capital assets owned by the dungeon also depreciated over a year. The furniture had a total value of INR 13,00,000 and depreciated by INR 1,30,000. The first INR 50,00,000 worth of machines depreciated by INR 10,00,000 in the first year, while the next INR 20,00,000 worth of machines depreciated by INR 2,00,000 in the 6 months since their purchase. The INR 16,00,000 worth of vehicles which the dungeon kept, depreciated by INR 4,00,000 over a year. While the newly purchased INR 5,00,000 vehicle depreciated by INR 31,250 in the 3 months since its purchase.

Financial Element Class	Journal Entry	Credit/Debit	Amount
Assets	Furniture contra account reduced by 1,30,000	Credit	₹ 1,30,000
Expenses	Furniture depreciation of 1,30,000 incurred	Debit	₹ 1,30,000
Assets	Machine contra account reduced by 12,00,000	Credit	₹ 12,00,000
Expenses	Machine depreciation of 12,00,000 incurred	Debit	₹ 12,00,000
Assets	Vehicle contra account reduced by 4,31,250	Credit	₹ 4,31,250
Expenses	Vehicle depreciation of 4,31,250 incurred	Debit	₹ 4,31,250

- Preliminary expenses were to be written off over 10 years.

Financial Element Class	Journal Entry	Credit/Debit	Amount
Assets	Preliminary expenses reduced by 10,000	Credit	₹10,000
Expenses	preliminary expenses of 10,000 incurred	Debit	₹10,000

Income Statement

Dungeon Laundry Private Limited		
Income statement for the Year Ended 31st March, 2022		
Particulars	Detail	Amount
Revenues and incomes		
Sales	11,00,00,000	
Profit on Sale of Investments	20,00,000	
Total revenues		11,20,00,000
Expenses		
Rent	(6,00,000)	
Manager Salaries	(48,00,000)	
Worker Salaries	(1,80,00,000)	
Repair & Maintenance	(4,00,000)	
Fuel	(5,00,000)	
Electricity	(20,00,000)	
Detergents Consumed	(50,00,000)	
Machines Depreciation	(12,00,000)	
Furniture Depreciation	(1,30,000)	
Loss on Sale of Vehicle	(1,00,000)	
Vehicle Depreciation	(4,81,250)	
Interest on Vehicle Loan	(10,000)	
Actual Bad Debt	(10,00,000)	
Doubtful (Bad) Debt Provision	(4,50,000)	
Interest on 10% Loan	(5,00,000)	
Preliminary Expenses Written Off	(10,000)	
Total expenses		(3,51,81,250)
Profit before tax		7,68,18,750
Income tax expenses		
Tax (21-22)	(60,00,000)	
Profit after tax (amount available for appropriations)		7,08,18,750
Appropriations		
Dividend Paid	(1,00,00,000)	
Balance carried to Balance Sheet		6,08,18,750

Balance Sheet

Particulars	31st March 2021	31st March 2022	
	Amount	Detail	Amount
Dungeon Laundry Private Limited			
Balance sheet as on: 31st March 2022			
ASSETS			
Current assets			
Cash/Bank	12,00,000		5,09,50,000
Pre-Paid Workers Salaries			15,00,000
Detergent Inventory			5,00,000
Accounts Receivable			90,00,000
Provision for Doubtful Debt			(4,50,000)
Advanced Tax + TDS (21-22)			1,10,00,000
Non-current assets			
Preliminary Expenses	1,00,000		90,000
Security Deposit	4,00,000		4,00,000
Furniture	13,00,000	13,00,000	
Furniture Contra Asset		(1,30,000)	11,70,000
Machines	50,00,000	70,00,000	
Machines Depreciation Contra Asset		(12,00,000)	58,00,000
Vehicles	20,00,000	21,00,000	
Vehicles Depreciation Contra Asset		(4,31,250)	16,68,750
Total	**1,00,00,000**		**8,16,28,750**
EQUITY AND LIABILITIES			
Current liabilities			
Managers Salaries Payable			4,00,000
Detergents Payable			5,00,000
Vehicle Loan Interest Accrued			40,000
Provision for Tax (21-22)			60,00,000
10% Loan Interest Accrued			5,00,000
Non-current liabilities			
10% Loan for 50,00,000	50,00,000		50,00,000
10% Vehicle Loan for 4,00,000			4,00,000
Equity			
A's Equity	30,00,000		30,00,000
B's Equity	20,00,000		20,00,000
Other Owner's Equity			40,00,000
Share Premium			20,00,000
P&L Balance Account			6,08,18,750
Total	**1,00,00,000**		**8,16,28,750**

Cash Flow Statement

Dungeon Laundry Private Limited		
Cash Flow Statement for the Year Ended 31st March 2022		
Particulars	Details	Amount
Cash from operating activities		
Profit before tax		7,68,18,750
Add: non cash expenses		32,71,250
Depreciation of Machines	12,00,000	
Depreciation of Furniture	1,30,000	
Depreciation of Vehicles	4,81,250	
Bad Debt & Doubtful Debt	14,50,000	
Preliminary Expenses Written Off	10,000	
Adj: Items belonging to other heads		(13,90,000)
Loss on Sale of Vehicle	1,00,000	
Profit on Sale of Investments	(20,00,000)	
Interest on Vehicle Loan	10,000	
Interest on 10% Loan	5,00,000	
Adj: Working capital changes		(1,11,00,000)
Pre-Paid Salaries	(15,00,000)	
Detergents Inventory	(5,00,000)	
Accounts Receivable	(1,00,00,000)	
Salaries Payable	4,00,000	
Detergents Payable	5,00,000	
Income tax paid		(1,10,00,000)
Income Tax Expense	(60,00,000)	
Advanced Tax (21-22)	(1,10,00,000)	
Provision for Tax (21-22)	60,00,000	
Cash Flow from operating activities		**5,66,00,000**
Particulars	Details	Amount
Cash from investing activities		
Sale of Vehicle	2,50,000	
Purchase of Vehicle	(1,00,000)	
Profit from Investments	20,00,000	
Purchase of Machines	(20,00,000)	
Cash flow from investing activities		**1,50,000**
Particulars	Details	Amount
Cash from financing activities		
Dividend Paid	(1,00,00,000)	
Owner's Equity	10,00,000	
Share Premium	20,00,000	
Cash flow from financing activities		**(70,00,000)**
Total cash flow during the year		**4,97,50,000**
Opening balance of cash and cash equivalent		12,00,000
Closing balance of cash and cash equivalent		**5,09,50,000**

From your analysis of the dungeon's financial reporting.

1. Which steps in the financial reporting process seem counter-intuitive?
2. Do you think those steps are technically right or wrong?
3. Can you come up with a justification for why this is the prescribed method of accounting?

Instead of just thinking on your own, I would encourage you to participate in a case discussion on the following Reddit thread. Through case discussion, your ideas may be validated or improved upon. You would also benefit from other people's viewpoints.

Chapter 18
Ratios & Metrics: Financial Health Check-up

We're just now getting into the most meaningful part of the finance section, the "so what" of it all. We already know how financial reporting happens. We also know the details of how to produce each of the financial reports, as well as some of the intricacies involved. We already have a decent idea of how to read a financial report. But having read the reports, it is important to understand the implication of each of the numbers. For just this reason, the experts have developed a few ratios and other metrics. These numbers can help give us an idea of whether the business is performing well, how profitable it is, whether investments are yielding appropriate returns and what the financial condition is.

Keep in mind that this chapter is going to contain a whole lot of formulae. They're all fairly easy to calculate, so there's no advanced math involved. As usual, one need not worry about learning all of the formulae. We will try and run through each of the metrics. The focus is on understanding what information each metric communicates, and why it is a good approximation of the information that we seek. As long as this is understood, the specifics of the math can be taken for granted and looked up as and when needed. Next to each of the values in the formulae, '(BS)', '(IS)' or '(CF)' may be mentioned, indicating that the value can be found in the balance sheet, income statement or cash flow statement respectively.

Overall performance

Before we get into the overall performance metrics which give us directional information, let's start with some basics. There are a few metrics which will be used in calculating a lot of other metrics. One of these is working capital. Working capital, as the name suggests is the amount of capital that a business has available to work with. This has to of course be a subset of the current assets because it must be available in the short term for us to use. Further, it has to be available for use even after addressing all of the short-term liabilities. Thus, working capital is calculated as current assets minus current liabilities (Desai, 2021).

Another metric used in some calculations is invested capital. This is an indicator of how much the company has invested into its operations and other long-term business activities. Simply put, this is everything that the business has borrowed from anyone, with the exception of the short-term liabilities. We aren't bothered about short-term liabilities because these tend to be more operational borrowings than invested capital (Gandhi, 2020).

The price:earnings ratio is a popular performance metric used by investors. This number gives us an idea of whether the business' stock is overvalued/undervalued. It can also be read as an indicator of whether the business' performance matches the investor's expectations or not. Obviously, a higher price:earnings ratio suggests that the company is overvalued or underperforming.

Return on assets, invested capital or shareholder's equity are all metrics which may be used to identify how useful each additional unit of investment (in/through each category) is. The return here is of course the net income that the company earns. The denominator in each case is whatever the return is expected to be on. The return itself may sometimes be exempted from the interest that the company has had to pay back. But these nuances need not be worried about too much. What matters is that when these metrics are compared from one business to another, the same formula is used uniformly (Gandhi, 2020).

Overall Performance		
• Working Capital	=	Current Assets (BS) – Current Liabilities (BS)
• Invested Capital	=	Owner's Equity (BS) + Long Term Liabilities (BS)
	=	Working Capital + Non-Current Assets (BS)
• Price:Earnings Ratio	=	Market Price per Share
		Net Income per Share (IS)
• Return on Assets	=	Net Income (IS) + Interest x (1 – Tax Rate) (IS)
		Total Assets (BS)
• Return on Invested Capital	=	Net Income (IS) + Interest x (1 – Tax Rate) (IS)
		Long-Term Liabilities (BS) + Shareholder's Equity (BS)
• Return on Shareholder's Equity	=	Net Income (IS)
		Shareholder's Equity (BS)

Profitability

Profitability metrics serve the core purpose of helping us understand whether a business is managing to retain the value that it has captured from customers. Essentially, it acts as a check to understand how much of what customers are paying for is the operational effort versus the value that the company gets to keep. In most of these metrics, the denominator is the total revenue collected by the company. Profitability metrics are broken down into various stages, to help diagnose which set of expenses might be impacting a company's profitability. This is useful because otherwise, we might know that our profit margin is low, but don't have information on why it's low and how to improve it.

Other metrics of profitability can look at how much profit the company is making as a function of other variables. One such metric is the earnings per share. This is a measure of how much profit the company is earning per share. Keep in mind that this is greater than or equal to, not necessarily equal to the dividend that will actually be paid out per share.

To take profitability metrics a step further, one can also look at how much actual cash flow is generated from operations, out of the total profit reported in the income statement (Gandhi, 2020).

Profitability		
• Gross Margin %	=	Gross Margin (IS) / Total Revenue (IS)
• Operating Margin (EBIT) %	=	EBIT (IS) / Total Revenue (IS)
• Cash Operating Margin (EBITDA) %	=	EBITDA (IS) / Total Revenue (IS)
• Profit Margin %	=	Net Income (IS) / Total Revenue (IS)
• Earnings per Share	=	Net Income (IS) / # Outstanding Shares
• Cash Realisation	=	Operating Cash Flow (CF) / Net Income (IS)

Investment utilisation

The next set of metrics is used to identify how well the company's investments are working out. Each investment serves a different purpose. Thus, some of them may be measured by the revenue earned, others by the amount of cash, receivables, inventory, assets, or even expenses incurred. At this stage, it's useful to remember that the metrics that we are looking at are just ones which are commonly used because they prove to be useful. Here also there are not too many right or wrong metrics. All of them can be changed a little bit if they provide more useful insights in the context of your business.

Asset turnover, for example, tells us how many times over in a year our average investment in assets provides return in the form of revenue. Invested capital turnover does the same with the invested capital as the base. This is also often calculated with the base as shareholder's equity or capital (some major non-current assets). None of these is definitively the best metric, because a combination of these bases leads to the final revenue. But each metric on its own gives us an idea of how well each base invested in is performing (Gandhi, 2020).

		Investment Utilisation
• Asset Turnover	=	$\dfrac{\text{Total Revenue (IS)}}{\text{Total Assets (BS)}}$
• Invested Capital Turnover	=	$\dfrac{\text{Total Revenue (IS)}}{\text{Long-Term Liabilities (BS) + Shareholder's Equity (BS)}}$
• Equity Turnover	=	$\dfrac{\text{Total Revenue (IS)}}{\text{Shareholder's Equity (BS)}}$
• Capital Intensity	=	$\dfrac{\text{Total Revenue (IS)}}{\text{Property + Plant + Equipment (BS)}}$
• Days' Cash	=	$\dfrac{\text{Cash (BS) x 365}}{\text{Cash Expenses (IS/CF)}}$
• Days' Receivables (Collection Period)	=	$\dfrac{\text{Accounts Receivable (BS) x 365}}{\text{Total Revenue (IS)}}$

Another way of looking at investments' performance involves looking at how much of an investment we have, rather than just looking at how much revenue it creates. There are some metrics which therefore look at how many days' worth of the investment we maintain on average. In this approach, the denominator represents the use of the investment or the total amount of that investment that would be required over a year. The numerator represents the amount of that investment currently being held on the balance sheet. This number is thought to represent the average amount of that investment that the company has at any given point of time in the year. This will of course lead to a fraction, less than 1, representing what portion of the year's requirement we maintain at any point in time. By multiplying this number by 365, we get the same answer in terms of the number of days' worth of investment that we maintain at any point.

Other metrics of interest may be the current ratio and the quick ratio. The current ratio simply tells us what percentage of the current liabilities we will be able to pay off with the help of our current assets. This might be greater than 100%, which is a great, healthy position to be in. If it's particularly low, that's a warning sign. Similarly, the quick ratio takes this a step further, by looking only at the monetary current assets, which is realistically, what we'll be using (Gandhi, 2020).

Investment Utilisation		
• Days' Inventory	=	$\dfrac{\text{Inventory (BS)} \times 365}{\text{Cost of Sales (IS)}}$
• Inventory Turnover	=	$\dfrac{\text{Cost of Sales (IS)}}{\text{Inventory (BS)}}$
• Working Capital Turnover	=	$\dfrac{\text{Total Revenue (IS)}}{\text{Working Capital}}$
• Current Ratio	=	$\dfrac{\text{Current Assets (BS)}}{\text{Current Liabilities (BS)}}$
• Quick Ratio	=	$\dfrac{\text{Monetary Current Assets (BS)}}{\text{Current Liabilities (BS)}}$

Financial condition

Of course, every financial metric that we have looked at so far tells us something about the financial condition of the company. Still, there are some ratios which give us information which really can only be described as relating to the financial condition of the company. At this stage, I doubt that much explanation is needed of how to read the formulae. Have a look at each of the financial condition metrics and see if you can make sense of why it's useful and calculated in a given way. If you get stuck somewhere, the internet always has the answers (Gandhi, 2020).

Financial Condition		
• Financial Leverage Ratio	=	$\dfrac{\text{Total Assets (BS)}}{\text{Shareholder's Equity (BS)}}$
• Debt:Equity Ratio	=	$\dfrac{\text{Total Liabilities (BS)}}{\text{Shareholder's Equity (BS)}}$
• Debt:Capitalisation Ratio	=	$\dfrac{\text{Total Liabilities (BS)}}{\text{Long-Term Liabilities (BS)} + \text{Shareholder's Equity (BS)}}$
• Interest Cover	=	$\dfrac{\text{Pre-Tax Operating Profit (IS)} + \text{Interest (IS)}}{\text{Interest (IS)}}$
• Cash Flow:Debt Ratio	=	$\dfrac{\text{Operating Cash Flow (CF)}}{\text{Total Debt (IS)}}$

Dividend policy

Finally, now that we have looked at a company's overall performance, profitability, investment and operations, we can look at how its investors stand to gain. For this, we want to understand how fair or otherwise their dividend policy is. For one thing, one might be interested in understanding the investor's return on investment. This is the amount that they gain through dividends on the market price that they must pay per share.

One may also be interested in what percentage of the company's profits gets distributed amongst the shareholders. For this, we look at the dividend over the net income.

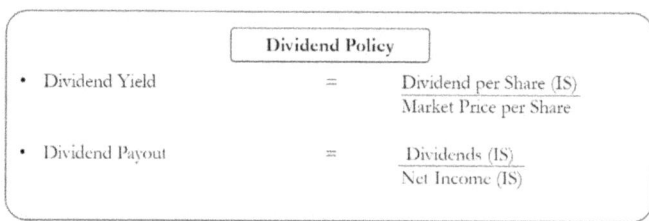

Dividend Policy		
• Dividend Yield	=	$\dfrac{\text{Dividend per Share (IS)}}{\text{Market Price per Share}}$
• Dividend Payout	=	$\dfrac{\text{Dividends (IS)}}{\text{Net Income (IS)}}$

Recap

In our attempt to understand how to manage a business, we have thus far learnt:

- Management thinking. We have extensively been using convergent thinking, structuring in particular and divergent thinking along the way.
- We got started with 4 steps of business value creation so that we can capture value from customers in return. We are capable of understanding the marketplace, positioning our brand to target the right customers, designing an effective market mix and managing relevant relationships along the way.
- To understand the language of finance, we have understood:
    o The financial reporting process.
    o What the 3 key financial reports are.
    o Basic concepts and accounting principles.
- Next, we understood the components of the balance sheet (assets, liabilities and owner's equity). We also understood how they relate to each other.

182

- Then, we understood how to read an income statement, with an emphasis on what intermediate numbers are of significance, and what some of the important line items are.
- Finally, we learnt how to construct and read a cash flow statement, to supplement our understanding of the business' performance. We understood each of the 3 types of transactions and how to map out the specific cash flows within each bucket, through the direct or indirect method.
- Over and above that we learnt about a few nuances which make financial reporting more complicated, powerful and useful.
- After that, we began to use our understanding of the financial reports to arrive at useful metrics and ratios. Through these metrics, we can diagnose how the business is performing on a range of parameters of interest.

With that, we have pretty much covered all of the basics of how to report, study and diagnose a business through financials. We have understood the jargon, the processes and the analysis. Before we can close up, we need to see what else we haven't yet explored in the world of finance.

Chapter 19
But There's More: Other Financial Ideas

So far, we have had a look at financial reporting alone. For managers who don't work in finance, that's the bulk of what we need to understand. Financial reporting of our own business and maybe some other related businesses gives us all the information that we need to manage most functions within the company.

However, when we traditionally think of finance, we think of rich investment bankers who are trading stocks and making profits or crashing markets. Nothing that we have looked at so far makes it obvious how their world works. Independent of whether you are a manager, or just trying to go about living your life, this world of finance will impact your life too.

And so, in this chapter, we shall take a quick glance at some of the basics that frame how the financial world works. This chapter of course should not even be thought of as an introduction to finance. There are thick and daunting books which can be thought of as an introduction to finance. This chapter is at best a list of some ideas to keep in mind if you decide that you want to learn more about finance.

Why is there a financial sector?

On the one hand, this is the sort of question that one asks when they suspect that we can do away with the financial sector. But in this context, we aim to reaffirm its existence and explain its real goal.

The reason that a financial sector came into existence long ago was to make borrowing money easier and better directed. There has always been a divide between those people who have money and those who do not. The financial sector aims to make it easier for 'worthy' causes to borrow money, grow it and return it. In a sense, the financial sector, therefore, aims to help us as a civilisation better allocate our resources amongst different causes (Pandey, 2020).

The question then arises as to what causes are 'worthy' and which ones are less so. There are many different ideologies that one could take up, and each would result in a slightly different kind of financial market. Within the market that we currently have, the deciding factor seems to be return on investment. Those borrowers or

184

investments which lead to the maximum growth of one's money are what investors favour. This lens is understandable, for when money is the currency, everyone is looking for more. There is also a new strain of thinking in which people invest in causes which they believe in, with profitability and growth as a secondary objective (but still of importance).

Debt, equity and other complications

Since the financial sector's goals are centred around allocating resources and enabling borrowing towards 'worthy' goals, borrowing is clearly an important part of the sector. In the oldest financial markets borrowing was a straightforward process. This straightforward borrowing where interest accumulates and the principal along with the accumulated interest must be paid back is called debt.

However, with time more complex instruments to fund 'worthy' causes were developed. One such instrument which should be familiar by this point is equity. Here the investor isn't promised returns in the form of interest. Rather, dividends are the promised form of return (in some cases). And this is only the beginning of complexity.

Often, investors purchase stocks of companies that they expect to perform well and grow. At a later stage, as a result of this growth, the stock value appreciates and investors sell the stock to profit. However, sometimes the reverse happens. Investors may also bet on companies failing. In these cases, they may 'short' a stock. This is effectively the same thing as selling the stock today (even though they don't own it yet), and then buying it at a later stage, when its price is lower. This reversal and convolution of timelines are enabled by financial markets through very thorough bookkeeping. This thorough bookkeeping makes sure that at a later stage we don't have multiple people claiming to own the same stock, or an unplanned increase in the number of stocks.

Now that we have touched upon debt, equity and shorting, let's discuss 3 other strange ways of transacting. Specifically, in the context of purchasing foreign currency, we know that there is such a thing as an exchange rate. The exchange rate is subject to a lot of variation and keeps going up and down. I won't attempt to explain why and how these variations happen. But there are a few approaches through which we can try to purchase foreign currency at lower rates. Some of these approaches are forwards, futures and options. Through each of these, we arrive at agreements through which we can purchase foreign currency at a future date (Pandey, 2020).

Forwards can be customised as long as one finds a bank agreeing to the currency, amount and date.

Futures are more standardised than forwards.

Options don't involve a fixed commitment (which futures and forwards do), but an option for future transactions instead.

We haven't even attempted to explain here the details of any of these complex transactions. We have just outlined some of the complexity and how the financial sector works. All of this complexity is of course not unfounded. The complexity came about because the simplest form of borrowing didn't match the complex requirements of the complex world that we live in. As such, each of these instruments that we have touched upon (and those that we haven't) serve to create more ways for funds to flow. The idea behind creating more ways of transacting is primarily to allow the market to decide which ways to use and when. A central idea in finance (and economics) is the wisdom of the crowd and the belief that the market will arrive at good decisions (Chatterjee, 2020).

Compounding and present value

We have touched upon why financial markets exist and have looked at some of the instruments that are used to help achieve their objective. In the midst of all this complexity, you might have gathered that there is an expectation that lending money to the right people helps create growth. Fundamentally this growth comes from the fact that the right resources, dedicated to 'worthy' causes, helps move society towards a better position. Now that we have philosophically outlined where financial growth comes from, let's have a look at how it manifests.

It is understandably tedious to analyse after each transaction whether society is better off and by how much. So, we allow the market to decide. When money is lent, the borrower does something with the borrowed money to generate more money than they borrowed. At least this is what happens on average. Some borrowers default and some companies fail. This sort of growth and return from financial instruments creates a compounding effect.

The idea of compounding shouldn't be new, since we study it in high school mathematics. The important takeaways are that larger principals create larger returns and that larger periods of investment create exponentially higher returns. Another important result of this compounding effect is that no asset, not even money has a singular value. The value of money is different one year from what it is in another year. As an example of this, ask your grandparents what a one rupee coin used to buy in their time. Compare that with the struggle that is to still find a candy that one can purchase for one rupee today (Housel, 2020).

This shifting value of money gives us an important concept of the present value of investments. At the centre of this concept is the assumption that we can estimate the rate at which money will be devalued or discounted in the future. We call this rate the discount rate. For any given investment, we then assume that we can predict how much it will cost us, as well as how much cash it will help us generate in each subsequent year. Each year's cash flow should be discounted by the discount rate, to arrive at the effective value of the investment today. This series of discounted cash flows together is what we call the present value of an investment. The comparison of net present values of different investments is prudently considered to be the best way of comparing investments which have different costs, return rates and time frames (Sinha S. , 2021).

$$\text{Present Value} = -\text{Investment} + \frac{1^{st}\ \text{year's cash flow}}{(1+\text{discount rate})^1} + \frac{2^{nd}\ \text{year's cash flow}}{(1+\text{discount rate})^2} + \ldots + \frac{n^{th}\ \text{year's cash flow}}{(1+\text{discount rate})^n}$$

Over and above this we have the concept of internal rate of return. When we are analysing an investment, and we have a rough idea of how much it might cost us, as well as the expected series of cash flows, we might want to understand whether or not it is profitable. The internal rate of return is the discount rate at which the net present value comes out to be zero. If the discount rate proves to be lower than the internal rate of return, the project is profitable, if it's higher, it's unprofitable.

Expected returns

The investor or lender has some expectations that the money that they provide should grow. We also know that this happens on average, or on expectation. But that implicitly means that this doesn't happen sometimes. There are risks and probabilities involved. With business projects and with loans, there are easy enough ways of predicting the expected cash flow. Thus, we have seen how we can use the net present value and internal rate of return to decide whether such a venture is worthy or not. However, in the case of the stock market, we need to apply a slightly different approach.

We start by assuming that there is some rate of return that we could get without taking on any risk at all. This risk-free return rate is calculated by taking the return rate from treasury bonds and subtracting the rate of return which is due to inflation alone. For any stock, the expected rate of return is the sum of the risk-free rate of return and something that we call the normal risk premium. The normal risk premium is the expected additional return that we get for taking on a riskier investment. By virtue of this investment being risky, this risk premium isn't guaranteed but is what we expect over an extended period.

We still need to have an approach to estimating the normal risk premium of a given stock. For that, we believe that the normal risk premium of a stock is correlated to the difference between the return rate of the entire stock market and the risk-free return rate. There is a constant called beta which tells us the extent to which a given stock is correlated to this difference between the market and the risk-free return rates. We won't get into the details of how exactly this beta is arrived at.

Another lens through which we can look at and estimate stock return is the sum of the portfolio's (of stocks) dividend yield and the rate of growth of dividend. In this lens, we assume that all value of the stock is derived from the dividend that it provides today, and in the future. We take the combination of these values and estimate the effective rate of return (Pandey, 2020).

$$R_{(stock)} = R_{(risk-free)} + R_{(normal\ risk\ premium)}$$

$$R_{(normal\ risk\ premium\ for\ stock\ i)} = \beta_{(for\ stock\ i)} \times (R_{(market)} - R_{(risk\ free)})$$

$$R_{(portfolio)} = \text{Portfolio Dividend Yield} + R_{(dividend\ growth)}$$

Having been acquainted with the idea of risk, it is useful to also understand that all bonds are given a risk rating by various authorities. These ratings start at AAA, which are bonds which are reliable and have the least risk. AA and A bonds are slightly riskier. Insurance companies are generally not allowed to invest in A bonds or lower. BBB bonds and above are referred to as investment-grade bonds. BB bonds and below are usually referred to as junk bonds. And these ratings go down all the way to D.

Market efficiency

For the very first time in this book, we have spoken about financial markets, the instruments they contain, how they get complicated, how the value of money changes and how one can expect returns to evolve. We have spoken about all of these complex subjects briefly, and as if there are definitive answers to them. Now is a good time to remember that in management, we often don't have right or wrong answers, just directionally useful ones. Even in an area as mathematical as finance, we don't necessarily have definitive answers.

The stock market for example is studied and analysed with a lot of detailed math. Thousands of super smart people are tracking and trying to predict how it will evolve. Some of them succeed and some of them fail. And which of these smart people fall into which bucket changes from one day to another. The fact is that the stock market follows a random walk. This statement doesn't mean that it's all random and it's not worth trying to figure it out. A random walk is a mathematical model, where a given day's happenings (step in the walk) are dependent only on the current market position, and not all of the history. The current market position is in and of itself a super complicated state, which is in and of itself a function of a lot of the history. But, at any point in time, investors make their decisions based on the information that they have today. This is a good thing because it has 2 implications (Pandey, 2020):

1.   Looking at just today's information, we can figure out what will happen.
2.   If we are in the exact same position, the exact same result will follow.

These implications may make it sound like the market should be perfectly predictable. But there are caveats. Today's information doesn't just mean stock prices. It means all information which could possibly have a bearing on what happens. This includes all financial reports for the company and all companies. This includes the weather forecast and the news. This could even include the mood that a particular person is in when they choose to make a stock market transaction. 'Just today's information' is a lot. The same position creating the same result also means that the position includes all of these thousands of variables. Thus 2 positions may look similar on a lot of dimensions but lead to very different results because on some less visible, but important dimensions, the situations were drastically different.

Clearly, in an ideal world, all of this important information could be simplified and represented easily. In a more realistic world, that is difficult. This idea of the markets working perfectly smoothly, because all the information is known to everyone is what we call market efficiency. To this end, we say that we have weak efficiency when all historic price information is available and reflected in how the stock market works. Semi-strong efficiency is when in addition to price information, all publicly known information is also reflected in how the stock market works. Strong efficiency is when all information which exists, and detailed analyses reflect in the stock market position. This is a situation in which everything has the absolute right price at each point. This type of market is one where society's resources are being perfectly matched to society's worthy causes optimally (Pandey, 2020).

We have a pretty good idea that our markets are not perfectly efficient. But where exactly in the spectrum are we?

Valuation

To end this chapter, I'm going to pose an important and difficult question, and I'm not going to answer it. The big question at hand is how do we value a company?

From the previous sub-section, we know that our markets are not perfectly efficient. This means that at least not everyone is valuing all companies the same way. Realistically, we can also say that we do not have a perfect method for valuation. But as managers we must come up with directionally useful methods. Finance experts will tell you that they have exceptionally accurate methods for valuation. Maybe they do. I am not an expert, so I will not comment on this. There are courses far more detailed than this entire book, which can teach you about the valuation of companies.

For now, I will name 3 different approaches which exist to valuation (Sinha S., 2021).

1. Dividend discount model
2. Earnings per share & present value growth opportunities
3. Free cash flow method

As promised, I'm not going to be giving you very useful answers in this section. But I have already named 3 different fairly accepted approaches to valuation of firms. The free cash flow method is generally considered to be the best. The free cash flow method uses the series of free cash flow of the company to arrive at what its value is. This intuitively makes sense, because it looks at all of the cash (absolute value) available to the company, and uses it to understand how valuable it is.

More precisely, the free cash flow method uses a formula very similar to our formula for the net present value of an investment (the company). Each year's cash flow (expected) is divided by a discount rate to arrive at how valuable this investment is in today's money. To decide what discount rate to use, we look at the rate of return for the company's own debt, equity and investments. This amount is called the weighted average cost of capital. There are of course layers upon layers of intricacies within this method alone. And this method on its own barely scratches the surface. I will therefore choose to leave you with this vague idea of how valuation works. Hopefully, this can lead you down more interesting and informative rabbit holes on the internet, if you are interested.

Recap

In our attempt to understand how to manage a business, we have thus far learnt:

- Management thinking. We have extensively been using convergent thinking, structuring in particular and divergent thinking along the way.
- We got started with 4 steps of business value creation so that we can capture value from customers in return. We are capable of understanding the marketplace, positioning our brand to target the right customers, designing an effective market mix and managing relevant relationships along the way.
- To understand the language of finance, we have understood:
  - o The financial reporting process.
  - o What the 3 key financial reports are.
  - o Basic concepts and accounting principles.
- Next, we understood the components of the balance sheet (assets, liabilities and owner's equity). We also understood how they relate to each other.
- Then, we understood how to read an income statement, with an emphasis on what intermediate numbers are of significance, and what some of the important line items are.

- Finally, we learnt how to construct and read a cash flow statement, to supplement our understanding of the business' performance. We understood each of the 3 types of transactions and how to map out the specific cash flows within each bucket, through the direct or indirect method.
- Over and above that we learnt about a few nuances which make financial reporting more complicated, powerful and useful.
- After that, we began to use our understanding of the financial reports to arrive at useful metrics and ratios. Through these metrics, we can diagnose how the business is performing on a range of parameters of interest.
- Finally, we have understood at a very broad level what else exists in the world of finance, ranging from why it exists to how we can value firms.

We therefore now understand how to think like a manager, the overall business process, and are capable of translating our vague ideas into more definitive financial models. Next, we hope to take our objectivity a step further, by working out the math and operations. Further, having discussed a lot of theory, it would help to understand the human side of business, which after all is what runs businesses. And finally, it will be useful to learn how to study the outside world to improve our business.

Section IV

Operations, Math and Technology

Now it's time to get our hands dirty. The side of management that we have seen so far has helped us take top level decisions. We know how to think like a manager, we have understood the overall business process, and are equipped to take objective decisions on what to do with the business. All of this gives us direction. In the space of operations, we need to translate these decisions into efficient action. After all, operations begins with a clear objective and helps translate the objective into a plan and the plan into action and results.

Before we learn more about operations, let's have a brief look at where our understanding of operations comes from. On the one hand, during the industrial revolution, for the very first time, goods were being mass produced. The big step-change in mass production was not only the volume of production but also the fact that each product came out identically. Today, luxury goods are probably the only space where small imperfections in a product are thought of as part of the artistic element, which makes it valuable. Large American corporations like Ford and General Motors are often associated with introducing the biggest changes in modern supply chains. Other mammoths from old industries, such as German and Japanese car manufacturers are also commonplace names in the space of optimising operations.

On the other hand, an interesting way of looking at operations is from the point of view of the 2 world wars. In addition to a lot of business analogies and operational thinking having been adopted from war time, there is also a lot of mathematical development which happened during the war. Most of this math would later help catalyse the development of computer science and the technology which we are very dependent on today. This is a lens which I think is particularly important to note. A lot of operational excellence in the twentieth century was thought of as patented brilliance of one or two companies. However, today's widespread knowledge of mathematics and the massive adoption of technology has made it much easier for every company to aim to perfect their operations. This is therefore one of the few domains of management where there may often be perfect answers, not just directionally useful ones. It is also a space where there is an immense body of scientific work which we can rely on, without expecting managers to solve everything from scratch.

Now we should be clear that operations is an age-old subject, where a lot of the answers and tools are being developed by people who are much better equipped than I am. Of course, what this means is that I'm not going to delve into each and every detail of operations management. I will try to outline some of the important concepts, terminology and developments over the last century. I will also make sure to detail where and how one can find or develop answers to any problem in operations management. With that crisp and simple understanding, one should be able to understand, approach and solve most problems in operations.

To begin with, in the first chapter we will have a look at a long laundry list of operations terms, concepts and frameworks. This should act as a sampler of the world of operations and also introduce you to some of the important concepts that will be recycled.

In the next chapter, we will try to get a little more mathematical. Within the same context, we shall pick up a few more formulae and illustrate how operations are optimised. Much like the other chapters in this section, this is not going to provide a comprehensive list of optimisation approaches. Rather it will illustrate how a mathematical and scientific outlook is applied in business. For any given situation, Google will prove to be a useful ally in operations management, as long as one understands how to frame a problem and search for a solution. This framing and searching is the focus of the chapter.

In the third chapter, we take another step towards mathematics. Without getting into the theory or problem solving, we shall outline some mathematical subject areas which have traditionally been particularly useful in management. The expectation is that they will continue to be indispensable in the field of management. None of this math will be very difficult. It ranges from concepts that we learn in high school to the sort of math that one uses in business school admission tests. What's more, we will have plenty of time, and the assistance of Microsoft excel this time around.

In the final chapter of this section, we shall have a look at the result of the application of all of this mathematics to operations. We shall explore some facets of technology which are especially hot in the business world right now. There are some ideas of what technology can be used for in the near future to solve some of the biggest challenges of the recent past in operations management.

Chapter 20
Operations Glossary: Tricks of the Trade

We are now ready to figure out how to take the directional answers from the first 3 sections of this book and draw out a plan of action to get results. We have decided that operations management is the science that we will use in this endeavour of ours. And, we are ready to find out what all of that means.

But as promised, I will continue to do the bare minimum to support you in this pursuit of understanding how to manage a business. Therefore, to begin with, I shall try to introduce you to the supply chain. The supply chain in some way or form ends up being the object that operations managers aim to manage. Beyond that, we shall look at some terms which will be thrown around as a part of operations management. Finally, we shall have a look at how these pieces are put together to manage large-scale projects and the quality of operations. This overview should hopefully give you an idea of both how operations works, and how you can learn any of the missing pieces of the puzzle.

Supply chain

The name more or less says it all. The supply chain is a series of processes through which a company aims to capture a supply of raw materials, do all of the needed activities in between, and supply finished goods to the customer. All supply chains in the economy, across all companies, can be thought of as a whole bunch of wildly flowing streams of different materials. The beauty of well-designed supply chains is that they can transform this image into one of neat pipes going from here to there. These pipes, in an ideal world, should ensure the perfect flow, independent of any externalities, so that a customer can just turn on a tap, and have their flow of the required good reach them. A good supply chain is low-cost, well maintained and effective in delivering the end result without delays.

Depending on the industry and specific purpose in focus, supply chains can look dramatically different. But for the most part, they start by sourcing the raw materials or other inputs required. A logical next step would be to combine these inputs and manufacture or create something. Post manufacturing, goods usually go through a few steps of logistics (transportation) and storage, until they reach a final depot, close enough to the end customer. Afterwards, the supply chain goes into the 'last mile', of delivery to the customer. Somewhere in this process, the customer places an order. If all of this is done without the customer placing an order, we enter the territory of unsolicited telemarketing calls, but I digress. Customers may place an order which prompts material acquisition or manufacturing, in very low volume products. In more fast-moving products the customer usually places an order, after which the company only needs to complete the last mile logistics and delivery.

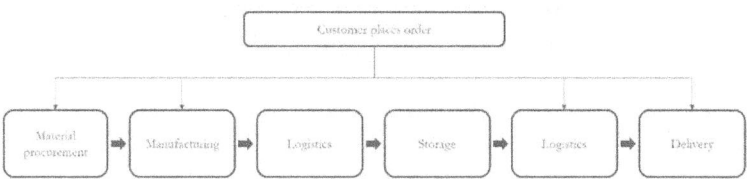

Independent of the exact supply chain, a lot of operations management involves taking a deeper look at the supply chain in part, to make sure that it works as efficiently and effectively as possible.

Operations terms

In this subsection of the chapter, the aim is to ensure you understand the language of operations. Most of the words used in operations management are pretty intuitive. On the off chance that you haven't heard a phrase being used before, the words it contains will probably tell you what it means. And so, I will now simply run through a long list of key definitions. These definitions might not be the best way of describing and explaining the terms in question. If you feel confused after reading the definition, I urge you to ask google for a better explanation. Once we have covered this long, boring list of definitions, we shall put some of these terms together, in the form of a diagram. This diagram is a convenient way of remembering how these terms link together. More importantly, it is a good illustration of how we use the study of operations to piece by piece analyse each part of the supply chain (Soman, 2020).

Blocking – The situation when the next step in the process is not ready or has no storage, leading to the current step having to be halted.

Bottleneck – The resource that limits the capacity or output of the overall process.

Buffering – The addition of storage between steps in a process. This allows steps to operate more independently and reduces the chances of blocking.

Cycle Time – The average time between the output of successive units of the product from the process.

Efficiency – The ratio between the actual output versus the theoretically expected output or benchmark.

Make-to-stock – A manufacturing approach, where standardised products are made ahead of time and stored. When the customer places an order, the finished good only needs to be delivered.

Make-to-order – A manufacturing approach, where the products are customised and made as per order instructions, at the time of receiving the customer's order.

Operation time – The total time required to setup and complete all processes for a whole batch of units.

Velocity/throughput ratio – The ratio between the throughput time and the value-added time for a single unit. This ratio gives us an idea of how much time each unit is wasting in the process, waiting to be acted on. Larger ratios are worse.

Productivity – The value of the output (in monetary terms) divided by the value of the input. This gives us an idea of how many times over the process is increasing value.

Queue time – The amount of time that a unit spends in the queue, waiting to be processed.

Run time – The amount of time required for the process to run over all units in the batch (only the processing time).

Setup time – The time required to setup all machines and inputs, so that the process can begin.

Starving – The situation when a step in the process has no work because there is no input coming in for whatever reason.

Throughput time/lead time – The total time that a unit takes to be produced, starting from the queue time, and including the entire run time.

Throughput rate – The number of units of output that the process is expected to produce in unit time. This is mathematically the reciprocal of the cycle time.

Utilisation – The ratio of the time for which a resource is actually being used versus the total time for which it is available.

Value-added time – The amount of time for which the unit is actually being worked on by any step in the process.

Little's Law – This is a convenient formula which helps us understand how the throughput, lead time and average inventory in a system are related to each other. This formula should intuitively make sense if you spend some time thinking about it. The attached diagram should help speed up this process of making sense of the formula.

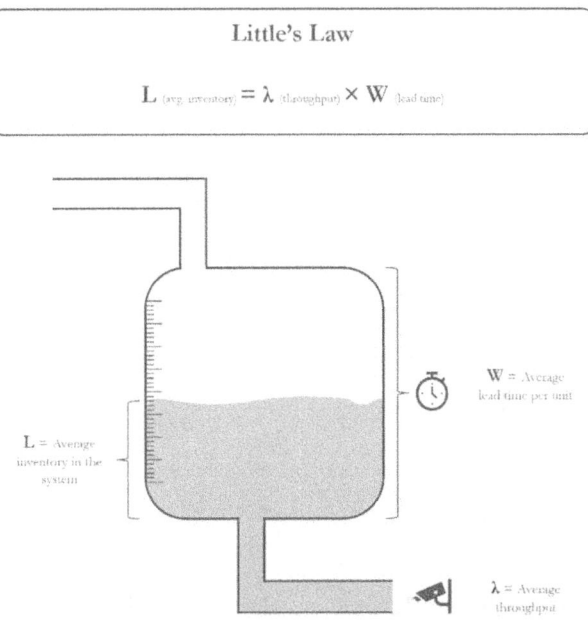

Case 9.1

The dungeon's management decides that they have dabbled in enough new and trendy businesses. They intend to acquire large, existing businesses to indicate that they are a large enterprise. This of course means that they will have to move towards more traditional industries, which are heavy on the operations side. As a starting point, they have acquired an FMCG (fast-moving consumer goods) company. Having studied many different courses on operations management, the dungeon's management is confident that they will be able to streamline and improve operations in the company.

However, as they are trying to understand the company's operations, they find themselves rather muddled up and confused about the many different operations terms and metrics being used. They think that it's best to first go back to the drawing board and understand how each term is related to the other. This understanding will enable them to analyse operations, without getting confused about different terminology used in each document (Sonnan, 2020).

Luckily, they have found an old diagram from their textbooks, which illustrates the relations between the different terms. Unfortunately, the book is so old, that the arrow marks remain, but the specific relation between terms has been erased.

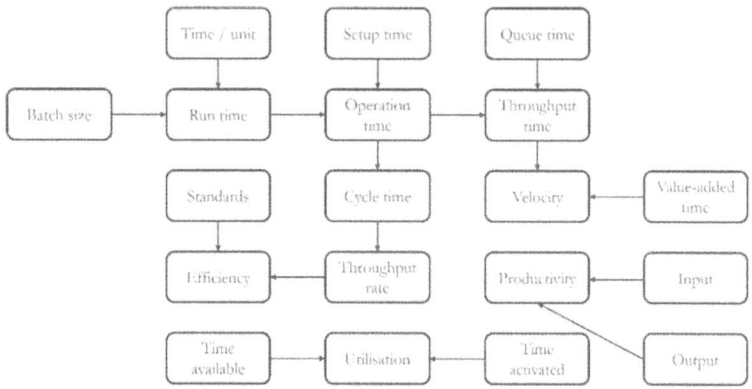

Case Questions

From your understanding of the diagram and the previously defined terms.

1. Are all of the arrow markings useful and correct?
2. What are the formulae through which each of the connected terms are related?

Instead of just thinking on your own, I would encourage you to participate in a case discussion on the following Reddit thread. Through case discussion, your ideas may be validated or improved upon. You would also benefit from other people's viewpoints.

Other operational details

From the list of terms that we have seen, it must be clear that a lot of operations involves figuring out how efficient processes are and whether our outputs are matching their potential. This is true, but it also makes it sound like operations is just looking at a dashboard and identifying disappointing metrics. In reality, once red flags are found, there is the exciting challenge of redesigning the process or improving execution to better the metric.

We can thus simplify operations down to the act of identifying inefficiencies, followed by the art of solving for the inefficiency. Because supply chains take many different shapes and forms, the list of possible problems and solutions in operations is far larger than what I can realistically cover in this book. However, most challenges in operations are old, well-documented and solved problems. Thus, I shall try to illustrate the process of identifying issues and matching them to established solutions in operations.

Case 9.2

Remember when the dungeon went and acquired an FMCG company? So, now the dungeon owns an old-school soap factory. Imagine that this factory is so old and small that we have very little automation, and just have 3 workers who make our soap. Currently, worker 1 completes step 1 in 8 minutes, then worker 2 completes step 2 in 7 minutes and worker 3 completes step 3 in 7 minutes.

Lead time = 20 min
Cycle time = 8 min

But dungeon's management is a bit smarter than this. They manage to come up with a brand-new approach to manufacturing this soap. In this new process, step 1 is worked on for only 3 minutes in the beginning and then repeated as step 4 for another 3 minutes right at the end. Thus, the same worker 1, now needs to work on each unit for only 6 minutes, not 8 minutes. The lead time per unit and the cycle time for the process are both reduced. This means that a unit of soap is produced every 7 minutes, instead of every 8 minutes. Of course, this means that the output has gone up.

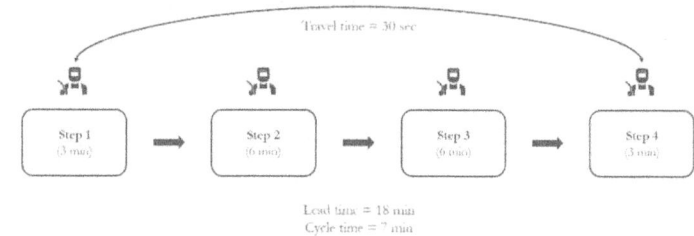

Travel time = 30 sec

Lead time = 18 min
Cycle time = 7 min

But dungeon's management was still surprised by this result. In the initial setup, the bottleneck step was step 1 at 8 minutes long. As a result of this, the cycle time was 8 minutes. The expectation was that in the new setup, the bottleneck step would be step 2 and step 3 and step 1 + step 4 together, all at 6 minutes long. However, it turns out that step 1 + step 4 + travel time each way is the bottleneck at a total of 7 minutes. Over and above this, worker 1, is working harder than the other 2 workers. Thus, whether the dungeon chooses to compensate worker 1 more, or hire an extra worker for step 4, costs will go up.

Even so, the increase in output is probably greater than the corresponding increase in costs. However, what if the design of the layout changed from a linear shape to a U shape, such that worker 1 need not walk between stations. This situation better matches our expectation, where each worker is equally the bottleneck at only 6 minutes long. Further, because all workers are still working just as hard, there is no need to increase anyone's pay. Thus, the u-shaped assembly line in this case helps improve efficiency, as compared to the straightforward line assembly (Soman, 2020).

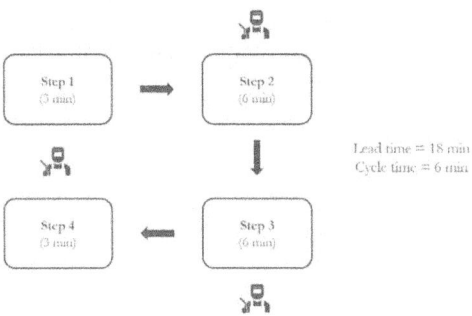

In another factory, where the dungeon manufactures toothpaste, each tube of toothpaste also goes through 3 steps. The first step takes 10 minutes per unit, the second takes 0.1 minutes per unit and the third also takes 10 minutes per unit. The factory currently uniformly operates on batch sizes of 100 units. Thus, 100 units are processed through the first step in 1,000 minutes, they are then processed through the second step in the next 10 minutes, and finally through the last step in the last 1,000 minutes. The overall process for 100 units is therefore completed within 2,010 minutes (Soman, 2020).

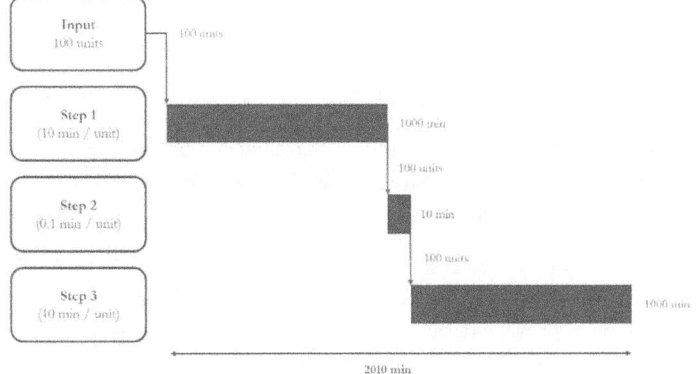

Dungeon's management decides to improve the efficiency of this factory as well. They notice that the first and third steps take a large amount of time, and are thus the reason that major machinery is idle for long periods. They thus decide to reduce the batch size from 100 to 10. In the resulting new setup, every 100 minutes, 10 units move from step 1 to step 2. Within 101 minutes, step 3 receives its first batch of 10 units to process. From there on out, every 100 minutes, step 3 receives batches of 10 units to process. Thus, within just 1,101 minutes the factory is now able to produce 100 units of toothpaste (Soman, 2020).

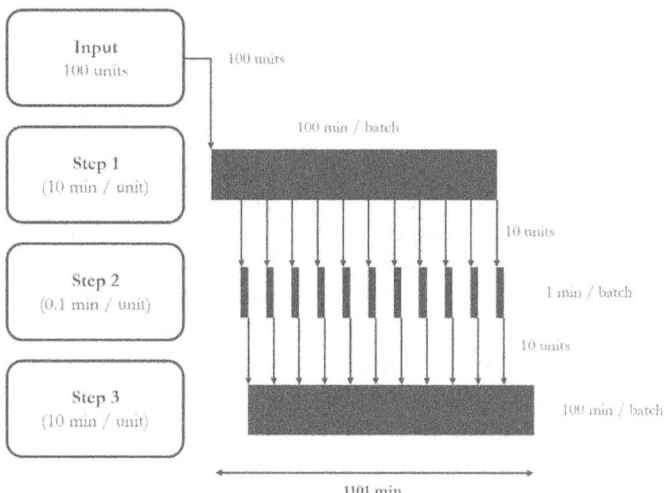

Case Questions

From your understanding of the operational changes introduced by the dungeon.

1. How does one go about identifying bottlenecks and sources of inefficiency?
2. Once a bottleneck is identified, how should one go about searching for ways to solve the problem?

Instead of just thinking on your own, I would encourage you to participate in a case discussion on the following Reddit thread. Through case discussion, your ideas may be validated or improved upon. You would also benefit from other people's viewpoints.

Project management

So far in the chapter, we have seen that there are many measures of efficiency at each step. We have also seen that once a source of inefficiency has been spotted, we can creatively come up with more efficient alternative approaches. I have vaguely promised you that these sources of inefficiency, as well as the solutions to them, fall into templates, which can be picked up from google or books on operations management. However, at this stage, I would like to point out that operations managers aren't usually just studying their supply chain and looking for sources of inefficiency. Sure, that also happens routinely. But, for the most part, they are in charge of projects and are tasked with executing them as efficiently as possible.

Once again, there are many aspects of project management which are of importance. If you aim to become a good operations manager, this chapter and this book are not going to get you across the line. But I shall try to provide an illustration, which will give you a good idea of how projects are planned and watched over.

Case 9.3

The dungeon has decided that it is time for them to open a new factory to produce ice creams. Since the dungeon is an ambitious business house, they would like to have their new factory up and running within 9 weeks. This goal has been provided by the dungeon's marketing team which believes that they would be able to capitalise on the summer season demand for ice creams if their new factory is operational within 9 weeks. The finance team has also arrived at a total budget of INR 3,50,000 for this project.

The operations team, while involved in these discussions, has now got to the drawing board to assess whether and how they can setup an ice cream factory within 9 weeks, with INR 3,50,000. To begin with they identify what activities they would need to complete in order to successfully open a new factory. They identify 7 activities that need to be completed, as well as the expected duration of each and the constraints in terms of which activities must be completed before any given activity can start.

Activity	Weeks	Pre-requisites
Purchase Land (A)	3	
Design Factory (B)	6	
Contract Builders (C)	4	
Register Land & Business (D)	5	A
Environmental Assessment (E)	7	A
Construct Factory (F)	4	B, C, D

Because tables are sometimes a little difficult to understand, they translate this table into a network diagram. In this diagram, we can see which activities happen in which order. The arrows mark the constraints of which activities must be completed before others can begin. Using this network diagram, management first completes a forward pass to identify the earliest week by which each activity can begin and finish. Then, they complete a backward pass (from the last node) to identify the latest week each activity can finish and therefore begin, without having any impact on the completion date. In case this example isn't in itself clear, you might want to google how to construct a precedence diagram and specifically look at the forward and backward pass calculations.

Within this diagram, management then calculated how much slack existed at each step. The slack in any given activity is the difference between the late start and early start or between the late finish and early finish. The slack represents the amount of delay which that activity can withstand, without impacting the project's timeline (Soman, 2020).

206

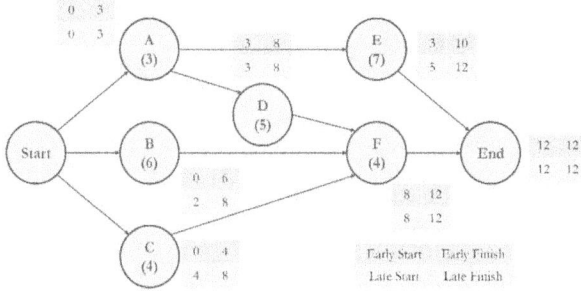

Thus, the activities with no slack, are bottleneck steps, whose duration can be reduced or increased to impact the project's timeline. Management then identified that the critical path in this project is A-D-F. This means that if any of these steps are shortened in duration, that would directly shorten the duration of the project. This is in fact necessary since the project currently looks like it will take 12 weeks, rather than 9 (Soman, 2020).

Luckily, some of these activities can be sped up to some extent. However, this additional speed comes at a cost. Thus, management studied the current costs of each activity, as well as the cost that would be incurred to speed up each activity.

Activity	Weeks	Pre-requisites	Current Cost	Cost / Week Reduced	Max Weeks Reducible
Purchase Land (A)	3		1,20,000	30,000	1
Design Factory (B)	6		20,000	15,000	2
Contract Builders (C)	4		40,000	10,000	2
Register Land & Business (D)	5	A	20,000	10,000	2
Environmental Assessment (E)	7	A	10,000	10,000	3
Construct Factory (F)	4	B, C, D	90,000	20,000	1

The project would currently cost INR 3,00,000 to be completed within 12 weeks. This leaves the dungeon with INR 50,000 to shave off 3 weeks from the project's timeline. Along the critical path A-D-F, it, therefore, makes sense to reduce 2 weeks from activity D for INR 20,000. This activity has the lowest cost per week reduced and is the only activity which can be sped up by 2 weeks. The resulting precedence diagram therefore changes.

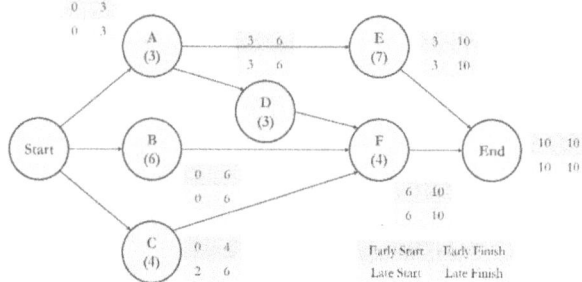

In the new situation, only activity C still has any slack. Thus, the new critical paths are B-F, A-D-F and A-F. Each of these critical paths must be reduced in duration for the overall project's timeline to be reduced from 10 weeks to 9. The most economical way of completing this reduction proves to be reducing the duration of E and F, each by 1 week, at a total cost of INR 30,000. This would result in the project being completed in exactly 9 weeks, at a cost of exactly INR 3,50,000.

Case Questions

From your understanding of the project managed by the dungeon.

1. What purpose was served by the drawing of a precedence diagram?
2. In what step were bottlenecks identified and how?
3. How does one decide which activity to focus on improving?
4. Find out what a Gantt chart is, and plot the final project timeline in the form of a Gantt chart.

Instead of just thinking on your own, I would encourage you to participate in a case discussion on the following Reddit thread. Through case discussion, your ideas may be validated or improved upon. You would also benefit from other people's viewpoints.

Quality management

So far, we have seen that a big part of operations management is ensuring that our supply chain processes are churning out maximum output with the help of minimum input and in the minimum amount of time possible. To bring about this efficiency, we have seen some metrics that can be monitored, examples of design changes which improve efficiency, and how projects can be managed efficiently.

However, in addition to maintaining the efficiency of the supply chain, operations managers are responsible for the quality of output. However efficiently a supply chain runs, a defective unit is the worst possible outcome. Not only does it not count towards our output, but it costs the company too. So, a big part of operations management is quality management. Remember, when we spoke about how the pioneers of operations management managed to standardise the quality of output? In this subsection, we shall see some of the techniques that they introduced to the world of manufacturing and quality management.

Service Quality

A lot of what we have covered in operations has related purely to manufacturing. This is largely because manufacturing and logistics in a supply chain are easy spaces to apply mathematical operations management. However, all of the same principles still apply in the context of services, even if it is less immediately visible. In the space of quality management, there is a popular framework on the 5 potential gaps in service quality. In case customers are not happy with service quality, one or more of these 5 gaps are likely present (Parasuraman, Zeithaml, & Berry, 1985) (Amblee, 2021).

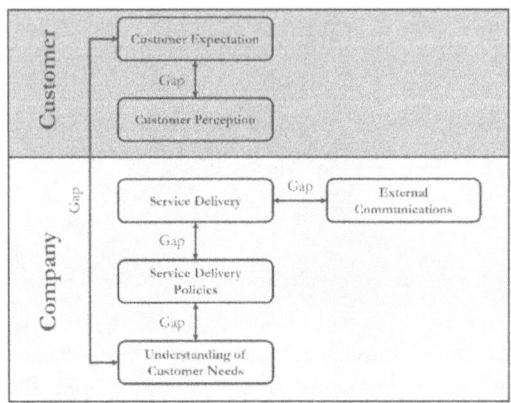

With this framework for identifying quality gaps in service in mind, let's move forward to other quality management measures. What we will see is also applicable in the context of services, but has been developed in the context of tangible products.

Control Charts

We have already seen that there are many metrics that operations managers look at to ensure the efficiency of their processes. Even in quality management, another set of metrics proves to be useful. This shouldn't be a surprise, since we have already noted that this is a space of management which is very scientific, where most problems have already been solved in some way or form.

The way in which operations managers watch over quality involves 2 key tools of control charts and acceptance tests. Control charts give us statistical information on large batches of units. Thus, at a glance, control charts can inform us as to whether something might be wrong with the process. This enables managers to allow the supply chain to flow at an industrial pace, until and unless something goes wrong. Acceptance tests are more manual processes of sampling and testing individual units. Once again here, we rely on statistics to tell us whether any deformities are within an acceptable range or not.

There are 2 control charts which are of particular interest to us. Both charts have time as their x-axis. This time could be represented in the form of a batch number, or literal time of manufacturing. The y-axis represents the measure of interest. This measure might relate to the size of the manufactured product, battery life or any other such feature (Soman, 2020).

- **x̄ charts** – These charts plot the average value of the measure of interest for a given batch on the y-axis.
- **R charts** – These charts plot the range (maximum – minimum) of the measure of interest for a given batch on the y-axis.

Notice that with these 2 charts together, we have an understanding of whether the batch on average is within expectation, as well as whether there is much variation within the batch. If both of these are within limits, we have no problems. However, if even one of these charts crosses the limits that we maintain, there may be excessively defective units.

Six Sigma

One of the most popular phrases to throw around in the space of quality management is "six sigma". So, what does it really mean and what's so special about it?

In a nutshell, six sigma is a statistical and data-driven process that companies and project managers can follow to improve efficiency and quality. The focus of the six-sigma method is to reduce occurrences of defects to less than 3.4 per million. This number of 3.4/million is where the name six sigma comes from (six standard deviations in a normal curve).

Of course, the six sigma approach is much more extensive, and I shall not attempt to explain it in this book. There are various levels of six sigma certification that one can apply for and earn. Those programmes are much better places to learn about six sigma. Nonetheless, there are a few takeaways, which are useful to understand. Operations managers in your organisation may be using the six sigma approach, so, it is best to understand at a broad level what that means.

The approach is centred around the DMAIC problem solving method. This approach requires us to define who our customers are and what our objective is, Measure our process and its performance, Analyse the cause of defects, Improve upon the causes of the defects, and Control the process, to maintain quality. Of course, each letter on the acronym can be delved into in much more depth, with a range of powerful frameworks, but I shall leave that task to six sigma courses (Soman, 2020).

There are also a few charts and techniques which are useful to analyse and solve for operational problems. Many of these will not be new to you, so I shall just list them out as a checklist (Soman, 2020).

- Check sheets
- Control charts
- Fishbone diagram
- Flow charts
- Histograms
- Pareto analyses
- Run charts

Learning from Japan

During the industrial and operations revolution, Japanese car manufacturers, especially Toyota introduced many changes to how quality is managed and efficiency is promoted. In addition to the more technical concepts that we have covered, are a few project management and design ideas which are fun, and find a prominent place in the modern world.

One such idea is that of a Kanban board. Kanban boards help us track many different modules in a project. Each part of the board belongs to a specific department/function/activity. Each post-it corresponds to a specific module or task. As one department finishes a certain task, they move the corresponding post-it to the next department which needs to work on it. Thus, we can visually track the progress, backlogs and bottlenecks. Kanban boards are a particularly popular way of organising work in software development in today's start-ups. Or at least it looks cool in TV shows about them (Kanbanize).

Poka Yoke is a popular design idea. It means idiot-proofing whatever we develop. USB C as a connector type is a big design step up from its predecessors. The design improvement in USB C essentially employs poka yoke. I won't even attempt to explain the concept beyond this. Google poka yoke examples to look at some very satisfying design solutions instead (Daniel, 2021).

Recap

In our attempt to understand how to manage a business, we have thus far learnt:

- Management thinking. We have extensively been using convergent thinking, structuring in particular and divergent thinking along the way.
- We got started with 4 steps of business value creation so that we can capture value from customers in return. We are capable of understanding the marketplace, positioning our brand to target the right customers, designing an effective market mix and managing relevant relationships along the way.
- To understand the language of finance, we have understood:
    o The financial reporting process.
    o How to build and analyse the 3 key financial reports.
    o Basic concepts, accounting principles and nuances.
    o Metrics and ratios for financial analysis.
    o What else can be learnt from financial markets to valuation of firms.
- Most recently, we have attempted to understand how to manage and run operations. To this end, we have a basic understanding of:
    o What the supply chain is.
    o Operations terminology.
    o Design approaches used in operations.
    o Project management in operations.
    o Quality management approaches.

We therefore now understand how to think like a manager, the overall business process, and are capable of translating our ideas into clear financial objectives. We are currently in the process of understanding how to translate clear objectives into definite action. Having already seen some of the tricks of the trade, we shall take a more mathematical look at how operations are optimised.

Chapter 21
Detailing with Math: Optimising Operations

From the first chapter of this section, hopefully, you have an overview of the types of problems that we aim to tackle in operations. We have had a look at a few illustrations of how operations managers may try to make processes more efficient, may redesign them, may manage large projects and maintain the quality of output. However, through all of this, to spare you some of the gruelling details, we have only had a look at simple illustrations. In operations, unlike many other domains of management, we can arrive at scientifically validated, optimal solutions, not just directionally useful ones. This chapter is dedicated to convincing you of the mathematical foundations of the optimisation possible in this space.

You may say that you are already convinced, but don't want to do the math on your own. As long as you're not an operations manager, you may not need to routinely do a lot of this math. However, the aim of this chapter isn't to delve into the mathematical details of operations. Rather, it is to help shift our mindset from one of directional frameworks to one of exact formulae. So, we shall take a glance at the kind of optimisation that can be done in operations.

Optimal ordering

In most industries, there are some sort of inputs which the company needs to maintain to provide customers with the final product or service. Let's simplify our lives by imagining that we are running a manufacturing plant, which requires raw materials for manufacturing. In a different context, an appropriate analogy can always be taken.

Ordering raw materials is a directionally simply task, which we took for granted in our previous sections. At most, we would have understood what type of raw materials make for a good product that customers would value, and we would have recorded the expected costs of raw materials. However, in operations, we aim to optimise this process of ordering and reordering raw materials.

To begin with, this process is more complex than meets the eye. There is the obvious cost per unit of raw material (let's call it C). Additionally, raw materials have a certain holding cost per item per year (let's call it H). This holding cost arises from the cost of renting warehouses and maintaining them. There is also a cost associated with each order placed (let's call it S). This order cost may be a function of the logistics cost of delivery or a service fee that a third-party charges. Despite these costs, we need to place orders, because there is a certain amount of the raw material which is demanded for manufacturing each year (let's call it D). Taking all of these factors into account, an operations manager needs to place orders for raw materials. But how many orders should they place in a given year? At what time interval should they place these orders? And for each order, how many items should they order in one go?

To answer these questions, we first centre around our main objective. In this context, the objective of the operations manager is to minimise the total cost of ordering (let's call it TC). The total annual demand for the material must be met, and that is a fixed constraint, not a goal. Further, we shall take the simplifying assumption here, that the raw material is uniformly consumed, so we don't have to worry about irregularity.

Let's begin by trying to figure out what the optimal order quantity is each time (let's call it Q*). Notice that, if we know what Q* is, we know that the number of orders we should place in a year is D/Q*. Further, because of uniform consumption, we know that these orders should be uniformly spaced out through the year (Sinha A., 2021).

Without going too deeply into the math, we start by trying to figure out how to represent the total cost incurred. In case the formula isn't clear, any textbook on operations or a google search for the derivation of optimal order quantity should explain it in much more detail.

$$TC = (C \times D) + ((Q^*/2) \times H) + ((D/Q^*) \times S)$$

(total cost) = ((cost per unit)×(annual demand)) + ((average inventory)×(annual holding cost)) + ((number of orders)×(ordering cost))

With a little simple differential calculus, we can arrive at the optimal order quantity to place, to minimise the total cost. It's easy to notice that the optimal order quantity is proportional to the total demand and the cost per order. More demand means that we will have to order more. And a higher cost per order means that we want to minimise orders, by ordering larger quantities in one go. Similarly, a higher holding cost, means that we want to minimise order quantity and thus average inventory (Sinha A., 2021).

$$Q^* = \sqrt{(2 \times D \times S) / H}$$

(optimal order quantity) $= \sqrt{(2 \times (\text{annual demand}) \times (\text{ordering cost}) / (\text{annual holding cost}))}$

Slightly more advanced approaches are used in contexts where we don't use unrealistic assumptions of uniform consumption. With this more advanced math, we get precise answers for when an order should be placed (in terms of remaining inventory). The point to be driven home here isn't the math that we went through here. Rather, the key idea is that most of the critical problems in operations are old and solved ones, where very precise answers are available.

As a manager what one needs to learn is:

- What sort of mathematical approaches are taken to optimise operations.
- Every manager should be familiar with this math, and the common results which are relevant to their business. Familiarity with this math would only mean that they should understand the contents of such a discussion, and be able to verify important insights if need be.
- Operations managers should know the operational details and the underlying math inside out. This means that they would often need to derive answers for what the optimal solution is. They are generally expected to have studied operations management in enough detail, to be able to reuse known results, rather than derive them from scratch every day.

Sequencing of jobs

Since the main objective of this chapter is to help us shift our mindsets, and learn to think mathematically when we have to, let's take another example. Not that this example is super critical, compared to other examples that we could look at. I just picked this one. So, let's have a look at how operations optimisation can help us with sequencing jobs.

Case 10

Back in the dungeon's head office, management is trying to work through some paperwork. Ever since the dungeon got into the FMCG space, many corporate clients have been eager to sign a long-term supply contract with us. As a result, a lot of paperwork has piled up. Some of the paperwork is more important than the rest, some of it takes longer than the rest, and neither of these is related to the order in which it has come in.

With all of the operations knowledge that they have, combined with ideas from the internet, dungeon's management is sure that they can find a way of optimising this.

Job	Processing Time	Due Date	Value
A	5	7	2
B	1	9	1
C	7	12	3
D	3	12	1
E	4	15	2
F	3	15	3

After a quick glance at a textbook, management arrives at 4 different strategies that they can apply. They are sure that in any scenario, one of these will prove to be the most effective approach.

First Come First Serve

One suggested approach is to just pick up the first task that came in, and complete that, then move on to the next. The rationale behind this approach is that the total time to complete the full list of tasks will remain the same. This approach is fair to the other stakeholders, who would expect to benefit from providing their task earlier. It is also the easiest to implement, and therefore adds no execution overhead.

Order	Job	Processing Time	Due Date	Value	Flow Time	Tardiness
1	A	5	7	2	5	0
2	B	1	9	1	6	0
3	C	7	12	3	13	1
4	D	3	15	1	16	1
5	E	4	18	2	20	2
6	F	3	17	3	23	6

This approach can make no guarantees as to the most valuable tasks being taken care of without hiccups, deadlines being met or tardiness being minimised.

In this approach, the task which will take the minimum time to get done is scheduled next. In case of a tie, any other method such as FCFS can be used to break ties. This approach will minimise the number of tasks in process at any point in time. It will also ensure that the average flow time (time from submission till completion) is minimum across all jobs.

Order	Job	Processing Time	Due Date	Value	Flow Time	Tardiness
1	B	1	9	1	1	0
2	D	3	15	1	4	0
3	F	3	17	3	7	0
4	E	4	18	2	11	0
5	A	5	7	2	16	9
6	C	7	12	3	23	11

Clearly, this is a good approach to reduce the number of pending tasks and make the average time per task look good and low. However, this doesn't necessarily mean that tardiness (delay on jobs) is minimised, nor does it ensure that the most valuable jobs are dealt with well.

Earliest Due Date

In this approach, the task which is due soonest is to be scheduled first, and so on. Once again, ties can be broken through any method. This approach reduces the number and extent of tardiness on jobs. On the whole, this is the best approach to minimise tardiness.

Order	Job	Processing Time	Due Date	Value	Flow Time	Tardiness
1	A	5	7	2	5	0
2	B	1	9	1	6	0
3	C	7	12	3	13	1
4	D	3	15	1	16	1
5	F	3	17	3	19	2
6	E	4	18	2	23	5

However, this doesn't guarantee the minimum average flow time, nor does it give any precedence to valuable projects.

Shortest Weighted Processing Time

There are clearly benefits to ordering basis processing time. However, in order to ensure that important tasks are given priority over unimportant but quick tasks, we weight the processing time with the value of the task. Thus, the weighted processing time is the processing time, divided by the value of the job. This gives us a measure of the processing time per unit of value.

Order	Job	Processing Time	Due Date	Value	WPT	Flow Time	Tardiness
1	B	1	9	1	1	1	0
2	F	3	17	3	1	4	0
3	E	4	18	2	2	8	0
4	C	7	12	3	2.33	15	3
5	A	5	7	2	2.5	20	13
6	D	3	15	1	3	23	8

This approach isn't necessarily the best on any one metric. However, much like the shortest processing time approach, it reduces the average flow time and the number of work-in-process tasks. However, unlike that approach, it ensures that important, high-value tasks aren't too tardy. It, therefore, provides a more balanced approach.

Other Approaches
There are of course many other ways of scheduling tasks, which the dungeon has not looked into for this problem. For example, there is Hodgson's rule, which would enable them to minimise the number of tardy jobs. There is also Johnson's rule, which they could use in case they have multiple people available to go through the paperwork (Sinha A., 2021).

For the time being, they believe that one of these 4 approaches would be a good start.

Case Questions
From your understanding of the job scheduling problem.

1. What are some realistic objectives and constraints that the dungeon might be working with?
2. Given the goal and constraints, which of the above 4 methods is the best to use?
3. In what circumstance, if any, will a different scheduling approach work? Explain which scheduling approach would work in which situation.

Instead of just thinking on your own, I would encourage you to participate in a case discussion on the following Reddit thread. Through case discussion, your ideas may be validated or improved upon. You would also benefit from other people's viewpoints.

Recap

In our attempt to understand how to manage a business, we have thus far learnt:

- Management thinking. We have extensively been using convergent thinking, structuring in particular and divergent thinking along the way.
- We got started with 4 steps of business value creation so that we can capture value from customers in return. We are capable of understanding the marketplace, positioning our brand to target the right customers, designing an effective market mix and managing relevant relationships along the way.
- To understand the language of finance, we have understood:
    - The financial reporting process.
    - How to build and analyse the 3 key financial reports.
    - Basic concepts, accounting principles and nuances.
    - Metrics and ratios for financial analysis.
    - What else can be learnt from financial markets to valuation of firms.
- We then picked up the basics of operations, including:
    - What the supply chain is.
    - Operations terminology.
    - Design approaches used in operations.
    - Project management in operations.
    - Quality management approaches.

- Just now, we immersed ourselves in some mathematics to optimise operations. Without learning any new math, we have accepted that it has already been used to solve most of the challenging operations problems.

We have understood the different types of questions that operations deals with, and have accepted that there are established mathematical ways to solve most of them. Since I have already bored you by stating that I won't delve into the details, I shall point you in a useful direction. Next, we shall list out the different types of math that one would have to be comfortable with as a manager. With that in your arsenal, everything that I have glossed over so far in this section will become easy for you to work out on your own, if and when you have to.

Chapter 22
Math for Managers: The New ABC

Through the last 2 chapters, while I have used a great many words, I have conveyed rather little. All that I have told you is that operations is a subject area where people smarter than me have solved all of our problems. Now, we need to equip ourselves to understand how to frame any problem, and then how to look for existing solutions to that problem. If we are able to do this, all of the operational challenges that we face are as good as solved.

This task of framing problems and searching for solutions requires us to understand the language workings of a little bit of math. We as managers need not develop a deep understanding, since we are rarely the ones deriving complex solutions. But a working understanding, to make sure that we aren't completely in the dark is necessary.

I'm going to assume that a lot of people reading this were not necessarily excited about math during school and college. The good news is that the math that you need to know as a manager is pretty simple, and I'm going to cover all of it in 5 quick steps.

Arithmetic

The first thing that you need to be comfortable with is basic arithmetic. Not just as a manager, but this is a useful life skill. When one is looking at sales numbers or pricing, a little bit of addition, subtraction multiplication, division and calculating percentages is always handy. A lot of these numbers will come your way multiple times in a day as a manager.

While quick mental math is useful and looks cool in a meeting, it's not absolutely necessary. But once one is equipped with a calculator or MS Excel, the expectation is that arithmetic errors should not be made. This is relatively simple to do. In case you have forgotten, you might want to brush up on your BODMAS. But with just that, you are through with the first of 5 mathematical steps to solve any operations problem. Over and above this if you understand orders of magnitude, exponentiation and logarithms, business should be a piece of cake.

Probabilities

Now that we are comfortable with simple, arithmetic, it's time to accept that there are no guarantees in the business world. Because a lot of important decisions are hinged on unknowns, we need to become good at estimating probabilities and then working with them.

For one thing, it's important to understand the concept of events, experiments and sample spaces. From there, it is important to be clear on simple probabilities, conditional probabilities and how they work when events intersect, are subsets of each other and so on. If this is starting to sound complicated, remember that all the answers, formulae and rules are available on the internet. You as a manager need to train yourself to understand the concepts so that you can frame the question and ask the internet for help.

While we're listing out concepts, it's useful if your understanding of probability extends to random variables, distributions, correlation and covariance. The reason that all of this is helpful, is that we are surrounded by data in business. If we understand the data, we can use it to predict outcomes and plan for them. Of course, as a manager, your role might not be the analysis of data. But because it will likely have an impact on your decisions, it is important to remain mathematically literate.

Statistics

A natural extension to an understanding of probability is an understanding of statistics. We have already accepted that we live in a world of unknowns, where probability helps us predict the future. We now have the benefit of big data. With an understanding of statistics, we can translate millions of data points into precise probabilities. In a later mathematical step, we will use big data to arrive at highly accurate answers, not just probabilities.

So, how does one leverage the power of statistics? To begin with, we need to make sure that we're looking at useful and relevant data. So, one needs to be clear on the idea of sampling, and when and how it should be done. Once one has understood the different sampling techniques, and which one fits in a context, they would have a lot of useful information at their fingertips. Developing a hypothesis, and learning how to test it is critical, and was therefore included in our 4 steps to manage any situation. Hypothesis testing, and using p values is a super powerful statistical tool. Finally, an understanding of regression, and how we can use it to predict trends and uncover patterns is very useful.

We have now covered 3 out of 5 mathematical steps that can give us the answer to any operational challenge. These 3 steps alone are immensely powerful. Until a couple of decades back, the manufacturing giants of the world were able to use just these to run near perfect operations. However, humans do have their limitations, and so the next 2 mathematical steps help us overcome them.

At this stage, some readers may be a little lost and might believe that these 3 steps alone are excessive. In fairness, many of the best managers are far from experts in arithmetic, probability and statistics. However, I'm sure that they run businesses which use these concepts effectively. It is always useful to understand at the very least what these concepts are, how they are used and why they work. Even if someone else is doing the grunt work, if it makes a difference to the business, you as a manager should understand what it is. No math is needed here, you just need to google all the new terms you have seen and read a little about them.

While you're going about googling, understand a little bit about calculus. Calculus is often used to translate our simple results for small discrete cases to effective solutions in massive, continuous scenarios. Often times this makes the difference between a good idea in theory, to one which works in the real world.

Better with MS Excel

Through the first 3 mathematical steps, we have already seen how we can put 2 and 2 together, arrive at decisions in uncertainty and use the power of big data to make the unknown known. There really isn't much else that a manager needs out of mathematics. But, all of this math is tricky or tedious at the very least. Luckily, amongst the many brilliant pieces of software written to tackle this problem is MS Excel.

There is of course other software used for analytics and insight derivation. Many of them are friendlier and easier to use. However, excel is sort of an industry standard and is immensely powerful. Whether you are looking to simply collate your data, do basic arithmetic, map out flow charts of probability, or run statistical operations, excel has you covered. Rather than understanding the details of the math from the first 3 steps, if you understand the input and the output, you can get the job done on excel.

There are many ways in which one could go about getting comfortable with MS Excel. If you have absolutely no background in using it, you might want to check out a few videos which introduce you to the software. However, most users who are comfortable with the basics, usually just consult the internet when there is an operation that they don't know how to complete. It's a pretty low-effort way of picking up what you need to know, without putting the rest of your work on pause.

Logic and computer science

Our fifth and final mathematical step is counterintuitively the simplest and also the most powerful. At the heart of borrowing mathematical solutions for operational problems is the study of logic. It is with the help of basic logic that we are able to frame our problem statements and constraints. It's with the help of logic that we are able to rule out some options and identify the best solution.

As we have seen in step 4, we can use a computer to run through the first 3 steps of math, rather than burdening ourselves. Similarly, with the power of code, anything that we can logically think through in the form of rules or instructions can be automated. This not only frees up our time but makes the process much faster and more error-free.

You might be sold on the benefits of code, but it doesn't help you unless you know how to code. Of course, in most organisations, there is an IT team or an analyst who will do the bulk of the coding work for managers. However, much like with the first 3 mathematical steps, it always helps to understand at a top level, at least how things work. To this end, it helps to understand the differences between back-end and front-end languages, as well as what database your company uses. These might all sound like gibberish. But just knowing these things, allows you to understand what parts of a conversation with IT you need to pay attention to.

As a next step, if you understand what variables, loops, conditions, functions and data structures are in a programming language, a lot of code would suddenly start looking like English. You need not understand any of these concepts well enough to code on your own. But understanding a little bit about the tech world may put you in a much better place to manage any business.

As a final touch to the fifth mathematical step, we have the dazzling world of machine learning. On the one hand, this is much like coding. But what's special about it is the fact that we as humans don't even need to come up with all of the logic and instructions to make it work. In areas where we don't yet have all the math that we need to solve a problem, smart machine learning algorithms can recognise patterns and come up with solutions, which humans haven't yet formulated or understood. But more on cutting-edge technology in the next chapter.

Recap

In our attempt to understand how to manage a business, we have thus far learnt:

- Management thinking. We have extensively been using convergent thinking, structuring in particular and divergent thinking along the way.
- We got started with 4 steps of business value creation so that we can capture value from customers in return. We are capable of understanding the marketplace, positioning our brand to target the right customers, designing an effective market mix and managing relevant relationships along the way.
- To understand the language of finance, we have understood:
  o The financial reporting process.
  o How to build and analyse the 3 key financial reports.
  o Basic concepts, accounting principles and nuances.
  o Metrics and ratios for financial analysis.
  o What else can be learnt from financial markets to valuation of firms.
- We then picked up the basics of operations, including:
  o What the supply chain is.
  o Operations terminology.
  o Design approaches used in operations.
  o Project management in operations.
  o Quality management approaches.
- As a next step, we immersed ourselves in some mathematics to optimise operations. Without learning any new math, we have accepted that it has already been used to solve most of the challenging operations problems.
- Because I had to put my money where my mouth is, we saw 5 areas of math which would help us solve all of our operational needs. We convinced ourselves that a combination of arithmetic, probability, statistics, excel and logic/coding could solve all of our problems.

Within just 3 quick chapters we have come up with a strategy through which we can frame any operations problem, and then borrow ready-made solutions from smarter people. Now that all of our operations problems have been solved, what could

226

possibly remain? Technology is constantly changing. Therefore, the best solutions are constantly getting better. What's more, technology often leaks outside of the scope of operations and changes business models. For that matter, technology is literally changing the world that we live in. So, let's have a look at what some of the biggest trends in technology are today, and what managers need to educate themselves on.

Chapter 23
Tech Trends: Thank God for Technology

In this section, unlike the previous few, it is quite possible that you have not yet read a single thing that you didn't know. I have only communicated that all the answers in operations already exist, and that one needs to be mathematically literate to access them. Towards the end of the previous chapter, I gave you a little hope, by promising that advancing technology may eliminate the need for us to even understand the underlying math.

Those statements are pretty loaded, so, let's try to unpack them with a few references to pop culture. The things that used to drive business yesterday, are not necessarily the same as what is driving business today, or what will drive it tomorrow. Take for example a scene from 2 states or modern family, depending on which one you're more interested in. In 2 states, Krish is able to help Ananya's father with a PowerPoint presentation. Not because he understands the business better, but just because the skills that make day-to-day business work have changed. On the funnier side, take the scene from modern family, where Jay, who has successfully run a business for years is struggling to double click.

Aside from acting as comic fodder, these scenes provide us with deep-rooted insights. Using a typewriter, language skills, math skills and selling skills used to be indispensable just a few decades back. Fundamentally, most of these skills still are. But each of them is evolving along with our world. Being able to type fast, or use a computer with ease is indispensable. Being fluent in language, and being able to express one's self over email or on social media is still valuable. Being comfortable with excel, code and data analytics is just as useful or more than basic math was. And selling remains important, even if it is now done more through digital marketing than face-to-face.

The conclusion is that technology is changing every part of our world and our work. So, let's have a look at some of the big technology frontiers one can expect to come up against in the workplace.

MS Office suite

In any white-collar work environment, one can safely expect there to be some combination of documents, spreadsheets, presentations and emails involved. For a lot of such jobs, this is almost all there is. I don't mean this in a work is boring and pointless kind of way. I mean this in the sense that an enormous amount of information is communicated, distilled and acted upon through these few streamlined tools.

The company that has nearly monopolised this market is Microsoft. Starting off as the operating system that most companies work on to providing the office suite that most employees use. Very few people have the express job of making documents and presentations look better. But for any manager, because work involves using these tools, understanding how to make the most of them can have a profound impact.

Mastery over MS Office today can have the same impact as a combination of language, persuasion and mathematical skills had in previous years. That being said, MS Office isn't the only software package in the industry. The Google suite is also a cutting-edge competitor. Whatever software suite your business uses, managers must learn how to use it well.

As for how one can learn all of this, the approach remains the same as what we discussed in the previous chapter. The very introductory skills can be learnt from videos and online courses. But most upskilling will happen only by trial and error, along with consultation of the internet. No matter what you are trying to achieve on MS Office, the odds are that someone else has also struggled and asked a web forum for help. You will likely either find detailed instructions, or ready-made solutions.

Company-wide software

Many knowledge workers use MS Office and similar suites a fair bit. However, many employees are tasked with more specialised labour who use email, but not excel, word or powerpoint. So, what are they doing through the day? Depending on the nature of one's work, they may be directly managing operations on the ground, they may be directly handling backend infrastructure, they may be in charge of projects, they may be in charge of arriving at insights from data, or they may be in charge of people. Of course, there are many other things that employees may be in charge of. Clearly, some roles don't require one to communicate through ppts and docs or to organise information in spreadsheets.

For this very diverse set of employees, whose work impacts the entire company, there is a range of other company software. Some of these software are not as well known as MS Office since they aren't used by as many people. However, they are still largely company-wide software, because, in some way or form, every department uses the output from these software.

CRM (customer relationship management) software is a popular example. Any company that sells at scale (most all of them), needs to keep a track of their customers, past purchases, behaviour, offers etc. CRMs like salesforce and newspage are particularly popular. CRMs are used predominantly by sales teams. However, the information held in CRMs is often very useful for departments like marketing, finance and supply. The IT team is required to work on the CRM, and the legal team will routinely have to review how the data is stored and used. As such, CRMs are central to how most companies operate.

SQL or SAP databases often make up the backend database where companies store all of their transaction, inventory, billing and other information. These databases are a treasure trove, which can reveal the history, growth, successes and failures of a company. Because these databases are so important, and also complex, they are usually directly operated on and accessed by a limited set of individuals. However, the information within these databases is useful to every employee in some way or form. Many companies have other software built on top of SQL and SAP databases. The purpose of this software is to allow analysts access to data, without putting valuable data at risk. They also serve to reduce complex, powerful commands to simpler, intuitive and user-friendly operations.

In addition to this, depending on the business, there may be a range of other software used for cloud storage of files, remote access to the company's server, ERPs, data analytics suites and other collaboration tools.

As long as you're not working in IT, you might not need to know the technology infrastructure inside out. However, for every employee and manager, understanding what software is available, and how to use it effectively helps unlock a lot of productivity. After all, no one wants to be stuck in a position where your software isn't working, and you're waiting for someone from IT to come help you out.

So, how does one get up to speed on this wide range of software, which varies from one company to another? Once again, the answer is just trial and error. Try using the tools which you are given. Ask people within the company who seem faster and sharper with the tools how they do it. Spend some time with the data analyst in your team, or with someone from IT to understand what technology infrastructure exists and how to use it. Without a little bit of curiosity, the constantly changing technology can be a big burden. But with a little bit of curiosity, it could be a wonderland of tools which are constantly making your workload a little bit lighter.

Technology trends

By now, we have a rough idea of the key software that we as managers would have to work with as well as the other major software that will be used across the company. However, technology's impact on our business extends beyond the software that we subscribe to today. Every forward-looking company is always looking to capitalise on changes in society, the market and technology. Technology happens to be changing the fastest and impacting both society and the market. Thus, we as managers are expected to understand how the world around us might keep changing, and to plan for how to make the most of it.

It is therefore imperative that we understand a little about how technology has shaped business in recent years, and how it might go on to in the future. So, let's have a look at some of today's tech buzz words, and try and get a grip on what they mean, in English.

AI and ML

Artificial Intelligence and Machine Learning have been hot words in business and technology for a while now. In very common parlance, artificial intelligence is a computer doing anything that mimics human intelligence. This can include even some of the simplest and least intelligent tasks. Of course, we are impressed by AI because it extends up to the most complex tasks, which would be rather taxing, for a skilled human as well.

231

On the one hand, this can be done by providing a computer with a long list of detailed instructions, through code. This isn't great, but it's still better than teaching humans through detailed instructions. It's better because computers can often act on these instructions faster and with fewer errors. Further, once the first computer has been taught these instructions, we can easily have another 1,000 doing the same. Scaling is easier with AI.

But, what is particularly interesting in the space of AI is machine learning. Rather than providing a long list of instructions, we only write code to instruct the computer on how to learn. From there on out, the computer can train itself on a set called the training data. There are many different approaches used in ML, and each ML algorithm is better tuned to learn different skills. But going into the depths of the latest techniques in ML might be a little too advanced for this book. Let me instead list out some ML buzzwords that I like, such as artificial neural networks, reinforcement learning, support vector machine, decision forest, k nearest neighbours, bayes algorithm and gradient boosting algorithm. If you're interested, feel free to google these approaches and understand how some of them work.

More to the point, ML is a game-changer because:

- The same or similar code for a machine to learn a certain skill can be reused, so that it can find patterns and learn different skills.
- Through ML algorithms, computers can detect patterns and pick up skills that humans are incapable of.
- The accuracy of the results from ML algorithms is astonishingly good.

Thus, AI and specifically ML are changing the boundaries of what are human and machine tasks. This change can boost productivity and even change the kind of services that companies can offer customers. The broad expected changes are new and improved quality of service, faster and less expensive production, and shifting in jobs handled by humans.

Blockchain

If AI and ML were easy enough to understand, let's shift to a technology whose name doesn't explain exactly what it does. Let's begin with understanding a fundamental challenge in operations and bookkeeping. Sometimes one loses track of records or there are mismatches between 2 sets of records. Sometimes, third parties have a vested interest in tampering with records, to benefit from a mismatch. And sometimes, customers want to maintain anonymity in a transaction, but usually, this worsens the first 2 problems.

To understand blockchain, it is best to google bitcoin and understand more about how it came to be, how it works, and why it's interesting. There are youtube videos which do a much better job of explaining this than I can.

But in summary, blockchain is a technology through which we are able to keep track of a series of records or transactions. This is generally done through a public, distributed ledger. This just means that every user of the blockchain technology has a copy of all the records and transactions. That isn't normally enough to prevent a few people from colluding and forging their records to put the whole ledger into question. But, with blockchain technology, each user has a public key (like a user name) and a private key (like a password) which are used in a hashing algorithm to update the ledger with each transaction. Suffice to say that advanced cryptography is used here to prevent any sort of illegal alteration of the ledger.

Thus, the selling point of blockchain technology is that it helps keep immutable and accurate records of transactions, shipments or anything else of importance. This can be pretty useful technology in spaces where the loss of records is a concern or the value of one record is very high. The downside to blockchain technology is that it consumes a lot of energy to maintain multiple copies of these immutable ledgers.

Cloud Computing

Cloud computing once again brings us into the domain where the name of the technology is sort of self-explanatory. The big question is, what this cloud is.

Most companies own a large amount of valuable data. This could be data on their customers, competition, the market, their own products and so on. We have already seen that AI, ML and really any computation on big data provides valuable returns. Unfortunately, the cost of storing all of this data and computing on it tends to be expensive. Service providers like Amazon, Microsoft and Google who offer web server space and cloud computing functionality are able to provide significantly lower prices because of the scale at which they provide infrastructure as a service. Further, this relieves the company of the burden of operating a large server and maintaining it.

For these reasons, cloud computing is a technology which for the last few years has been enabling businesses to make much better decisions, and reap greater revenues, without incurring much of an additional expense.

AR, VR and XR

This seemingly strange string of letters is the technology which is most rooted in our physical world. Before you read ahead, if this is the first that you're hearing of AR and VR, I would strongly recommend that you watch a few videos online, which illustrate what the coolest AR and VR headsets can do today.

I don't believe that I could describe the benefits of this technology any better than the above video has. It's precisely this power of visuals over text which make AR, VR and XR so powerful. Let's have a quick look at the distinction between the three. Virtual Reality headsets take the user into an entirely virtual reality. Everything that the user sees and interacts with exists only digitally, and not in the real world. Augmented Reality headsets focus on adding layers to the real world. Thus, the user is looking at and interacting with the physical world. However, augmented layers of information, applications and tools help the user to navigate the physical world and possibly complete tasks more successfully. Extended Reality is a combination of AR and VR. Here, the user could transition between viewing an augmented physical world and a completely virtual digital world.

Platformisation

We started off with the plan of having a look at the big technology frontiers that we expect to interact with at the workplace. To this end, we have already had a look at the software through which most employees complete their work, the big software applications used in running many companies and the technology trends which are shaping the industry. We will finally touch upon how businesses are themselves moving into a digital world, via platforms.

From tech start-ups to tech giants, increasingly as customers, we interact with businesses through our phones or our computers. As customers, we begin to demand online platforms from the businesses that we frequent. This is understandable since it provides us with convenience, price and specification comparison and transparency, and even aggregation of services. Businesses too have a vested interest in platformisation. It enables them to collect more information on customers, better retain them, cross-sell, up-sell, price-target and so on. With all parties seeing some potential benefit, almost all industries are rapidly shifting to an online marketplace.

At the extreme end, platforms might take us to an all-encompassing version of the internet. You can think of this as something in the range between the matrix and the proposed metaverse.

Recap

In our attempt to understand how to manage a business, we have thus far learnt:

- Management thinking. We have extensively been using convergent thinking, structuring in particular and divergent thinking along the way.
- We got started with 4 steps of business value creation so that we can capture value from customers in return. We are capable of understanding the marketplace, positioning our brand to target the right customers, designing an effective market mix and managing relevant relationships along the way.
- To understand the language of finance, we have understood:
    o The financial reporting process.
    o How to build and analyse the 3 key financial reports.
    o Basic concepts, accounting principles and nuances.
    o Metrics and ratios for financial analysis.

- o What else can be learnt from financial markets to valuation of firms.
- We then picked up the basics of operations, including:
  - o What the supply chain is.
  - o Operations terminology.
  - o Design approaches used in operations.
  - o Project management in operations.
  - o Quality management approaches.
- As a next step, we immersed ourselves in some mathematics to optimise operations. Without learning any new math, we have accepted that it has already been used to solve most of the challenging operations problems.
- For closure, we convinced ourselves that a combination of arithmetic, probability, statistics, excel and logic/coding could solve all of our problems.
- Finally, we moved from the solved to the developing space of technology. From software that companies use regularly, to the latest trends to the possible extended reality in which we might exist in the future.

We therefore now understand how to think like a manager, know the overall business process, can financially model the business, and can objectively use math and tech to run operations. Next, we hope to understand the human side of business, which after all is what runs business. And finally, it will be useful to learn how to study the outside world to improve our business.

Section V

HR and Communication

After 4 very distinct sections on very different subject areas, we have finally made it to the section about people. When one thinks of a manager, one usually thinks of someone who is handling complex business situations and has a team of smart and specialised people reporting to them. Or at least that's my first impression of a manager.

Of course, this idea isn't strictly true in any sense. One of the important ways in which it isn't true is that many entry-level managers don't have people reporting to them. Managers who do have reportees are often called people managers. But, as one rises up the ranks in a company, they will have more and more employees reporting to them. In CXO level positions a manager's main tasks are making important and difficult long-term decisions, and managing the people who report to them. The importance of managing the people in an organisation grows in importance as managers grow in importance.

In this section, we shall try to build up a set of ideas and frameworks, which will help us become better people managers. While this is only one of six sections, this can also be thought of as half the job, as a people manager.

In the first chapter in this section, we shall explore communication. I think everyone in the world can benefit from becoming a good communicator. So, we shall have a look at what the key elements of communication are, and try to find some direction through which we can constantly improve our business communication.

In the second chapter, we shall try to understand the psychology of individuals. I am of course no psychology expert. But we will have a look at some of the experts' frameworks to get a better grip on understanding any individual that we interact with, or ourselves for that matter.

In the third chapter, we shall scale up by a step. Having understood what makes individuals tick, we shall study group behaviour and the levers which make groups work the way they do.

In the fourth chapter, we shall scale up once again. Now that we understand, small groups and individuals, we shall study the dynamics of large organisations, how they are organised and how they can be moved in a direction.

In the fifth and final chapter, we will try to bring all that we have understood about people back to the workplace. Human resource management, like the other 4 disciplines we have looked at is a pretty old one. Many frameworks already exist, stemming from the psychology that we looked at in the first few chapters. There are other, entirely different frameworks which are also of importance. We shall look at all of them, to form our mental model of people management.

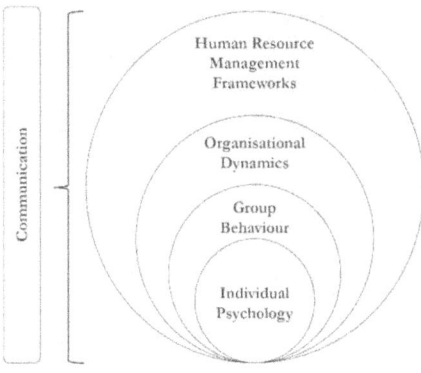

Chapter 24
Communication: Words Are All We Have?

This should come as no surprise, but communication is possibly one of the single most powerful skills that one can pick up as a manager. In fact, maybe communication is one of the most useful skills that an individual could pick up altogether. The range of famous people in history whose important speeches we have read and listened to stands testament to this idea. But communication isn't just about grand speeches. And that's a good thing because most of us can't capture the attention of a large audience for long enough to deliver a world-changing speech. Rather, communication is happening every minute of every day. As humans, we find it difficult to accomplish anything without communicating.

I'll assume that you're sold on the importance of communication. The key question at hand now is what we can do to leverage this powerful tool. To begin with, I propose that each of us can constantly improve our ability to communicate effectively. And I assume that we can all agree that if this is true, this means that each of us can constantly improve our ability as managers by doing so.

So, we're all in agreement that communication is super useful, and that we can become better managers, by constantly improving our ability to communicate. Therefore, in this chapter, let's try to understand why we want to communicate, and what the major levers are that we have at our disposal. And, you guessed it, words are in fact not all that we have at our disposal while communicating. Next, we'll have a look at a few quick models which are particularly useful in a business context, while communicating. Finally, we'll have a look at how we can constantly improve our ability to communicate.

Objectives and levers of communication

In the process of communication, more often than not, we have a certain end goal that we're working towards. We might want to convince the other party of something, we might simply be requesting information, just strengthening or maintaining a relationship etc. To have this required impact, we aim to deliver our communication effectively. This means everything ranging from saying the right words to using the right form of communication, to using the right style of delivery and so on. To successfully deliver our communication, one needs to understand the audience well.

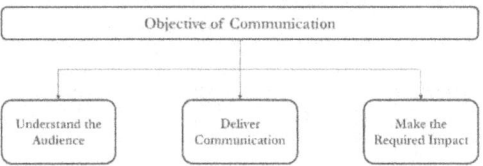

This complex, multifaceted objective is easy to wrap into a simpler objective of getting our message across to the listener. However, good communication involves much more than that. Because we are all constantly communicating, we end up brushing this task off as trivial. To ensure that we are less likely to do so, let's break up each of the 3 steps in the objective of communication a little further.

Let's begin with understanding our audience. There are a great many things that we could learn about our audience. The better we know them, the easier it would be to communicate with them, so that they are easily swayed. One such key thing to know is what their predisposition is towards the topic of communication (Kulkarni, 2020).

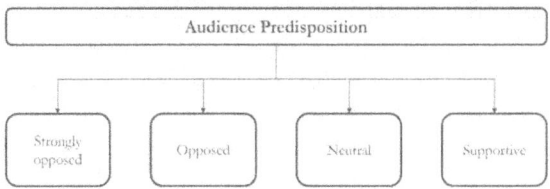

In case the audience is strongly opposed to the idea we are trying to sell, it may be unrealistic to expect to win them over. Creating a little bit of doubt, and scope to rethink is perhaps a better aim. For an audience which is opposed to the idea, reducing the resistance in their minds, so that we may be able to convert them soon is a reasonable goal. Neutral audiences should ideally be shifted towards our way of thinking and won over. And for those audiences who are already supportive, we should create a stronger sense of support and excitement. Thus, the audience's predisposition affects even what the goal of our communication is. The more we understand about our audience the more we will be able to effectively communicate with them (Kulkarni, 2020).

Next, let's look at how we can deliver our communication. This is of course a pretty large topic to break down. Even over the course of the entire chapter, we will only be touching the tip of the iceberg. So, let's just make sure that we're clear on what sort of elements are involved in delivering communication. For one thing, the communication that is received by the party that we are communicating to isn't just a function of the words that we say to them. Some of the other factors involved are context, history, tone of voice, body language etc. Some of these elements are within our control. For example, let's imagine that we are writing content to convince an audience of a point of view. We would find that presenting both sides of the argument, along with their merits, and then providing justification for one side being superior, and then countering key claims by the other side is the best approach. Next to that might be presenting just one side thoroughly, along with its key benefits. The worst content would include a strong presentation for both sides, without providing any counterargument against any side.

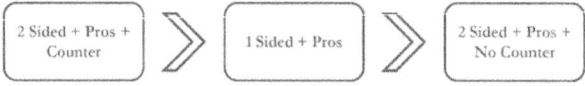

Other elements, such as the context and history (of the topic or between people) are not under our control. To effectively deliver communication, one must work around and work with the factors which are outside of their control as well. Of course, this list isn't exhaustive but should shine some light on the factors involved in delivering communication.

Over some time, each of us develops our own style of communication. Some facets of this style have an important effect on the success of our communication. These factors should be worked on and improved. Other factors don't have a strong first-time impact but can come to be associated with our brand of communication. In the long run, developing a characteristic style of communication can be a big positive, as long as it doesn't annoy the audience.

Finally, coming to achieving the required impact of communication. Unfortunately, this last step is not directly within our control. Communication isn't just an activity completed by the speaker. The audience has a key role in receiving the communication. The best we can aim for is to do a good job of the first 2 steps, in order to maximise the chances of our communication being received as planned.

Business communication

There is no shortage of communication tips which would come in handy during any business interaction. The surest way to pick up a new tip is by doing something dramatically wrong while communicating in a business setting. Here, I shall attempt to outline 6 such tips that I think provide a solid base for ensuring strong communication in a business context.

Summarise

It is normal human nature to get attached to one's work. We are responsible for each of the intricacies. And only we know how time-consuming and involved each of them is. However, we often need to communicate the progress on our work to higher-ups, clients or anyone whose time with us is in short supply. In these situations, the audience neither has the time for nor is interested in all of the details. It is a good practise to routinely summarise the work that we have done. Any documents that we make, updates that we prepare, or communication that we intend to send out should be subject to summarisation routinely. Most of our work can be summed up in 3 sentences. It is therefore useful to be equipped with a 3-sentence version, a 10-sentence version, and an elaborated version with all of the details.

Elaborating in (<=3) Points

All managers will find themselves in meetings where they need to convince others of a viewpoint or justify a recommended course of action. In such settings, assuming that we have done our homework, we would likely have a detailed thought process to share with them. In these situations, it is always recommended that we elaborate our thought process in points. And ideally, one should restrict the number of points that they make to 3 key points or less. The reasoning behind this approach is:

1. Elaborating in points allows one to showcase their thought process and structured approach. This helps win over the audience's favour or at least minimises their scepticism.
2. Succinct and distinct points are easier to follow and keep track of than a long-drawn speech.
3. A limited number of points is easier to keep track of, and therefore more likely to be remembered and impactful, than a long list.

To this end, to ensure that one keep's their audience's attention, it is useful to inform them of the number of supporting points that one has. It is also useful to call out the point number before beginning, to ensure that they are on the same page as you.

Given that we are sold on the benefits of summarising, and elaborating in points, this just combines the 2 ideas. It is always useful to begin with a crisp answer first. After that, one can elaborate on their pillars of support in succinct points. This top-down approach ensures that the most important information is conveyed before the audience loses attention. It is then easier to maintain their attention as one justifies their standpoint, in a structured and simple manner.

A top-down approach is particularly useful in emails because it helps cater to an audience which is paying limited attention, as well as to an audience that is actively engrossed. That being said, a top-down approach is also very powerful in just about any business setting.

Process Driven

In some situations, we have the luxury of time to communicate. In these situations, the audience is actively interested in the details. However, this also means that we must be very clear and organised in our communication, so as to not confuse the audience. A process driven approach to communication prescribes going step by step. This may involve following a clear order, such as a chronological order of events. It is once again important to call out each step that we are discussing before we delve into it. This makes it easier for the audience to follow, without getting lost in the details.

Synthesis and Confirm

Communication is a two-way street. It is therefore often important to ensure that we are also understanding what the other party is communicating to us. To this end, it is useful to routinely synthesise what we have heard, and make sure that we have understood it correctly. This ensures that communication was not in vain and that we have correctly understood what we have been told.

Pausing and Pacing

A big part of communication is knowing what we want to say and why. Thus, it is important to pause now and then. This doesn't mean a large gap where one brainlessly buffers in the middle of a meeting. A pause could mean taking 5 minutes to think through what we want to say before walking into a meeting. It could also mean asking for a few seconds to think before responding to a question. This often seems daunting but is truly useful. It ensures that you don't blurt out something irrelevant. Usually, the other party (yes, even your boss) would also appreciate that you are deliberating over your answer to them, and not just saying the first thing that comes to mind.

Pacing is always a tool that needs to be kept in mind. Especially while we are talking about our work, it is easy to talk at runaway speed. This can make it difficult for others to understand and follow the conversation. Talking a little slowly ensures that we are understood, but this obviously shouldn't be taken too far. A little variation in pace allows us to stress on the key points while glossing over details.

I have also covered these 6 business communication tips in a little more detail, in the context of consulting case interviews in a youtube video.

Personal communication style

So, how can one improve their style of communication? The simple answer is to just go ahead and communicate, check how effective you are, and then diagnose what you could improve upon.

But because this is a tad bit boring, at least in the early stages, one could use role models as a benchmark, rather than just making incremental improvements on their own style. In this process, it is important to keep in mind that one cannot just copy their role model's communication style. It might make for fun impersonations at a party but won't get you too far as a manager.

Rather, the key lies in picking out a few tricks that they use, and then deliberately trying to incorporate some of those tricks in your communication. When done right, your communication will visibly improve. In fact, why stop at one role model. Pick and choose what you like from a range of speakers, and that's how one can create their own, unique, effective style of communication.

As a starting point, here is an analysis of Obama's style of speaking that I particularly enjoy.

Recap

In our attempt to understand how to manage a business, we have thus far learnt:

- Management thinking. We have extensively been using convergent thinking, structuring in particular and divergent thinking along the way.
- We got started with 4 steps of business value creation so that we can capture value from customers in return. We are capable of understanding the marketplace, positioning our brand to target the right customers, designing an effective market mix and managing relevant relationships along the way.
- To understand the language of finance, we have understood:
    - The financial reporting process.
    - How to build and analyse the 3 key financial reports.
    - Basic concepts, accounting principles and nuances.
    - Metrics and ratios for financial analysis.
    - What else can be learnt from financial markets to valuation of firms.
- To tackle any operational challenge, we had a look at:
    - The basics and terminology of operations.
    - The mathematical nature of operations.
    - The specific math managers need to know.
    - The scope of technology in business.
- Just now, we realised that a large chunk of management lies in getting people to work on all of the fancy things we have just learnt. To this end, we learnt about:

o The major levers that we have in communication.
o 6 tips for communicating in business situations.
o Improving our personal style of communication.

Chapter 25
Individual Psychology: Know Thyself

Now that we're well educated on a range of management topics, we have started to see the importance of being able to mobilise the people in our business. We have had a glance at how we can become better communicators, enabling us to get more out of the people that we work with. This seems like an appropriate time to take a monk like pause and look within. For only if we are able to manage ourselves can we manage others.

Now, let's look at the truth in that statement in a more objective business-like fashion. In most companies, entry-level jobs require an employee to only manage their own work and responsibilities, before they are promoted to the point of managing others. Even at this stage, for many years, one is expected to manage their own work first and foremost, before managing their reportees. Thus, being able to understand how one thinks, behaves, reacts and performs is a key first step.

Over and above understanding one's self, a manager needs to also understand the psychology of other individuals. Whether or not you manage people, you will certainly interact with them at the workplace. A basic understanding of human psychology can make a confusing workplace seem a lot more sensible.

As we go through some useful frameworks from psychology, keep in mind that managers aren't expected to be experts in this field. So, a lot of key frameworks may be missing here, but put together, this should provide a useful view of how people work.

Managing one's self

Learning how to manage one's self is probably a lifelong effort. Of course, the hope is that you will get good enough at it through your early 20s to hold down a full-time job and manage your personal life. But, the scope for improvement and growth will probably persist for decades after. Given that this is a long-drawn task, which almost no one has perfected, what can we hope to pick up from this sub-section of the chapter?

I think that a good starting point is having a system of review. A few questions that one can ask one's self to figure out where they stand. With the help of these routine questions, if we are able to review, self-correct and grow, that's the best that we can hope for. Of course, each of these questions has a ton of frameworks associated with them, to help us do a better job of answering them effectively and truly. I might not be able to help with very many of these frameworks. But, as a starting point, I shall try to present some of these pertinent questions.

- What are my strengths and weaknesses? How should I get feedback to develop a clearer and less biased opinion on the same?
- How well do I perform my job? When and where (what sort of environment) do I perform well and poorly in? How can I improve upon this?
- What are my values, beliefs, attitudes, hopes and dreams? How do these affect how I live my life and carry out my work?
- Where do I belong and what is my purpose? Using the answers to the above questions, can I arrive at a stronger answer to this question?
- What should I contribute? What is the need of the hour and what is needed of me in the long run and by who?
- Whom and what am I responsible for? In my relationships, what must I do, and how can I help the people around me achieve their purpose as well?
- Beyond my career, what do I hope for? What in my personal life matters and am I making time for that? What should the second half of my life look like, and am I on track?

Notice that not all of these questions are strictly about work. That's because managing one's self means stretching past boundaries that exist in the workplace. Our feelings and attitudes at home and work end up crossing these boundaries despite our best efforts. A well-oiled machine (individual) must be fully functional on all dimensions, to function well on even one dimension.

Each of these questions has been dealt with by many experts, who have put years of research into it. And they have come up with useful frameworks and processes that can make our lives easier. As always, a simple google search against any of these questions will provide powerful insights. I shall, however, illustrate a couple of frameworks before moving forward.

The Johari window is a popular framework used to map out our qualities against how well we and the people around us know about them. A great deal can be learnt about our personality and how people feel about us, as a function of the extent to which we live in a given quadrant. I'm sure that a lot must be self-evident by looking at the framework. But, because I am not the best person to teach you more about it, this is a framework worth googling (Theory, 2021) (Gupta, 2020).

	Known to Self	Unknown to Self
Unknown to Others	Hidden Self (Facade)	Unknown Self (Unknown)
Known to Others	Open Self (Arena)	Blind Self (Blind Spot)

Feedback

A lot of the questions that we need to ask ourselves are at the end of the day going to be answered only by ourselves. It is always useful to get feedback from other people so that we don't falsely assume and then build up our personality on lies. We similarly have a responsibility to provide others with useful and sensitive feedback. To this end, there are a few useful and easily actionable dos and don't of feedback. Making a habit of adhering to them can help us and the people around us easily self-improve (Gupta, 2020).

	Feedback Dos	Feedback Don'ts
Giving Feedback	• Feedback on their behaviour • Discuss the controllable • Specific feedback • Data based feedback • Timely feedback • Negatives with positives • Suggestive • Actionable and helpful	• Feedback about the person • Discuss the uncontrollable • General feedback • Impression based feedback • Late feedback • Only negatives • Prescriptive • Criticism
Receiving Feedback	• Elicit feedback • Listen and self-analyse • Clarify meaning	• Wait for feedback • Deny and rationalise • Assume meaning

Learning and convincing

A big part of managing ourselves, or any individual is the process of learning and teaching. As with most other topics in this book, learning and teaching are far too big to be dealt with here. So, let's touch the tip of the iceberg with some learning theories (Gupta, 2020).

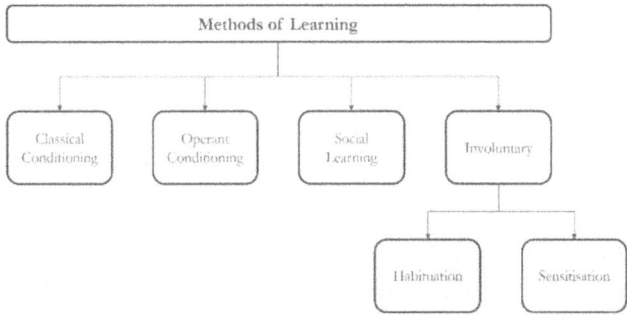

Classical conditioning is best captured in Pavlov's experiment. In case this is the first that you are hearing of it, I would strongly encourage you to watch a video about it. Classical conditioning is essentially about learning through the association of certain stimuli with other events.

Operant conditioning is also a conditioning method of learning but is focused instead on consequences being tied to actions. This ensures that the learner picks up some behaviours (better consequences) over others (worse consequences).

Social learning doesn't use association, but rather relies on the learner to observe others and attempt to mimic them. The decision to mimic may arise from a desire for similar outcomes. But most importantly, the learning process is through social mimicry.

There are also a few types of involuntary learning. Habitual learning stems from something which becomes a habit or a routine. Sensitisation on the other hand arises from singular events, which make one's behaviour change in a certain way. For example, an accident may make one more sensitised to loud noises of any sort (Gupta, 2020).

There is of course much more that one could learn about learning techniques. But, it is important for us as managers to not focus purely on learning and on trying to teach other people, but to also convince people. This is of utmost importance, as most of us are reasonably rigid by the time we are well into our careers. As we have seen in the chapter on communication, the ability to convince is a very powerful one. Let's look at a simple 3 step process that helps us convert any no into a yes (Gupta, 2020).

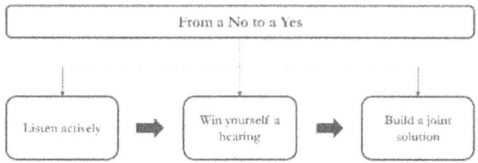

While listening actively, it is important to not just pay attention, but to also show the speaker that you understand how they feel and why they feel so strongly. In the critical second step, one should always avoid asserting themselves or contradicting the points made by the other person, as that becomes combative. Rather, the usage of doubts and questions is a better way to build towards information that both parties can agree on. While referring back to the other person's points, one should then aim to put their points across clearly, but in a friendly manner. To seal the deal, ask for input, build on their ideas and provide your own ideas to arrive at a solution which solves everyone's problems (Gupta, 2020).

This of course is much easier in theory than in practise. The other person might not be following these same principles. The other person may be particularly unreasonable and combative. But with time and experience, this is a good process to follow.

Perception

You might find that even if you are great at learning, teaching and convincing, not everyone is going to be on the same page as you. This isn't necessarily just because you're smarter than everyone else. One of the many factors at play here is that people perceive things differently. Some of the factors that affect how we perceive the information we are shown, and the information that stays with us are (Gupta, 2020):

- Size of stimulus – If we are given much more information about one option than about others, we are more likely to remember and select this option.
- Intensity – In a presentation, a topic which is covered with a video, a song, sample food and fragrances is likely to leave a much stronger impression than one which is covered with a text slide.
- Repetition – Constant repetition has a tendency of engraving information in our minds. This is after all how we learnt our ABCs.
- Novelty – The very first time we experience something new often stays with us for much longer than a run-of-the-mill experience.
- Familiarity – On the other hand, we are often inclined to prefer familiar experiences, that contain no surprises. Have a look at your Zomato/Swiggy order history, if you need convincing.
- Contrast – When all options look similar, and one stands out, we are likely to be drawn towards it. This works like the novelty effect, even if the unique option isn't novel.

If these were the only factors at play, as long as the same information is presented to different people, in the same way, everyone should have the same perception. This of course doesn't happen. One of the main reasons is that we carry biases. I will leave you to google each of the following biases to learn more about them. But, I shall provide you with a list of different types of biases (Gupta, 2020).

- Projection
- Preoccupation
- Perceptual Readiness

- Halo Effect
- Beliefs
- Perceptual Defence
- Primacy Effect
- Recency Effect

Attitude, values and stereotypes

Having just thought about our biases and how they affect our perception, a natural next step is to evaluate our attitudes, values and the stereotypes that we hold.

Because I have completed my MBA, rather than explain what an attitude is in a sentence, I shall unnecessarily use a diagram which is basically a sentence.

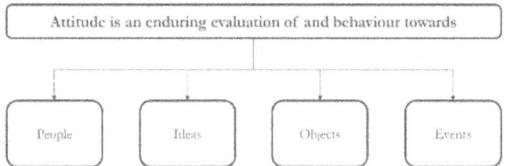

Attitude has a few different components to it. They affect our feelings. As a function of this, they affect how we think about things. And finally, this impacts how we behave. People's attitudes may be in the same or different directions, they may be stronger or weaker than others, and they may be more general or more specific than others. This difference in people's attitudes finally differentiates how they may react to similar situations (Gupta, 2020).

A value is a little different from an attitude. Rather than being directed towards something external, a value is a belief that a certain way of living, a certain behaviour or end-state is preferable for you. A value thus indicates one's preferences, what one prioritises or even what one believes to be right or wrong.

Values are developed in a similar fashion to how attitudes are developed, through experiences and through what we are taught. However, values tend to be ingrained in us over a longer period, through stronger experiences (Gupta, 2020).

Stereotypes are different from attitudes and values in a couple of ways. For one, stereotypes are less personal, since they are held by large groups of people, and are less personally formed. Secondly, they are generalisations that we make about groups of people, rather than any other object, event or behaviour. Stereotypes are usually formed by the media, within a community or family.

Stereotypes aren't inherently bad. In a setting where one has very limited information, stereotypes act as heuristics to help us better guess how one might behave. However, it is very important to remember that it is only a heuristic. In a lot of settings, we can and should spend the time understanding each individual and their actual behaviour, rather than fitting them into a pigeonhole (Gupta, 2020).

Decision making

Having understood how perception, biases, attitudes, values and stereotypes are formed, let's now understand how we finally make decisions. As we have seen briefly in marketing, the psychology behind decision making is intricate and complex. We shall therefore restrict ourselves to how managers make decisions.

They may be authoritarian, and unilaterally take decisions. They may consult a few other team members, to keep them involved, while they make the final decision. Or they may allow everyone to participate and arrive at a decision together. Of course, this is a spectrum of decision-making styles.

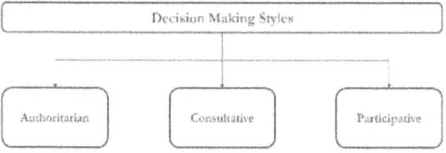

How managers can decide which style works best for the scenario is a function of 3 factors (Gupta, 2020):

- Quality of the decision that will come out of each style.
- Acceptance of the decision by the final stakeholders, as a function of which method of decision making was used.
- Time available to arrive at a decision.

Motivation

Thus far, we should have a decent idea of how we as individuals process information and arrive at decisions. Looking back at how we can better manage ourselves, this tells us a lot about how we perform and how we can improve. But, to find out what our purpose is, where we should be, and even to diagnose our underlying behaviour, it is important to understand our motivations.

While dissecting consumer behaviour as a part of marketing, we have already touched upon what I believe to be one of the most shockingly powerful frameworks, Maslow's hierarchy of needs (Maslow, 1943).

This is far from the only framework that deals with motivation. This too is a field which has been studied in great depth, because controlling our motivation enables us to get the most out of ourselves and our lives.

A few of the other competing (and sometimes complimentary) theories of motivation are:

- Alderfer's ERG – This theory also has 3 levels of motivation (existence, relatedness and growth), which correspond to Maslow's 5. However, these 3 needs are believed to arise in any combination together, unlike Maslow's hierarchy which can only arise one after the other (Alderfer, 1969).
- McClelland's Need Theory – This theory suggests that we have 3 basic needs for achievement, power and affiliation. These 3 needs in combination are used to explain all of our actions (McClelland, 1988).
- Herzberg's 2 Factor Theory – This theory suggests that we have motivators such as achievement, challenge, recognition etc. which drive us to act. Additionally, there are hygiene factors such as working conditions, interpersonal relations, job security etc. which if not satisfactory, can demotivate us from acting (Herzberg, Mausner, & Snydermann, 1959).
- Vroom's expectancy theory and Stacey Adam's equity theory are also useful frameworks in the space of understanding motivation. These are also worth googling, in case you are interested in this space.

Stress

Anyone who is working their way towards becoming a manager or is already a manager is no stranger to the idea of stress. I'm probably not in the best position to advise anyone on how to deal with or get rid of stress. Rather, I shall only share a simple framework which is worth keeping in mind while handling the natural stresses of managing a business.

The 2 key things about stress are (Gupta, 2020):

- A manageable amount of stress is a motivator.
- Stress won't simply disappear because it is dealt with once. Stress is likely a bit of a constant. One must learn to manage and minimise it.

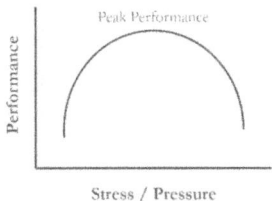

Leadership

At the beginning of this chapter on individual psychology, we had stated that it is worth understanding both as working individuals, as well as managers of individuals. To take this a step further, if we rise up the ranks as managers, we will become leaders of the business. As leaders, we are expected to have a rather strong sense of understanding of ourselves and of the people that we lead. For that matter, impressive individuals begin leading from early on, even before they rise up the ranks officially.

Let's, therefore, take a small look at what leadership is. This is once again a well-researched area. However, this one seems to be fairly subjective. Everyone has their own idea of what leadership is and where to draw the line between management and leadership. I don't have a right answer, but some ideas to get you thinking are:

- Leaders, don't just get a team to achieve goals. They set a vision in place.

- Manager is designation. Leadership on the other hand doesn't need a designation, it is a role that one plays.
- Leadership involved influencing people in the direction of a goal or purpose.
- Leadership involves helping others recognise their full potential.
- Leaders are not born. Anyone can develop into a leader through the right experiences, but mainly by having the courage to take the right actions, and inspire others to do the same.

But, because this is a book on business management, let's not get too carried away with just lofty ideals. We must also ground some of this in objective theory. One of the interesting and useful theories in the space of leadership is McGregor's theory x and theory y. According to this, managers and leaders may believe in theory x or theory y. Theory x takes a more pessimistic view of the average employee, believing that they need to be monitored and driven at each step. Theory y is more optimistic, believing that employees inherently want to work well, and just need to be enabled the right way. Depending on which theory a manager subscribes to, their leadership style varies dramatically (McGregor, 1960).

Theory X	Theory Y
• Inherently lazy	• Self motivated & self
• Dislike work	controlled
• Shirk responsibilities	• Enjoy work like they do
• Limited creativity capacity	play
• Little Ambition	• Seek responsibilities
• Seek direction wherever	• Have creativity/capacity
possible	• Are Ambitious
• Primarily motivated by	• Primarily motivated by
lower level needs	higher level needs

Hersey and Blanchard's situational leadership model too helps group leadership styles into 4 basic types. The 2 dimensions of importance here are task behaviour and relationship emphasis. Leaders who are task-oriented are very focused on getting the job done, whereas those who are relationship-oriented are focused on breeding talent. The ideal leader is able to blend the 2, and eventually move to a stage where their followers don't need too much instruction (task behaviour) or hand-holding (relationship emphasis).

As such, the ideal leader in this framework may have to start by giving detail-oriented instructions. However, the expectation is that they groom followers to first start thinking for themselves, then start taking action for themselves, to the point where work can be delegated (Hersey & Blanchard, 1972).

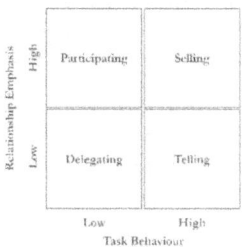

This of course begs the important question of how can one successfully delegate. There are broadly 4 key factors to be taken care of in delegation (Gupta, 2020):

- Select a capable and ready individual.
- Explain the objectives and constraints.
- Enable them with the means to get the job done.
- Arrange to keep in contact and support if need be.

Recap

In our attempt to understand how to manage a business, we have thus far learnt:

- Management thinking. We have extensively been using convergent thinking, structuring in particular and divergent thinking along the way.
- We got started with 4 steps of business value creation so that we can capture value from customers in return. We are capable of understanding the marketplace, positioning our brand to target the right customers, designing an effective market mix and managing relevant relationships along the way.
- To understand the language of finance, we have understood:
    - The financial reporting process.
    - How to build and analyse the 3 key financial reports.
    - Basic concepts, accounting principles and nuances.
    - Metrics and ratios for financial analysis.

259

- o What else can be learnt from financial markets to valuation of firms.
- To tackle any operational challenge, we had a look at:
  - o The basics and terminology of operations.
  - o The mathematical nature of operations.
  - o The specific math managers need to know.
  - o The scope of technology in business.
- We learnt how to better communicate by understanding:
  - o The major levers that we have in communication.
  - o 6 tips for communicating in business situations.
  - o Improving our personal style of communication.
- To manage people, we learnt how individuals think, behave and perform by learning:
  - o How to manage one's self.
  - o How to learn and convince.
  - o About perceptions, attitudes, values and stereotypes.
  - o About motivation and stress.
  - o How to lead.

Chapter 26
Group Behaviour: Working with Humans

Since we have been working on improving our communication and understanding of how individuals work, we are ready to take the next natural step, understanding group behaviour. On the one hand, understanding a group involves putting together our understanding of many individuals and how they interact (communicate) with each other. On the other hand, there are a few new dimensions which get introduced with scale.

In addition to understanding how individual personalities fit together, we must be prepared for when things don't go perfectly, and conflict arises. In addition to this, as managers, we don't want to just manage any group that we're added to but want to have some degree of control over the kinds of groups that form. Finally, while a group is alright, we strive to convert groups of people into cohesive teams, that work together.

Through this chapter, we shall make use of another set of frameworks which help us understand how to go from managing individuals to managing groups of people.

Personalities

Everyone has their own unique personality, and that shapes how they behave, get along with people and respond to situations. Understanding someone's personality well, likely means that you would be better equipped to manage them, or even interact with them. Even something as subjective as personality must be broken down objectively for us to gain something out of it as managers.

To this end, one useful framework is the big 5 personality traits. Here, we look at 5 major dimensions of personality, being Openness to change, Conscientiousness (work ethic), Extraversion, Agreeableness and Neuroticism. Each of these 5 words, spelling OCEAN should be fairly self-explanatory. But, in case you're unsure about what any of the words means in this context, someone on the internet must have explained this framework in a good amount of detail (Cherry, 2021).

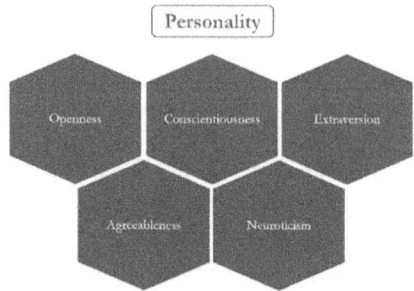

Clearly, some of these traits are generally positive, while some of them are better in smaller proportions. However, as managers, we have limited capacity to change the personalities of the people we work with and manage. And perhaps we shouldn't aspire to change people's personalities anyway.

But, understanding people's personalities helps in ensuring better compatibility, and in preparing for clashes. For example, extroverts and introverts will likely have distinct styles of socialising and working. This is an area of possible friction. Too many people who are high on neuroticism can lead to high tensions within a team. As a manager, we may be in a position to choose the sort of personalities that we include in our team, or can definitely be aware of the potential hazards, and the strengths that the team has.

While a manager may or may not have their team members' personality scores available, they should be able to get a decent read on each person's personality, simply through interactions.

Managing conflict

We all know conflict to mean some sort of disagreement, usually between people. However, here, we will take a slightly broader view of conflict, as something not sitting right within the team, or even just for select individuals in the team.

From this point of view, we may look at conflict as a drop in concern either for one's own interests or of the interest of others in the team (Gopakumar, 2021).

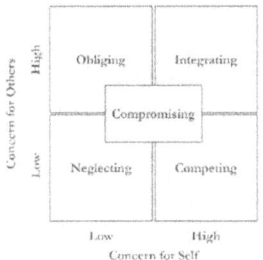

Clearly, integrating is a great state to be in, while each of the others is less ideal in at least one way.

However, this is not the only view of conflict that one can take. Looking at just the individual employee, we can also look at conflict as a lack of fit in some way or the other. As an employee in an organisation, there are several constructs that we hope to fit into. And lack of fit on even one dimension creates some amount of conflict (Gopakumar, 2021).

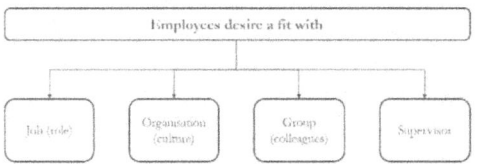

We can also view conflict from the angle of what one chooses to do in the situation. Hirschman's EVLN model suggests that there are 4 courses of action that an individual may choose (Hirschman, 1970).

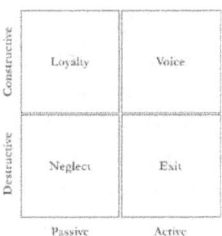

263

We have thus far used a few lenses to look at the idea of conflict. You might say that we have thus understood a few different types of conflict which could potentially exist. Let's take this a step further and outline some potential reasons for conflict.

- Incompatible goals.
- Differences in outlook or approach.
- Interdependent tasks (high expectations of each other).
- Limited resources (excess demand and low supply).

There are likely more potential sources of conflict, but this should cover some of the most common ones.

Closely linked to the idea of conflict is that of power. The reason is that with power, one can influence how others behave, and therefore potentially resolve conflicts. It is also true that the quest for power in itself creates a lot of conflict, but we shall stay focused for now on the question of how we can use power to resolve conflict. More precisely, we shall look at the different types of power one could hold in a business setting. Each of these different types of power can be used to ease tensions in some way or the other (Gopakumar, 2021).

- Positional Power – This type of power is bestowed upon someone as a function of the position that they are in. 'Position' in this context could mean a variety of things, and each meaning grants a different type of power.
    - o Coercive Power – This arises because others fear the consequences that the possessor of the power could bring upon them.
    - o Reward Power – This arises because others hope to receive benefits that the possessor of the power could bestow upon them.
    - o Legitimate power – This arises because the organisation formally recognises the authority or designation of the possessor.
- Personal Power – Personal power is derived from one's unique abilities or personality traits. As a function of what these abilities are, personal power may be either:
    - o Expert Power – This arises from unique expertise, which provides the individual with a sort of scarcity power.

264

- o Referent Power – This arises from influence over other individuals who may possess other forms of power.
- Relational Power – This type of power is created by maintaining strong relationships and acting as a central node in the flow of information and resources.

Abuse of Power

Having seen that power is a source of influence, which can solve different types of conflict, let's have a look at the flip side. Power is also abused, causing conflict in the first place. One may expect that organisations would have mechanisms in place to prevent this from happening. If a manager is found abusing their power, there are in fact mechanisms in place to prevent them from doing so, and even to revoke their power, and remove them from the organisation. With such high stakes, abuse of power ought to be rare, if ever it happens.

However, this is all dependent on the abuse of power being found out or reported in some form. This is a pretty heavy requirement, because it requires a few people to call out the abuse of power, and then for the relevant authorities to recognise it. It's easy to blame the failure of reporting and recognition down to cowardice or corruption, but this is a complex space. Without delving into the quality research which has gone into this space, some reasons why individuals may not speak up range from their personal disposition (the matter seeming too trivial) to fear of organisational perception or backlash (Gopakumar, 2021).

Creating groups

By now, we have understood how to look at the different personalities within a group. We have also appreciated that conflict is a concern to be taken care of and that power can be a double-edged sword.

With these constraints in mind, as managers, we are still responsible for creating the groups which we work in and improving our position within these groups.

Social Network

The first idea that comes to mind today, when one talks about a social network is the online social networks which we are all a part of. These are, however, a useful tool to imagine the social networks which we are talking about in the business world. Here too we are connected to several people, and through them, indirectly connected to more. Each connection has a certain strength, has existed for a certain period and so on.

There is a lot that can be reused from graph theory and other math to model social networks. For our limited purpose in this chapter, we won't be touching upon graph theory to a great extent. Instead, let's talk about some interesting patterns that we might see in social networks in a much simpler fashion.

Amongst the patterns that one aims to avoid in groups is an echo chamber. An echo chamber can be visualised as a group of people who are connected to each other, but not so much to people outside of the group. This may look as innocent as a group of people who are close to each other. However, the key concern with an echo chamber is each member's lack of connection to people outside the group. Echo chambers repeat and amplify the same set of ideas and views, without bringing in more holistic points of view.

More desirable patterns tend to include higher degrees of connectedness. What this means is that the individual is connected to a large number of people. Purely from the point of view of exposure and social influence, this is desirable for anyone. Especially a manager should have some of these benefits from their social network.

Further, if one aims to possess relational and referent power, it isn't sufficient to simply be connected to a large number of people, though this is a necessity. Additionally, one should aim to be connected to people who are not connected to each other. This is what makes one's connections unique and valuable (Gopakumar, 2021).

In case you are interested in furthering your own social network, there are as usual better resources than this one. A personal favourite of mine and an all-time classic is "How to Win Friends and Influence People" by Dale Carnegie.

Diversity, Inclusion and Discrimination
Those of us living in the 21st century are presumably not new to the idea of diversity and inclusion. As managers, it is important to remember that diversity is an outcome, and a desirable one. Desirable largely because a team that is well equipped to deal with a range of scenarios and is representative of the world within which we live is usually a diverse one.

In striving for diversity, one wants to steer clear of token diversity, which is simply for the sake of show, without actual involvement. We similarly want to avoid discrimination in order to enforce diversity. A fair and effective approach to ensuring diversity is that of inclusion. Inclusion is nothing more than valuing ideas and perspectives from a wide range of sources and appreciating the distinct capabilities that diverse individuals bring to the table.

All of this sounds both easy and obvious. The challenge that arises is that each of us usually carries our own set of stereotypes, biases and attitudes. This is why it is key to first master the art of managing one's self before we can effectively manage groups inclusively .

At the other end of the spectrum, when inclusion and therefore diversity is not valued, we end up discriminating. Discrimination itself has a wide range of possible outcomes (Gopakumar, 2021).

Allport's scale of prejudice shows the possible outcomes that arise from discrimination and prejudice. What is particularly insightful about this scale is that most of us can recognise that something as extreme as extermination or physical attack is a clear display of prejudice and bigotry. However, at the lower end, simple bad-mouthing is more often given a pass. This, however, is the starting point of a rather dangerous cycle. As a member of any organisation, it is useful to keep this scale in mind to ensure that one does not enable this sort of maltreatment of individuals of any group (Allport, 1954).

Team forming

We have just now understood that as managers, we are responsible for bringing groups of people together and creating a conducive environment for work. However, good managers are likely to more than simply bring people together.

There is a distinction between a group and a team. Spoiler alert, a team is preferable and is what we're aiming to build.

There are more technical definitions of what makes a group of people a team, but the crux of it is (Gopakumar, 2021):

- Teams work towards common goals.
- They have interdependent tasks and activities.
- They share a large amount of social interaction.
- Members may have specified roles, and be bound by certain rules and boundaries.

There is also a lot of literature on what makes good teams, and how one can be an effective leader. Rather than trying to cover that ground here, it is split up and distributed across the chapters of this section. However, one concept worth dissecting at this point is the very frequently used word "synergy".

Synergy refers to any interaction of individuals in which the outcome of cooperation is greater than the sum of separate effects. The more pertinent question is how one can bring about synergy. I'm not equipped to give you a detailed and well-studied answer. However, the simple answer comes in 2 parts:

- Tap into inherent synergy – When 2 or more groups have been carefully selected to cooperate and produce a certain outcome, there tend to be some complementary capabilities and skills. Complementary skills tend to exponentially multiply each other's effect, unlike similar skills which only linearly add on. By identifying these complementary capabilities, brand new opportunities are availed and exponential growth becomes possible.
- Minimise process losses – Interactions between groups tend to come with a little bit of friction, as we have already seen while studying conflict. The cost of conflict is a loss in productivity and potential. Minimising this loss enables us to reap the benefits of more synergy.

Recap

In our attempt to understand how to manage a business, we have thus far learnt:

- Management thinking. We have extensively been using convergent thinking, structuring in particular and divergent thinking along the way.

- We got started with 4 steps of business value creation so that we can capture value from customers in return. We are capable of understanding the marketplace, positioning our brand to target the right customers, designing an effective market mix and managing relevant relationships along the way.
- To understand the language of finance, we have understood:
  - The financial reporting process.
  - How to build and analyse the 3 key financial reports.
  - Basic concepts, accounting principles and nuances.
  - Metrics and ratios for financial analysis.
  - What else can be learnt from financial markets to valuation of firms.
- To tackle any operational challenge, we had a look at:
  - The basics and terminology of operations.
  - The mathematical nature of operations.
  - The specific math managers need to know.
  - The scope of technology in business.
- We learnt how to better communicate by understanding:
  - The major levers that we have in communication.
  - 6 tips for communicating in business situations.
  - Improving our personal style of communication.
- To manage people, we learnt how individuals think, behave and perform by learning:
  - How to manage one's self.
  - How to learn and convince.
  - About perceptions, attitudes, values and stereotypes.
  - About motivation and stress.
  - How to lead.
- To effectively manage groups, we saw that it is important to:
  - Understand the personalities involved.
  - Manage conflict through power.
  - Be inclusive and leverage social networks.
  - Form teams and tap into synergies.

Chapter 27
Organisational Dynamics: People and Politics

Throughout this section, we have been learning how to manage the all-important human element of businesses. We have largely been looking within the boundaries of the organisation, though the same principles can easily be extended to relationships with third parties, outside the organisation. In this exercise we have learnt the basics of communication, understood individual psychology and group behaviour. Since we have been scaling the same principles up and seeing how they change, let's scale them up one more time.

Organisations are made up of many groups of people, and in a way, a huge group of people. With scale, aspects of human behaviour change. More importantly, our ability to control and direct human behaviour changes. So, we shall aim to understand what organisations are and what sort of goals they work towards. While we haven't explicitly discussed this so far, you have likely developed an idea of this over the course of the book. We'll discuss the different organisation structures that may exist in a business. We will touch upon the dangerous topic of power and politics within an organisation, and how that scales up from a group setting.

Most interestingly, in this chapter we shall see how thinking and decision processes scale-up in organisations, and we shall see how culture is visible, affects the organisation and can be changed.

Organisations

The idea of an organisation is a rather intuitive one for us, and one which isn't inherently different from a group, except for the scale.

> *"Organisations are large groups of people who work together in a specific and deliberate structure, interacting with the outside world, in order to achieve a common goal."*

-Shreyas Harish, 2022

A definition of that sort probably wasn't necessary. But, since I haven't used as many definitions as I thought I might have, I decided to throw one in.

Some of the keywords of interest are the ideas of how people in an organisation might be structured, how they might work together, and what sort of goals they might work towards. For the time being, let's have a look at the simplest of the lot, the goals.

Goals

The nature of the goal that an organisation works towards could be almost anything. We have businesses which work towards profits by trying to produce products that make customers happy. We have NGOs which work towards public welfare in some space or the other. We even have fan groups, which work towards knowing as much as they can about the celebrities that they worship.

If we look at more formal organisations, amongst their goals there seem to be 2 dimensions, both of which we have already seen in the section on operations. Organisational goals are focused on effectiveness and efficiency. Effectiveness is in line with quality management, where we are concerned about successfully reaching our end goals. Efficiency is more in tune with a lot of the math that we do in operations, to ensure that we minimise the inputs while maximising outputs.

Importantly, when we put together the subgoals of effectiveness and efficiency, organisations aim for certain end states via the easiest and quickest path (Gopakumar, 2021).

Structures

You might recall that we had seen how salesforces are organised in the section on marketing and strategy. It should come as no surprise that organisations, on the whole, are also structured in largely similar ways.

Functional organisations are first structured on the basis of what role employees play. Sales and marketing is a function, as are research and development, finance, legal, HR and so on.

Divisional or product structures divide employees first and foremost based on which product or group of products their work is related to. This is sometimes useful in the cases of large companies like Unilever and P&G, where a group of products make up a large amount of business and need to be treated as if they are a company of their own.

Geographic structures are used in multinational companies where operations in one or a few countries is large and very distinct from the business in another geographic area.

Matrix structure is popular in both technology and consulting firms, where business is organised in the form of projects, with each project requiring employees with certain specialised roles (Gopakumar, 2021).

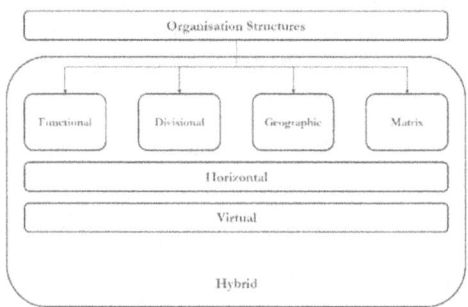

Horizontal structures are distinct from traditional organisation structures. In any horizontal structure, there is less of a reporting hierarchy, and each member of the team is given more authority to make decisions. A horizontal structure can be embedded in any of the 4 classical organisational structures.

Virtual structures are increasingly becoming the norm in a digital world. Virtual structures are also embedded in any of the traditional structures. They break geographic boundaries and allow sharing of employees and resources across any division that may exist in the organisational structure.

Hybrid structures are more realistically what we expect any organisation to have in place. Most organisations have some combination of the 4 traditional structures and may have some degree of a horizontal and virtual structure in place. This is called a hybrid structure (Gopakumar, 2021).

Power and politics

We have already seen how power exists in groups, and how it can be used to solve or create conflict. Most of the types of power that we saw in groups is what we call vertical sources of power. This name is chosen because the person with power is

272

usually hierarchically senior to the people over whom they exert their power. We also saw a few types of power which were horizontal.

In a large organisation, the scope for exerting power scales up exponentially. The types of horizontal power also blow up, because the number of people within the same hierarchical level scales up dramatically. This horizontal power may stem from (Gopakumar, 2021):

- Dependency – Often one is dependent on another person inside their team or outside to help complete a task. This dependence creates a source of power.
- Financial Resources – Some employees have access to certain resources, which are needed by other employees at the same level.
- Non-Substitutability – This source of power is similar to expert power, which is created through scarcity. However, in some cases the organisational structure forces non-substitutability, even if expert power is missing.
- Centrality – Points of contact are often set up which inherently gives the more central employee a source of power.

Politics in an organisation arises from the usage of power to influence decisions which should ideally be made through a more pristine decision process. This could include decisions about what the business should do in the market, how the organisation should be restructured, how resources should be allocated etc. Importantly, organisational politics is often at play when employees seek to increase their power in some way.

Organisational thinking

Ideally, organisations should be perfectly rational. After all, you have already read around 300 pages on how to manage a business, with the expectation that a lot of rational thought goes into this. Not to worry, rational and scientific thinking is what organisations strive to put behind all of their decisions. But the best businesses are also run only by humans, with limited resources. And so, sometimes, the business thinking process is a little less than ideal. We call this more realistic process one of bounded rationality.

Bounded rationality is in itself a spectrum (Gopakumar, 2021).

- Management Science – This is the approach that we have been trying to develop through this book. One which is not 100% precise, but still directionally useful and based on rational thought at each step.
- Carnegie Model – This model assumes that uncertainty and conflict are part and parcel of businesses in the real world. Thus, different teams of people, with clashing objectives form coalitions and try to arrive at solutions which are compromises but are still satisfactory.
- Incremental Approach – This approach accepts that solutions in the business world are often short of perfect. Thus, we start with whatever solution we have available, and in as scientific a manner as possible make incremental improvements until we end up with something satisfactory.
- Garbage Can Model – This model is far more pessimistic. Here, we believe that in the confusion of the corporate world, solutions may be proposed when there aren't problems, choices are made which are short of useful and many problems go unsolved. But some problems are still solved along the way.

As a function of how much uncertainty exists as to what problems we are solving and how to solve them, the business is constrained in terms of the realistic best approach available. Of course, we would love to live in a world of certainty. However, realistically sometimes that is either impossible or too expensive to achieve. As bad as some of the other models may sound, they often produce good enough results, which is all that really matters.

Culture

Culture is another word which is often thrown around, even though many people have contrasting views of what it means. So, to begin with, let me put out my understanding of what organisation culture is.

I think of organisation culture as consisting of a range of norms, symbols, behavioural patterns, traditions and more which exist across the organisation. These attributes of culture come to exist because at some time or the other they solve existing challenges and therefore are treated as useful or valid. From there on out, they are propagated by existing members of the organisation to new members of the organisation. At some stage the original reason for the culture having come about might be forgotten, whereas the visible attributes of it may remain.

You may agree or disagree with parts of my understanding of culture, but that is the one that we will be working with in this subsection since we aren't in a position to debate and agree on a definition.

The bulk of culture isn't visible. We can see the symptoms or the effects of an existing culture, such as a dress code, type of language used, traditions and so on. However, the important underlying factors in this culture are the organisational beliefs, values, attitudes and so on. These are not directly visible, even though a majority of the people in the organisation may hold them (Gopakumar, 2021).

Since we can only see parts of the culture, it would help if we knew what all to look out for, as that would help us form a clearer idea of what the organisation's underlying and invisible culture is as well. Luckily, we have a framework from Schien, which gives us 8 artefacts of corporate culture to look out for (Schien, 1984).

Norms	Language	Heroines & Heroes	Myths
• Expected behaviour • Standards • Dress code	• Jargon • Terminology	• Role models • Legendary visionaries • Motivating standards	• Frequently told stories • Setting real/fake standards
Symbols	**Ceremonies**	**Folkways**	**Others**
• Objects/events • Layers of implied meaning • Insider constructs	• Elaborate events • Reinforce values • Aspirational standards	• Customs • Unconscious acts	• Subcultures • Unsaid rules

While there are many such artefacts through which culture can be perceived, not all artefacts of culture are equivalent. There are 2 dimensions on which we can compare any artefact. The first dimension is how widely shared the attribute of culture is. More widely shared attributes are more visible, while more narrowly shared ones might be a part of a subculture. The second dimension is how deeply held the cultural attribute is. More deeply held attributes are enforced and indoctrinated more strongly, while weaker attributes of culture are more of a token (Gopakumar, 2021).

Now that we have understood what culture is, how it can be perceived and the difference between different attributes of culture, the question is what can we as leaders do about it?

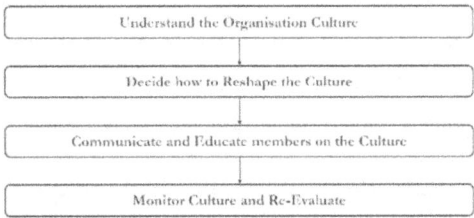

Before we rock the boat, we probably want to understand the existing culture, and then take a call on which parts of it are truly helping the organisation achieve its goals. After redefining the underlying parts of the culture that need some changing, it's through Schien's 8 artefacts of culture that one can incrementally make the required shifts needed. Of course, putting this in place is difficult, because culture is often ingrained, and difficult to change. Therefore constant monitoring and repetition of the effort may be needed.

Recap

In our attempt to understand how to manage a business, we have thus far learnt:

- Management thinking. We have extensively been using convergent thinking, structuring in particular and divergent thinking along the way.
- We got started with 4 steps of business value creation so that we can capture value from customers in return. We are capable of understanding the marketplace, positioning our brand to target the right customers, designing an effective market mix and managing relevant relationships along the way.
- To understand the language of finance, we have understood:
    o The financial reporting process.
    o How to build and analyse the 3 key financial reports.
    o Basic concepts, accounting principles and nuances.
    o Metrics and ratios for financial analysis.
    o What else can be learnt from financial markets to valuation of firms.
- To tackle any operational challenge, we had a look at:
    o The basics and terminology of operations.
    o The mathematical nature of operations.
    o The specific math managers need to know.

- o The scope of technology in business.
- We learnt how to better communicate by understanding:
    - o The major levers that we have in communication.
    - o 6 tips for communicating in business situations.
    - o Improving our personal style of communication.
- To manage people, we learnt how individuals think, behave and perform by learning:
    - o How to manage one's self.
    - o How to learn and convince.
    - o About perceptions, attitudes, values and stereotypes.
    - o About motivation and stress.
    - o How to lead.
- To effectively manage groups, we saw that it is important to:
    - o Understand the personalities involved.
    - o Manage conflict through power.
    - o Be inclusive and leverage social networks.
    - o Form teams and tap into synergies.
- To comprehend and control the dynamics of a large organisation, we learnt:
    - o What forms an organisation and its goals.
    - o The underlying structures of an organisation.
    - o How power and politics shape an organisation.
    - o How organisations think in different situations.
    - o How culture manifests in organisations.

Chapter 28
Human Resource Management: Building CEO Factories

We have already learnt how to communicate better in a business context, and have understood human behaviour at all scales ranging from the individual to groups to large organisations. As a manager, that should already help us work with and manage people in pretty much any situation.

Yet, there is one missing piece of the puzzle. Because there are so very many humans in a company. And because humans are rather important, companies have a single dedicated function called human resources which works on managing the human resources, amongst other things. That doesn't mean that all other managers are exempt from dealing with other people. You might then wonder if there is an unnecessary overlap of responsibilities.

The simple answer is that line managers (not HR managers) are responsible for managing how the people in and around their team get the work done. Whereas HR managers are responsible for pretty much everything else to do with the people in the business. In this chapter, we shall start by understanding what else is needed on the human front and therefore what HR's role is. We shall then have a look at some of these roles in more detail, understanding how HR can capture, retain and breed the best talent in an organisation.

HR's Role

Most of us are most familiar with HR's role in recruitment, promotions and raises. This is in fact an important role that HR plays. For us as employees, this may seem to be the most significant of roles. However, HR plays a broader range of roles. According to David Ulrich's HR model, the 4 key roles played by HR can be looked at along 2 dimensions. The first is one of process vs people orientation. The second is a function of whether the role is today's day-to-day operations or is more future-looking. Across these 2 dimensions, HR is expected to be a strategic partner, ensuring that the people and structures of the business are ready to face the needs of tomorrow. To this end, they must also act as change agents, bringing in the right people or helping them grow into those who will be required by the business in the future. HR also has a responsibility to the employees of the organisation and acts as their representative on a variety of counts. Finally, there is no shortage of administrative work which HR is responsible for (Ulrich, 1997).

A lot of the process-oriented work may not warrant discussion right now. Mainly because I don't know enough about it. But also, because what I do know has largely been covered in the section on strategy. And parts of what I don't will often vary with company and context. We will, however, be looking at how HR recruits, represents, retrains and retains employees through the rest of this chapter.

Managing human resources

As an employee, one can imagine that their line manager is the person that they go to in order to receive work, solve work-related challenges and get assistance in dealing with other employees or functions. Outside of this, any other challenges or queries that one has tend to be redirected to the HR manager in charge of one's team. Rather than looking at this from an employee's point of view, let's begin to view the process of managing human resources from HR's standpoint.

There are a variety of frameworks available to choose from. So, we shall have a look at a few to form our own idea of what HR must do to manage an effective set of human resources.

One view suggests that HR managers are responsible for ensuring that the people in the business are capable of performing their roles. Given that they are managers, they can't leave this vague statement as is, and therefore must structure it into smaller, more manageable tasks. Therefore, HR strives to ensure that the people in the business have the right set of abilities (through selective recruiting or training), are motivated to complete the task, and have the right set of opportunities.

Another view looks at the organisation as a whole and believes that if everything about the organisation is attractive, the right kind of people would want to work here and work well. The 3Cs model, therefore, aims to create an organisation which is a compelling place to:

- Shop
- Work
- Invest

What this means is that the business must be one which customers are interested in, potential employees are interested in and investors are interested in. As long as HR can nudge and influence the right decisions on all 3 of these factors, a virtuous cycle of getting the right employees, producing the right products and attracting investment shall ensue (Varkkey, 2020).

Yet another framework by Ready, Hill and Conger takes a view of the organisation as something which can have the right attributes to attract and retain the best talent. According to this framework, there are 4 key attributes which must be strong in an organisation (Ready, Hill, & Conger, 2008):

- Purpose – The mission and vision of the organisation should be clear, strong and attractive.
- Brand – The business' brand must be one recognised by customers, valued and appreciated.
- Culture – The company's culture must be meritocratic, but also inviting, safe and attractive for the required sort of talent.
- Opportunity – The work itself, the challenges and rewards must seem interesting and worthwhile to potential employees.

And finally, another view which can be implicitly seen through some of the other frameworks is spelt out in no uncertain terms in the ASA framework. HR aims to (Varkkey, 2020):

- Attract – Attract the best talent.
- Select – Select from the lot the best and most fitting talent.
- Attrition – Prevent attrition of the most valuable employees.

Performance Management Systems

Every company has its system of performance management. Broadly, this is the system through which one's goals/KPIs are set for the year. Over the year, through a series of activities execution of these tasks happens. By the end of the year, each employee's performance is evaluated, and they are duly rewarded for the same. Each of these steps in a generic performance management system has its associated frameworks, which help us improve them.

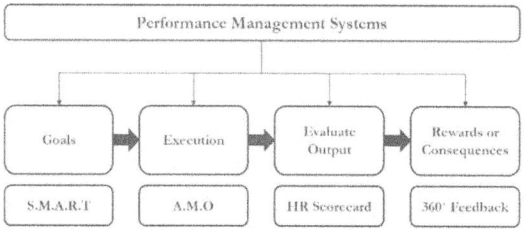

Training

Many other steps in the performance management system have previously been dealt with within this very book. Thus, we already know how to transform those subject areas into objective frameworks. Training, however, is a topic that we haven't covered yet. While we won't be going into the science of education and learning, we shall break down training in a business context. A useful and important split to remember is that almost all employees need to be trained on 2 key dimensions of (Moses, 2020):

- Technical – These aspects relate to their work and the skills required to carry the same out.
- Behavioural – These aspects relate to more of what we have covered in this section, on how to work with other people in the organisation, propagate the culture etc.

Legal aspects

For those employees not involved in HR, one of the least visible aspects of HR's work is that on the legal side. While most companies have their own legal departments, there are some aspects of labour law which HR must be well versed with. The government often passes legislation to ensure that working conditions across the country are satisfactory, and promote productivity. While HR no doubt strives to ensure this and more, this also creates additional administrative work.

It may be useful to note and read up a little on the 4 labour codes in India, which include also freelancers and the informal sector.

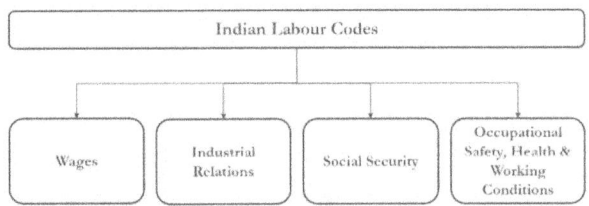

Thus, there are 3 sets of institutions which play a major role in the formal process of human resources management. There is the state, which puts in place boundaries and rules through legislation. There are unions which make employee demands known and ensure representation in some form. And there is the company which acts through its HR function, negotiating and lobbying to arrive at reasonable solutions (Varkkey, 2020).

On this note, it might be of interest to read up a little on the principal-agent problem. It is relevant in this context because of the levels of representation involved. Firstly, unions represent many individual employees, who may have different interests. Next, employees work for company shareholders and effectively represent their business interests. There is also a layer of a handful of government officials representing the interest of a diverse nation of employees.

Recap

In our attempt to understand how to manage a business, we have thus far learnt:

- Management thinking. We have extensively been using convergent thinking, structuring in particular and divergent thinking along the way.

- We got started with 4 steps of business value creation so that we can capture value from customers in return. We are capable of understanding the marketplace, positioning our brand to target the right customers, designing an effective market mix and managing relevant relationships along the way.
- To understand the language of finance, we have understood:
    o The financial reporting process.
    o How to build and analyse the 3 key financial reports.
    o Basic concepts, accounting principles and nuances.
    o Metrics and ratios for financial analysis.
    o What else can be learnt from financial markets to valuation of firms.
- To tackle any operational challenge, we had a look at:
    o The basics and terminology of operations.
    o The mathematical nature of operations.
    o The specific math managers need to know.
    o The scope of technology in business.
- We learnt how to better communicate by understanding:
    o The major levers that we have in communication.
    o 6 tips for communicating in business situations.
    o Improving our personal style of communication.
- To manage people, we learnt how individuals think, behave and perform by learning:
    o How to manage one's self.
    o How to learn and convince.
    o About perceptions, attitudes, values and stereotypes.
    o About motivation and stress.
    o How to lead.
- To effectively manage groups, we saw that it is important to:
    o Understand the personalities involved.
    o Manage conflict through power.
    o Be inclusive and leverage social networks.
    o Form teams and tap into synergies.
- To comprehend and control the dynamics of a large organisation, we learnt:
    o What forms an organisation and its goals.
    o The underlying structures of an organisation.

- How power and politics shape an organisation.
- How organisations think in different situations.
- How culture manifests in organisations.
- To understand where HR fits into the organisation we saw:
  - What HR's roles are.
  - A few lenses through which human resource management can be structured.
  - The legal aspects of employee management.

Section VI

Studying the Outside World

After a great amount of effort, you have covered more than 300 dense pages of management knowledge. At this point, you should know everything there is to know about managing a business, from inside the business. Or at least everything that I know, which is significantly less, but I'm sure you can make do with it.

That being said, there is still everything outside of the business, which we haven't even touched upon in this book. It may be a bit much to expect a business manager to know a lot about anything external to the business. After all, they have been employed to manage the business, not everything outside the business. However, in the inter-connected world that we live in, things that happen outside the organisation affect the organisation and vice versa. So, better-equipped managers have a rough idea of what is happening outside the organisation, as well as how it will affect their business.

In the first section of this chapter, we shall aim to understand how the law governs and regulates businesses. While we won't be able to detail all the intricacies, we should be able to build up an appreciation for how the legal framework fits in on the whole.

In the second chapter of the section, we shall understand some basics of microeconomics. Through this, we hope to be able to model and visualise market interactions of our business with other entities. In fact, we can even model interactions between other entities that might affect our business. This simplified model of microeconomics may seem familiar, since a lot of it is rather useful, and has been used in parts of the strategy and marketing frameworks that we have already understood.

In the final chapter in this section, we shall study a little bit of macroeconomics. Here we shall see what happens when these individual interactions scale up and compose an entire economy. We hope to become a little more literate with respect to the economy. In doing so, maybe the news will make more sense to us and will give us actionable information about how our business will be impacted by the world around us.

Chapter 29
Letter of the Law: Staying Out of Jail

As managers, we are now beginning to stray toward those topics which are at the fringe of our business. That doesn't mean that they are any less important than those topics which are squarely within the business domain. Think for example about how important the borders of a nation are from the point of view of a government.

Within a topic such as the law, one is required to have a very detailed understanding of its provisions and regulations. So, just a textbook or two on business law, and this book in particular, certainly won't equip you to handle the legal aspects of your business. It is important to have experts on the law, working within the legal department, and for the legal department to be routinely involved in decision making.

What any other manager can be expected to do is to have a basic understanding of how the law governs the actions of businesses and marketplace interactions. Without this basic understanding of the legal framework, managers may not understand the concerns raised by a legal team or may be incapable of working towards effective solutions. In this chapter, we, therefore, aim to cover some basics of business law. We won't be able to discuss intricacies but will understand what it takes to form a contract, communicate agreements, accept offers and break contracts. We shall also understand the importance of and difference between bonds, indemnities and guarantees, how sales contracts are different and how the law looks at companies.

Formation of contracts

The formation of contracts is of particular interest to businesses. This is a domain in which businesses benefit from a strong government, which can enforce the law. In case the law is not enforced by the government, businesses and individuals can be stolen from, and no property is protected. Understandably, there would be little incentive to setup successful businesses then. The law is much larger than simply contract law. Contract law is only that portion of the constitution which deals with the matter of contracts between individuals and businesses. However, the existence of and enforcement of contract law is also of great importance to businesses. If contracts can't be enforced, one party may decide not to provide promised services to another, after accepting payment. Far more trivially, if services aren't provided satisfactorily, there is no recourse that a business has available. Thus, contract law is of great importance.

Having stressed how important it is, let's now understand what a contract even is. Broadly a contract involves an agreement between 2 parties. A legally enforceable contract more specifically must also include "considerations" for the parties involved. A "consideration" is some sort of benefit that the party receives or a loss that the other party takes on for the benefit of one party. This just implies that a contract involves an agreement, in which both parties receive some benefit. If either party receives absolutely no benefit from the contract, then it is no longer recognisable as an enforceable contract and is perhaps closer to slavery (Mohan, 2020).

An agreement itself must consist of an offer being made by one party, and being accepted by the other party. This offer and its acceptance may be explicit, where written, spoken or electronic words clearly indicate the offer/acceptance. Offers and acceptance may also be implicit, where the offer/acceptance is judged by one's actions. This may sound concerning, but rest assured that offer or acceptance, explicit or implicit is considered only when it is objectively firm, clear and unambiguous (Mohan, 2020).

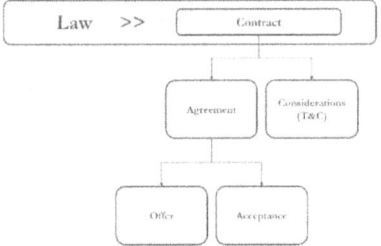

We shall develop a clearer idea of what does and doesn't make the cut, later in this chapter.

Communication

Communication in contracts is often thought to be complicated and particularly involved. After all, it is usually drawn up by legal experts and contracts extend into the hundreds of pages. In reality, however, while contractual communication is detail-oriented, it is quite comprehensible. The next time you click on 'I agree', try spending 5 minutes reading a little bit of what you're agreeing to. You definitely won't finish reading the entire agreement, but whatever you do read will most likely make complete sense to you.

Now that we have busted one myth about contractual communication, let's bust another. Contracts are formed not only through writing, but also orally. This shouldn't be surprising. Just earlier, we had said that offers/acceptance, in the agreement forming process can be explicit or even implicit. An oral agreement is usually quite explicit. Think about an instance when you walked to the grocery store, picked up a loaf of bread and put it on the counter, asking the shopkeeper how much it costs. They tell you, you pay, and leave with the bread. That is an agreement being reached and executed, without any writing. Thus, an oral contract was formed. Even if you didn't pay, but asked them to add it to your tab, an oral contract has been formed. These contracts are also enforceable by a court of law. However, as one might expect, purely oral contracts are tougher to enforce, because it is tougher to ensure that all the relevant information is available. If a written contract is available, courts are often hesitant to look at any oral agreements over and above this (Mohan, 2020).

At this stage, it is worth revisiting the assurance that I gave you, that independent of the form of communication, a court of law will interpret the objective meaning. Subjective meaning in this context is the meaning that an individual intended, which is known only to them. The objective meaning is the meaning that a rational and reasonable outsider interprets from the actions and words used. For example, let's imagine that a seller has emailed information about a product to a potential buyer and made an offer. In the email, the seller mistakenly mentions that the price is INR 4,000 instead of INR 5,000. The buyer accepts the offer. Now, if the seller tries to claim that the price to be paid is INR 5,000, it will not hold up in a court of law. Even if the seller can prove that the item is usually sold for Rs 5,000 and that the email was a genuine mistake, to the objective outsider, an offer for INR 4,000 was justly made and accepted.

Offers are also expected to be clear and definite. In the absence of this clear and definite information, rather than an offer, it may only be an invitation for an offer. For example, if a shop posts an advertisement saying "Mega Sale. Up to 50% off on merchandise.", this isn't an offer. The reason is that it isn't clear which items are being offered at what discount, or for how many units. It's an invitation for an offer, where customers are expected to pick up items in the shop, look at the new discounted price and then make an offer (take for billing) if they're interested. This distinction is important because it protects the shop from customers who see the ad, and then claim a 50% discount on any item of their choosing (Mohun, 2020).

Acceptance of offers

We have understood that forming contracts is a big part of business and that the communication involved has some nuances to it. As such, one would expect that accepting an offer is a pretty straightforward process. It usually is. However, this too has some nuances to it. One could fail to accept an offer in a multitude of ways. A long silence could imply rejection of an offer. Especially if an offer has a limited time validity, failing to respond within that time would lead to rejection. But even when a time frame is not specified, a failure to respond for months is reasonably treated as a rejection. Similarly, the party making an offer is free to revoke the offer at any point of time before acceptance is communicated, even if the offer is revoked almost immediately. If the other party chooses to accept the offer, but adds their own conditions or modifies some conditions, that is not considered to be an acceptance. Instead, that is treated as a rejection, followed by a counter-offer. The party that made the original offer is now in a position to either accept or reject it. And of course, express or implied rejection is another way in which offers are not accepted.

While there are many ways in which an offer is thus not accepted, offers are also often accepted. As mentioned earlier, express or implied acceptance isn't exactly difficult to successfully complete. One important factor here is the modality of communication. While making an offer, one can specify the mode of communication through which the acceptance must be communicated. For example, one is often required to make a payment, and then send an email with proof of payment, to communicate acceptance of an offer. However, sometimes this mode of communication isn't specified. In such cases, a mode of communication which is reasonable, with respect to the mode of communication of the offer, may be expected. For example, if one receives an offer on their mobile shopping app, it is unreasonable to accept it by faxing your acceptance to some phone number.

Now that we know how to successfully accept an offer, and what pitfalls to avoid, there is the matter of where the contract is formed, on acceptance. Usually, in any mode of communication, which is immediate (face-to-face, telephone, email, via the internet etc)the contract is formed wherever the offeror receives the acceptance. However, if the mode of communication is not immediate, like in the case of post, the contract is formed wherever the acceptor provides their acceptance or posts the mail in this case. This can of course be overridden by an explicit term in the contract. The reason that this is of importance is that each region and court of law may have its own set of rules in terms of how to enforce contracts, and this may impact the contract itself (Mohan, 2020).

Breaking contracts

Now that we know how to successfully form contracts, let's have a look at how contracts are broken. Once again, there are many ways in which contracts may be broken. Usually, when contracts are not fulfilled, there is one party at fault. If that is the case, and the other party has suffered some loss as a result, the suffering party is awarded "damages". Damages are a fair calculation of the benefit (usually monetary) that the suffering party must be awarded by the party at fault, in order to offset their loss. Damages are supposed to be compensatory, and not punitive. Thus, if the party not at fault somehow doesn't suffer, but profits as a result of the breach of contract, damages are not awarded.

Now that we have a rough idea of what happens when a contract is broken, let's have a look at how this can happen. One obvious way is when the contract is breached, or not fulfilled. Even here, there are different terms in a contract of differing importance. The core, most important parts of a contract are called the "condition". The subsidiary portions of less importance are called the "warranty". These terms may seem a little confusing since they have different meanings in common parlance but bear with me for a minute. When a condition of a contract is breached, usually damages are awarded and the party not at fault has the option of terminating the contract as a result of the breach. If they choose not to terminate the contract, they have the option of demanding "specific performance", which translates to demanding that the party at fault still somehow fulfil their contractual obligation. On the other hand, if only a warranty is breached, the suffering party is owed damages, but the contract is not terminated as a result.

Contracts may also be broken by mutual consent. If both parties intend to break the contract, this is similar to them arriving at an overriding contract, which declares the previous one void.

Sometimes, contracts must also be ended because the agreement reached proves to be impossible. The world is always changing, and some external events may make the agreed-upon activity impossible to carry forward. Once it has been made completely impossible, the parties involved may terminate the contract without the payment of damages. However, depending on the nature of the task involved, and the specifics of the contract, the termination may be handled differently. For example, in some cases, a force majeure clause may detail what actions should be taken in case of an impossibility of certain kinds (Mohan, 2020).

Bonds, indemnities and guarantees

We saw early on that all contracts must have some conditions for each of the parties involved. Bonds, indemnities and guarantees, however, are special contracts. These are all unilateral, meaning that one party stands to gain no benefit within the contract.

A bond is a contract where one party undertakes to pay (provide some benefit) another party. It's just that simple.

An indemnity is a contract where party A undertakes covering the losses that may arise to party B. Usually, the losses that are covered are those which may arise from a contract between party B and party C. Thus, in an indemnity, there are 2 contracts between 3 parties. If a loss arises in the main contract (between B & C), then as per the secondary contract (between A & B), A must cover the losses of B.

A guarantee is similar to an indemnity in structure. However, the payment in a guarantee is triggered not by a loss caused to B, but rather by a default in the contract. Here, party A undertakes to pay party B, in case party C defaults on a contract between B & C. Thus, there is a main contract between B & C. In case C defaults on this main contract, as per the secondary contract between A and B, A will pay B what is owed by C (up to some amount) (Mohan, 2020).

Companies

A large part of the law which is of importance to businesses is that portion which determines how companies should be treated and recognised. This is largely dealt with in the Companies Act 2013. Importantly, this act deals with:

- Incorporation of a company.
- Prospectus and allotment of securities.
- Share capital and debentures.
- Management and administration.
- Payment of dividend.

- Accounts.
- Appointment of directors.
- Meeting of the board.

The law usually deals with how individuals are supposed to act with one another, and how they should live in a society. Thus, the introduction of companies and organisations would be a bit of a departure from the regular nature and wording of the law. For this reason, a company, once registered is essentially treated as an individual, which is separate from the individuals who form it. A company can be thought of as a contract, which is formed through the memorandum of association and articles of association, thus creating a distinct entity.

The companies act allows for 3 different types of companies to exist. One-person companies have exactly one individual, who must be a real person (not a company), and a citizen of the country. Private companies have a limit on the number of people who may be members, and they aren't allowed to raise funds, like public companies. Public companies on the other hand need to have a minimum of 7 members involved (Mohan, 2020).

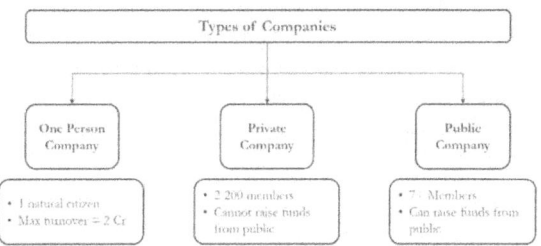

As we have already noted, one of the requirements in the process of registering a company is the creation of a memorandum of association. This is one of the foundational documents for any given company. Some of the information required in an MoA is (Mohan, 2020):

- The name of the company to be registered, along with the addition of limited/ private limited if required.
- The status of the company as a limited liability company (or not). As well as whether it will be registered as a one-person, private or public company.
- The state in which the main office of the company shall be.

- The comprehensive list of objectives which the company shall or may serve going forward.
- The total amount of share capital with which the company shall be registered, as well as the value of each share and the total number of shares to be attributed to each subscriber at the time of registration.

Case 11

As the dungeon expands from one industry to another, they find that it is important to have a strong legal advisor as a part of their team. With the assistance of the legal advisor, the dungeon's management was able to start closing the gap on some loopholes in their business practices. The dungeon had recently started an online television retailing portal. They had requested that the legal advisor carefully scrutinise and improve their business practices in this domain.

The service worked like most e-commerce websites. Customers could browse through arrange of available models, see the specifications, prices, delivery timelines and so on. Once the customer had selected a TV of their choice, they would make the purchase online. All the parameters of the agreement, such as the price, delivery date and contract regarding the delivery process were set by the dungeon. But the customer, in selecting the product, clicking the buy button and completing the payment is making the offer. The dungeon by processing the transaction and producing a "success page" is accepting the offer. The legal advisor helped tweak the included terms and conditions. For example, they ensured that once delivery has been completed and the customer is in possession, the dungeon will no longer be liable for any damages/repairs.

The dungeon used to purchase these TV sets from manufacturers and store them in their warehouse. Thus, once the customer purchases a product, the dungeon was in a position to transfer ownership, rather than simply acting as an intermediate agent. Unfortunately, the dungeon usually doesn't have the user manuals for these TV sets. They used to ask customers to download the digital manuals online. However, as advised by the legal advisor, the dungeon began explicitly mentioning in their contracts that the TV manuals are not included. Failure to mention even such a trivial thing could lead to a breach of contract.

The dungeon also offered an EMI option on their TVs. Through this option, the customer would immediately get possession of the TV but could continue to pay the EMI in the form of monthly instalments for 10 months. Failure to pay the monthly instalments would lead to a breach of the contract, in which case the dungeon would repossess the TV and refund the customer (minus damages). Only after all instalments have been paid would the customer become the owner of the TV.

One particular customer (A) had purchased such an LED TV from the dungeon through an EMI offer. After 4 monthly instalments were paid, this customer sold the TV to a friend (B) of theirs. The customer (A) continued paying the monthly instalments, and the dungeon of course was unaware of the fact that A was no longer in possession of the TV. 6 months after the purchase, the dungeon was called up by B, asking for a refund on the TV. B claims that they were expecting the TV to be a smart TV, with content streaming services available.

Case Questions

From your understanding of contract law, and the specific agreements in place.

1. Who is the current owner of the TV?
2. Is the sale of the TV from A to be legal and valid?
3. Is the claim for a refund from B valid?
4. Who is at fault and are any damages due?

Instead of just thinking on your own, I would encourage you to participate in a case discussion on the following Reddit thread. Through case discussion, your ideas may be validated or improved upon. You would also benefit from other people's viewpoints.

Recap

In our attempt to understand how to manage a business, we have thus far learnt:

- Management thinking. We have extensively been using convergent thinking, structuring in particular and divergent thinking along the way.

- We got started with 4 steps of business value creation so that we can capture value from customers in return. We are capable of understanding the marketplace, positioning our brand to target the right customers, designing an effective market mix and managing relevant relationships along the way.
- To understand the language of finance, we have understood:
  - The financial reporting process.
  - How to build and analyse the 3 key financial reports.
  - Basic concepts, accounting principles and nuances.
  - Metrics and ratios for financial analysis.
  - What else can be learnt from financial markets to valuation of firms.
- To tackle any operational challenge, we had a look at:
  - The basics and terminology of operations.
  - The mathematical nature of operations.
  - The specific math managers need to know.
  - The scope of technology in business.

- So that our technical knowledge can practically be put to use, we learnt how to communicate better with anyone involved. We spent sometime understanding how individuals, groups and large organisations may behave at scale. And we understood the role that HR plays in managing the human element of business.
- To understand how our business fits into the outside world, we had a glance at some of the basics of business law, including:
  o Offers, acceptance, formation and breaking of contracts.
  o Special types of unilateral contracts.
  o The fundamentals of the companies act.

Chapter 30
Microeconomics: Free Lunch and Other Imaginary Constructs

Having understood a little bit about the law, let's begin educating ourselves on economics. The good news is that the language and nature of economics should feel very similar to what we have been covering throughout the book. Economics is a study of the production, distribution, consumption and transfer of wealth. Business is after all a big part of all of this creation and movement of wealth. So, it should feel like we're back home, after a small detour into law.

However, while managing a business, most of the economic knowledge that you will need has most likely already been repackaged in the form of what we have studied in the first 5 sections of the book. In this chapter, we shall study a little microeconomics, which focuses on individual economic units of consumers and firms, rather than the entire large scale of the economy. This should be a useful subject to get a grip on especially while dealing with new situations. It should prove to be useful because it helps us develop our first principles-based thinking about how interactions in the market play out. This coupled with our first principles-based thinking from the first section should equip us to handle most situations.

While all topics in this book are individually covered better in books written by experts, the area of economics stands out in particular. There is no shortage of engaging, insightful and interesting books on microeconomics. What we shall try to cover in this chapter is a wide range of topics, to get a broad sense of the world of microeconomics. We'll start by learning about markets, prices, consumers, firms, costs and profits. We'll then get deeper into the territory of market regulation, game theory, externalities and information asymmetry.

Markets and prices

In economics, we talk a lot about markets. So, let's start with an oversimplification of what a market is. A market is just a group of firms that produce goods and people who buy them. In the market, they interact or even just potentially interact to set prices and determine the quantities of the products which will be traded. We are usually particularly interested in what we call perfectly competitive markets. These are markets which have a large enough number of buyers and sellers competing with each other so that no individual has a strong influence over the price. As you might have guessed, it's the competition in the market which helps set the price, and determine what will be sold, to whom and how.

Since we have spoken about markets and their competitiveness in terms of price setting, let's quickly discuss a few prices of interest. In a competitive market, we expect goods to be sold at what we call the market price. This is just the price that the specified good is usually sold at, as a function of market competition. Prices may be what we call nominal or real. A nominal price is the exact number or price value at which the product is sold. The real price gives us a better picture of what this number means. The real price is the nominal price, after adjustment for other factors, such as inflation. There are also price indices, such as the consumer price index and the producer price index, which give us a rough idea of what aggregate price levels are like across important goods in the market (Pindyck & Rubinfeld, 2013).

The key question is how competitive markets determine prices and quantities of sale. To model this, we imagine a demand curve and a supply curve.

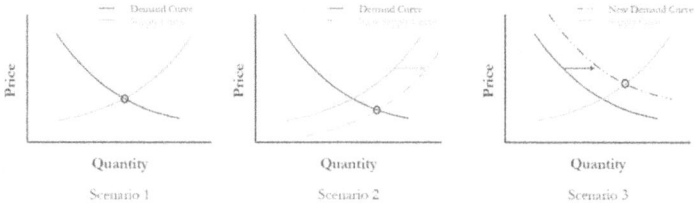

As can be seen in scenario 1, the demand is downward sloping. What this implies is that as prices go up, fewer consumers are interested in purchasing the product, or the same consumers are willing to purchase a lower quantity. Understandably the supply curve is therefore upward sloping. At higher prices, firms are willing to produce larger quantities and sell more. The point at which these 2 curves meet is the point which a competitive market gravitates towards. Hopefully, this makes intuitive sense. In case it doesn't let's use some basic math to lock ourselves into the idea. Consumers will refuse any point which is not on the demand curve. Suppliers will refuse any point which is not on their supply curve. That leaves us with exactly one possible option for price and quantity.

Demand and supply curves can be shifted though, by a range of factors. Think about how the telecom market in India started dropping prices when Jio entered the market and provided customers with more talk-time and data at the same price. Effectively the supply curve had been shifted towards the right. The demand remained pretty much the same (at least in the short term). And so, more customers were able to get more out of their service providers, at lower rates. This is visible in scenario 2.

Think now about how, as soon as lockdowns were announced, western markets started running out of toilet paper. Initially, and immediately, supply had not yet changed. However, in anticipation of this challenge, demand skyrocketed. As such, a larger quantity was purchased at higher prices. This can be seen in scenario 3. As and when the supply also shrunk, prices would have gone still further, while the quantity of sales would have dipped.

Hopefully, by this point, you see why the idea of economic modelling is fascinating. Through a simple model, we can explain and even predict pretty large-scale economic events.

Before we move past the idea of markets, let's touch upon the idea of surplus. Since we are modelling markets and trying to understand how buyers and sellers may interact, it's useful to ask if they are on the whole better of or not. The concept of surplus is an attempt at the same. Let's think of the demand curve as a series of buyers. The first buyer is willing to pay the highest price. The second buyer is willing to pay the next highest and so on. That would explain the shape of the curve, as a series of increasingly stingy buyers. We can similarly imagine the supply curve, but with each additional producer willing to sell one unit only at a higher price. The surplus for an individual buyer is the difference between the price they were willing to pay and the price at which the good is sold. Similarly, the surplus for a producer is the difference between the selling price and the price at which they were willing to produce and sell (Chatterjee, 2020).

Graphically, we can visualise that those buyers and sellers who do get involved in transactions are better off by some surplus amount.

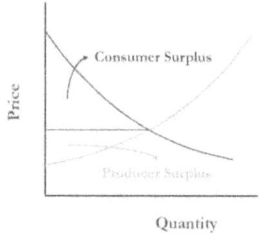

This idea of surplus is useful to see whether market actions are overall improving the situation for buyers, sellers, both or neither.

We have already seen how both consumers' and producers' behaviours are modelled in the supply and demand curve. One might look at this and think that it's a fair estimate at an overall level, but not very nuanced. It's a good thing that economists have been looking at these curves for much longer and have more solutions to this than I'll be able to cover.

One nuance is that there are multiple different products on offer to choose from. One might wonder how consumers would decide how much of each product to purchase when each of them has its own supply and demand curve. To this end, we have a new curve to answer our question. The indifference curve marks out all of the possible combinations of 2 goods which are equal in value (or satisfaction) to the consumer. Each indifference curve can have a different satisfaction value, but a consumer is indifferent between any 2 points on a given curve (Pindyck & Rubinfeld, 2017).

Take for example the case of sleep vs grades in college. We all want both, ideally, more of each is better. But there is a trade-off, and so we're often okay with a little more of one, in exchange for less of the other.

301

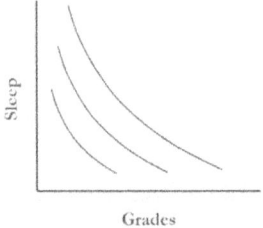

Similarly, the concept of perfect substitutes and complements is visually pleasing when depicted through indifference curves. Substitutes are products which can replace each other in a consumer's basket of choices. Complementary products are those which work together, and not as well individually.

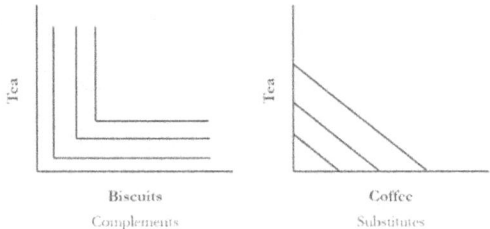

Underlying the idea of demand and indifference curves is a more fundamental idea that a consumer's preferences can be mathematically modelled. A utility function is one such mathematical formulation which assigns some sort of value to a basket of consumer purchases. It should be easy to see how a utility function can assign different values to each indifference curve while maintaining the same value along a single curve.

Now that we are assigning values to combinations of goods, an interesting question is whether the utility function tells us that more is always better. Simplistically, our answer could be "yes, of course". However, I'm sure that from experience we can all agree that a second and even a third scoop of ice cream is great. But a fourth, fifth and maybe at least a sixth would become more of a problem than a delight. This concept of us valuing each added unit a little less is called diminishing marginal utility. And this concept is the reason that utility curves will start with a great slope and then flatten out. So, more is still better, but beyond a point, the difference almost comes down to zero.

Just as consumers assign a certain value to any given basket, the market at large also assigns a certain price to the basket. Thus, a similar concept of budget lines can be imagined. A single budget line would mark out all the points (combinations of products) which amount to the same price. Different budget lines of different values would be able to hold different baskets.

Since we like putting curves together and seeing what we learn, let's put the budget line and indifference curves together. A given consumer has a specific budget, and therefore just one budget line of interest. As far as indifference curves are concerned, there are multiple to choose from. Each indifference curve has its own utility value, so some are better than others. We, therefore, want to find the best indifference curve that our budget line intersects. Amongst the points that it intersects with, on this best indifference curve, we are indifferent. The math tells us, that any budget line will tangentially intersect some indifference curve. This is the best indifference curve that it will intersect with, and luckily there's only one point of intersection (Chatterjee, 2020) (Pindyck & Rubinfeld, 2017).

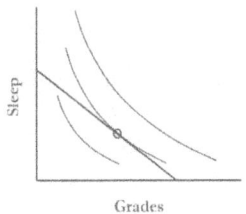

Grades

Thus, as consumers, if we can draw out our budget line and indifference curve, we will always know the best selection of products for us to buy. Unfortunately, the fact that we aren't mathematically driven robots makes this a little tough in practice.

While none of us is explicitly calculating utility and making hard-coded choices, there is some level of utility-seeking behaviour which is still modelled fairly through the various curves and functions that we have seen. However, this too is subject to classic human irrationality. One such source of irrationality is network externalities. A network externality is basically when people change their behaviour as a function of what other people (their network) are doing.

One such externality is the bandwagon effect. Here the demand (or perceived demand) for a product further drives up the demand for it. Think of any fad, where you don't know why it's valuable, but just that it is. The snob effect is the opposite. Once the demand for a product goes up, it's no longer niche and cool. And so, the demand for it ends up dropping. Many hipster fashion trends are impacted by the snob effect. The Veblen effect shows how we react to price changes, rather than quantity demand changes. In the context of luxury goods, a higher price makes consumers believe that the product is of greater quality, and so the demand for it goes up (Chatterjee, 2020).

Another nuance is that of price elasticity, which can be studied through the demand curve itself. But we have already touched upon that in the marketing section, in the chapter on the 4Ps (pricing in particular). With a basic understanding of price elasticity, infinite and completely inelastic demand, you might want to look up a few other variants of elasticity. Income elasticity, cross-price elasticity, point elasticity and arc elasticity are simple concepts to understand, with a quick google search.

Firms

Having seen how consumer behaviour can be modelled beyond just the demand curve, it is fair to expect that something similar can be done on the firm's side. Unsurprisingly, this is exactly the case, and we will see many analogies.

Similar to indifference curves, we have isoquants. Isoquants are curves which map out all possible combinations of inputs which will produce the same level of output. Just as we had a utility function, here we have a production function underlying the math. Just as marginal utility doesn't grow forever, we have a law of diminishing marginal product as well.

Costs

When we think of costs, the first thing that comes to mind is usually the amount of cash that we have spent out of our pockets. In addition to this most obvious of costs, there are several other costs and several sub-costs which are of interest to us in an economic analysis.

The most basic of costs that we discussed is what we call the accounting cost. Economic costs are more advanced, and they take into account what-if scenarios and appropriate probabilities. But both of these are costs which we have literally incurred or could reasonably expect to.

Opportunity costs are costs which come in the form of profits that we did not make, by picking one option instead of another. We don't actually incur this cost in an accounting sense. But not making this profit is as good as losing it, in an economic evaluation. Sunk costs on the other hand are costs that we have incurred, but can't recover. Thus, using sunk costs in any calculation is a pointless effort, since it only throws our evaluation off.

Amortisation and depreciation costs should be familiar from our section on finance. Marginal costs are the added costs incurred by producing one more unit. Fixed costs are the sum of all costs incurred before the production of any units has begun. Variable costs are the sum of all costs which are incurred as we start production. They are the costs which vary as the production level varies. The total cost is usually the costs included in fixed and variable costs (Chatterjee, 2020).

If there's one thing you should know about costs, it is to always ask what cost the other person is referring to, and then understand what it means and where the number comes from.

Some of these costs change depending on the scale and scope of production. The general expectation is that as we scale, the marginal cost should decrease. This situation is called an economy of scale. The reverse also happens beyond a certain scale, sometimes. This situation is called a diseconomy of scale. Similarly, when the range of products produced grows, we may have either economies of scope or diseconomies of scope (Pindyck & Rubinfeld, 2017).

Additionally, even at the same scale and scope of production, we might just get better at production. This improvement in costs through learning is represented through the learning curve.

Profits

Now that we have understood markets, consumers and firms in equal measure, it's time to focus on the business side of microeconomics. As business managers, we are often concerned first and foremost about our profits. Since we are dealing with the simplified world of microeconomics, and not the complex analysis of more advanced economics, let's make some simplifying assumptions. First, let's assume that we are working in a perfectly competitive market, where each producer is a price taker (has no individual influence on price) and where there is free entry and exit into the market. Let's also assume that whatever quantity we choose to produce, will be accepted by the consumers.

The key question is therefore how much we should produce to maximise our profits.

As we can see in the figure, and more generally, profits are maximum when the gap between revenue and costs is maximum. But more interestingly, this will always happen at the same point that the slope of the revenue curve is the same as the slope of the cost curve. This is true because just before the maximum difference, the cost curve will have a lower slope, and just after, it'll have a greater slope. This is true, even if the revenue curve isn't a straight line. Leaving the math aside, the key implication is that the quantity at which the marginal revenue is equal to the marginal cost is our profit maximising point (Pindyck & Rubinfeld, 2017).

$$\textbf{MR}_{\text{(marginal revenue)}} = \textbf{MC}_{\text{(marginal cost)}} => \textbf{Maximum Profit}$$

Regulation of markets

The regulation of the market, in general, is so broad and complex a topic, that all of microeconomics isn't enough to come up with clear answers. So, you can imagine how little of the topic we will touch upon. Even so, what we will touch upon is pretty wide-ranging. Before we jump into it, let's make sure we're clear on some of the relevant jargon.

To begin with, one of the metrics that we look at to judge regulations is the welfare effect or the deadweight loss. This is the increase or decrease in the sum of the consumer and producer surplus, as a result of the regulation. Economic efficiency is when this welfare is maximised, and market failure is when the prices in the market fails to provide proper signals to consumers and producers as to what action they should take. An externality is any action taken by a producer or consumer which affects others in the market but isn't reflected in the price. Price support is when the government sets the price above the free market price, and also buys the excess supply. An import quota limits the quantity of a good that can be imported, and an import tariff is a tax on imported goods.

Let's start with the case of a price ceiling. As we cap the price, the total amount that suppliers are willing to sell drops. With this reduced quantity and price, the surplus for consumers might increase or decrease. However, the surplus for suppliers decreases significantly. More importantly, there is a net decrease in surplus, and thus, there is a deadweight loss (Chatterjee, 2020).

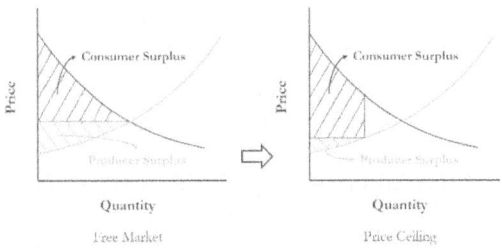

With a price floor, the reverse happens. There is a drop in demand. While the producer surplus might increase or decrease, there is a drop in consumer surplus and net surplus. Once again there is deadweight loss (Chatterjee, 2020).

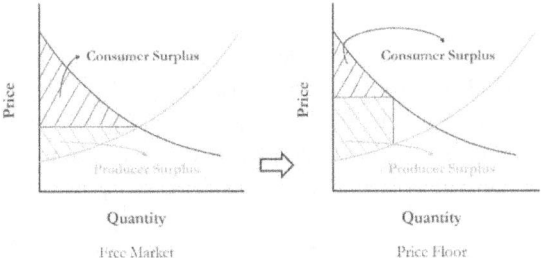

A production quota is like the converse of a price floor. The quantity is capped, so, producers can charge more. Producer surplus may increase or decrease. But consumer surplus and net surplus drop. Once again, there is deadweight loss (Chatterjee, 2020).

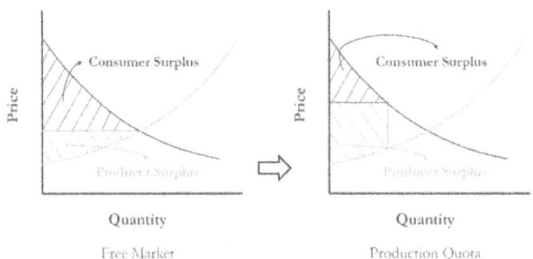

In a free market with imports, the overall surplus is higher than in a free market which is purely domestic. This makes sense since it is essentially a larger market. Let's now add a quota for the total amount of imported goods. Similar to the production quota situation, producer surplus increases, consumer surplus and net surplus decrease. No surprise, there is a deadweight loss (Chatterjee, 2020).

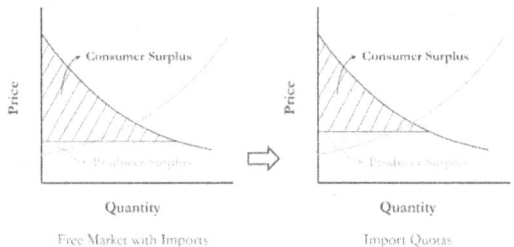

Instead of introducing an import quota, if there was an import tariff, some deadweight loss could be salvaged. In this case, the government gains through tax. But even including this gain in our net surplus, it drops a little bit compared to the free market with imports. This is because the government + suppliers don't regain as much surplus as consumers lose. So, even in the case of import tariffs, there is a deadweight loss (Chatterjee, 2020).

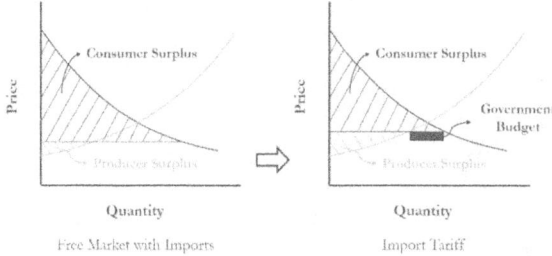

Free Market with Imports   Import Tariff

Let's now look at the context of the government introducing taxes in the conventional domestic market. For consumers, this is as if the price has gone up, and for suppliers, this is as if prices have come down. We can visualise this through a new supply curve which is shifted up by the tax amount. Consumer surplus reduces as if there is a new price floor. Producer surplus also goes down as if there is a price ceiling. And the government gains some of this surplus in the form of tax. However, all 3 of these put together still leads to a drop in net surplus, and therefore deadweight loss (Chatterjee, 2020).

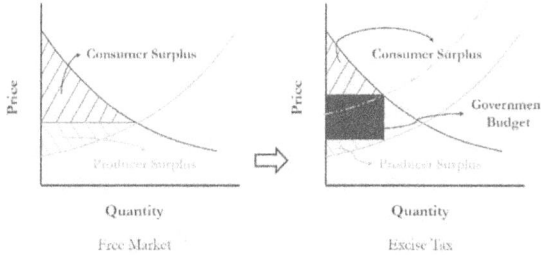

Free Market   Excise Tax

The important lesson from these six scenarios is that when the free market becomes less free, there is some deadweight loss. This should intuitively make sense because in a free market consumers and producers reach a spot of maximisation. Any intervention will impact one of them more than anyone else can gain.

There are other ways in which deadweight losses can arise. Economists often advocate for a perfectly competitive, free market. We have seen how less freedom in the market (through regulation) creates deadweight loss. Imperfect competition can also have a similar impact. Let's start by looking at how imperfect competition may exist.

Monopolies are markets where there is only one seller, and monopsonies are markets where there is only one buyer. In both of these cases, one individual has undue control over supply or demand, and can therefore manipulate prices and quantity. Unsurprisingly, this will lead to some deadweight loss.

In a cartel, a few firms collude, thereby setting the price and quantity to maximise their collective profits. The consumers end up losing surplus in the process, and of course, there is deadweight loss. In an oligopoly, there are only a few firms in the market. The entry of other firms is impeded. While there is no explicit collusion, the prevention of entry of other firms, makes it less competitive, and therefore, each of the firms still has more control over price and quantity. Once again there is deadweight loss.

In monopolistic competition, there is free entry of any number of firms. Each of the firms produces close substitutes of each other's products, but not perfect substitutes. This is pretty close to a lot of real-world scenarios, where there is some differentiation between the various products in the market. Because the substitutes aren't perfect, the competition is also not perfect, and so, even in this very reasonable scenario, there is some deadweight loss (Pindyck & Rubinfeld, 2017).

Game theory

Everything that we have seen thus far in microeconomics simplifies the world. One of the key simplifications is that we look at the market as a system which works in a fixed way, and will respond to our actions only. However, many players in the market are acting simultaneously. Our actions can not be expected to produce a fixed result, but will depend on the actions of others as well. Through game theory, we will try to factor in the possible actions of other players, to arrive at the best course of action.

The key elements in a game are (Chatterjee, 2020):

- Players – The other participants involved are what makes game theory different from the microeconomics we have seen so far.
- Payoffs & Outcomes – There are certain benefits that we would expect from making the right moves. The extent of gain or loss, as a function of our decisions and others' decisions, is an important variable in our calculations.

- Strategy – Taking into account the possible actions from other players, the payoffs and outcomes, we hope to come up with a strategy which will most likely maximise our benefit.

So far, I'm sure that all of this must make sense. But it doesn't yet give us any insight as to what to do when we are caught in such a situation. The first useful insight that we shall look at comes to us from the protagonist of the movie "A Beautiful Mind". The famous Nash equilibrium is a situation where each of the players chooses a strategy which will give them the highest benefit, given the strategy chosen by the other player. If that sounds vague, let's focus on the 2 main points of interest:

1. No player has any incentive to unilaterally change their strategy.
2. No player can improve their payoff by unilaterally changing their strategy.

Aside from Nash equilibriums, there may or may not be dominant and dominated strategies. A dominant strategy is always the best (winning) strategy. If identified, it will always be chosen. A dominated strategy is always a worst (losing) strategy and will be ignored.

Case 12.1

The dungeon has a study group of its own because aside from running many successful businesses, they are also trying to graduate. They are in a simplified class, where there are only 2 study groups, our own and another group, that we just refer to as 'them'.

This course has a version of relative grading. The grades that we receive are based on our relative performance and ranking within the class. But there is also some absolute component involved.

Before we start studying, we try to calculate whether it would be worthwhile or not. In doing so, we try to factor in whether or not the other study group might study. We have the following payoff matrix.

	They Study	They Don't Study
We Don't Study	We score 6/10 They score 10/10	We score 8/10 They score 8/10
We Study	We score 9/10 They score 9/10	We score 10/10 They score 6/10

Case Questions

From your understanding of the game at play.

1. Do we have a dominant strategy? If so, what?
2. Is there a Nash equilibrium? If so, what?
3. What would the other player do?

Instead of just thinking on your own, I would encourage you to participate in a case discussion on the following Reddit thread. Through case discussion, your ideas may be validated or improved upon. You would also benefit from other people's viewpoints.

Case 12.2

Let's complicate matters further. Because the academic schedule is packed with many different courses, it becomes difficult to study thoroughly and effectively for a single course. Instead, time must be split across a few courses. Given this situation, the dungeon has realised that out of the 3 tests in the course, they can study well for just 1. The remaining 2, they will pass, but might not perform well on. They now need to figure out which test to focus on.

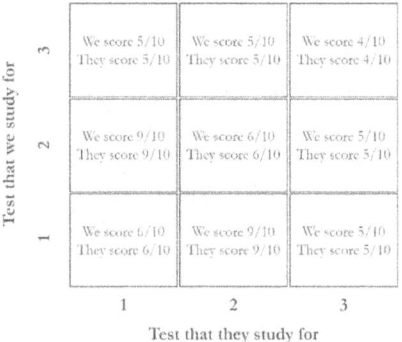

Test that they study for

The dungeon has understood that our results are better when we study for a different test from the other study group. They have also realised that the weightage for test 3 is the lowest. As such, studying for test 3 is a dominated strategy, which no one will follow. The simplified matrix is:

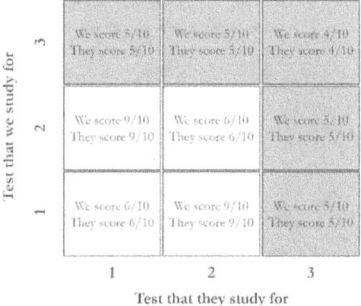

Test that they study for

However, the dungeon finds that they aren't sure what strategy to pursue.

Case Questions

From your understanding of the game at play.

1. Is there a Nash equilibrium? If so, how many?
2. What can the study group do?

Instead of just thinking on your own, I would encourage you to participate in a case discussion on the following Reddit thread. Through case discussion, your ideas may be validated or improved upon. You would also benefit from other people's viewpoints.

Case 12.3

As it turns out, while members of the dungeon were hard at work, a few students cheated instead. While the dungeon doesn't condone cheating and refused to provide any consultation, they were fascinated by the situation on hand. One member of management pointed out that the situation was similar to the famous prisoner's dilemma.

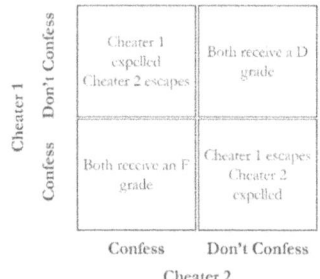

In this situation, the best outcome for both parties involved is for neither of them to confess. However, that is a risky move. It's risky particularly because the dominant strategy for both parties is to confess. And so, it is difficult for them to end up in the best possible situation. Of course, they can't collude here.

Case Questions
From your understanding of the game at play.

314

1. What is interesting about the prisoner's dilemma?

Instead of just thinking on your own, I would encourage you to participate in a case discussion on the following Reddit thread. Through case discussion, your ideas may be validated or improved upon. You would also benefit from other people's viewpoints.

In game theory, we are always looking at increasingly complicated scenarios. One such situation is the realistic setting of repeated games. For example, there are multiple courses that students have to take together. Thus, sometimes it is possible to over time reach an agreement for both parties to drop their dominant strategy in favour of cooperation, which leads to overall greater benefit. What is particularly interesting in this scenario is the cost-benefit calculation of defecting. We assume that we know the exact number of courses that we have together, and the exact grade that we stand to get by cooperating (both play dominated strategy), by defecting (we play dominant while they play dominated) and later as a result of defection (both play dominant). With this information in hand, we can take a call on which course we want to cooperate till, and at what stage we want to defect.

There is also the interesting case of sequential games, where one person must make their move before the other. This happens to be a convenient solution to situations where multiple, equal nash equilibriums exist.

A particularly useful and interesting instrument that game theory provides us with is auctions. Auctions can be an effective and efficient way of finding the best buyer/supplier, getting the best price, as well as quickly selling an item. While this book wouldn't suffice to cover auctions in detail, some interesting auctions to read about are the allocation of spectrum licenses in the United States, New Zeeland and the United Kingdom. These 3 auctions are covered very interestingly in the book "the undercover economist" by Tim Harford.

A few types of auctions that one might want to understand the differences between are:

- English auction
- Dutch auction
- Vickrey auction
- Sealed bid auction
- Yankee auction
- Reverse auction

Externalities

We already have a rough understanding of externalities. The problem with consumer or supplier actions which aren't reflected in the price is that the market will likely respond poorly. This is because the market, as per our model responds only to demand, supply and prices.

Let's take the example of greenhouse gases which are emitted from fossil fuel consumption. Fossil fuels are sold largely at the price that it takes to drill/mine them, refine them and distribute them. There is of course the supplier's margin and subsidies/taxes involved. However, those are small details in the grand mix. What is not taken into account is the social cost of fossil fuels and their greenhouse gas pollution. For each unit of this fuel used, the planet is dramatically damaged, and this impacts not just the user of the fuel, but society at large. Because this isn't reflected in the price, it's easy for suppliers and consumers to consume large volumes of fuel without thinking too hard about the consequences.

A potential solution to this problem is the idea of a Pigouvian tax. These taxes try to capture the additional social cost and transfer them to the person deciding to affect society. For example, let's say that we can calculate the social cost per litre of fuel used. This may be calculated through the cost of air clean-up, cost of health treatment for those affected and the general cost of global warming on other fronts. With this number in hand, we have an idea of the added social cost. The tax amount per litre of fuel sold should include this social cost. This would of course shift the market price and quantity, and increase government collection which can be used to tackle the lessened problem. On the whole, the expectation is that the introduction of a Pigouvian tax will eliminate the largely invisible deadweight loss (Chatterjee, 2020).

316

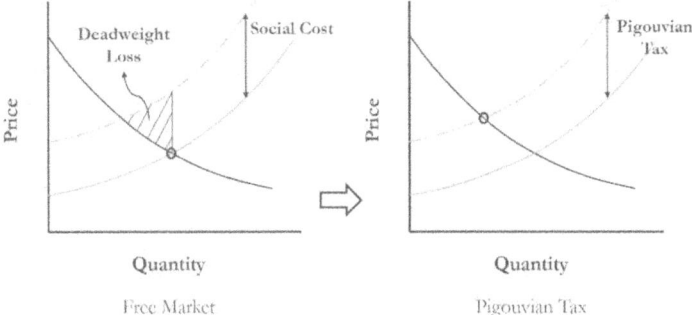

Free Market   Pigouvian Tax

Conversely, there are certain activities, such as the usage of solar panels, planting of trees, administration of vaccination or education etc, which create social benefits beyond the consumer. To encourage such activities, the government may introduce Pigouvian subsidies to effectively lower the price for consumers and increase the price for suppliers, and drive up quantities (Chatterjee, 2020).

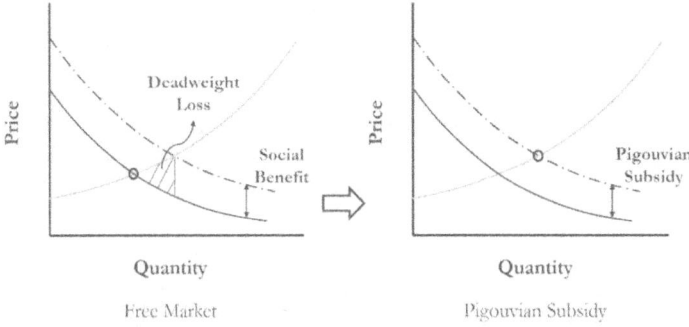

Free Market   Pigouvian Subsidy

Information asymmetry

An underlying assumption in a free and competitive market is that the price captures all of the relevant information. For this to be true, by looking at a product in the market, the consumer must know all the relevant information regarding it and therefore be able to judge their demand, willingness to pay and so on. As we have seen just now, there are certain social costs and benefits which aren't necessarily captured in the price. More dramatically, there is often vital information about the product itself which is known only to the seller, and not to the buyer.

In the case of used products, which are being sold the seller knows whether their product is an effective one (a plum) or a defective one (a lemon). This nomenclature of plums and lemons comes from George Akerlof's research paper on information asymmetry, which is the most popular resource on this topic (Akerlof, 1970).

The challenge that arises is that the consumer doesn't know whether they are getting a plum or a lemon. It is reasonable to assume that all consumers are interested only in purchasing plums.

Let's now take the example of water coolers, which are typically passed on from PGP2s (seniors) to PGP1s (juniors), in IIM-A. The activity of selling one's cooler to a PGP1 usually happens in March, as the Ahmedabad summer sets in, and the PGP2 batch graduates.

From the point of view of a PGP2 (seller), they know whether they have a plum (good) or a lemon (bad). A PGP2 owning a lemon is willing to sell it for any price above INR 0. Not wanting to signal that their cooler is a lemon, they will aim to sell it at whatever the market price is. A PGP2 owning a plum is willing to sell their cooler for INR 5,000 (for example). They are not willing to sell it for any lesser, as they would derive more value from transporting it back home with them.

A PGP1 is only interested in purchasing plums. But because they don't know whether the cooler is a plum or a lemon, they don't know what price to pay for it. They are willing to pay INR 5,000 for a plum and INR 0 for a lemon. The underlying assumption here is that there is no way to check the cooler to identify whether or not it will work well. Even lemons work well for the 15 minutes that it is tested out and then stop working once the purchase has been completed. The probability of a cooler being a plum or a lemon is 50%-50%. So, a PGP1 is willing to INR 2,500 for any cooler.

The issue is that at this price only lemons are available in the market. Thus, we have a market which simply doesn't work because of the information asymmetry within it.

The idea of information asymmetry is closely related to the idea of moral hazard. When there is information asymmetry, it may prompt one party to engage in fraudulent activity to gain some financial incentive. The problems of information asymmetry and moral hazard are particularly rampant in the insurance industry. Various authors with an economics background have done a much better job of writing about this than I can.

One way of solving the problem of information asymmetry is through signalling. Signalling is any method used to pass on information that one party has and the other party cannot observe. For example, if PGP2s offered PGP1s a guarantee of a 100% refund, in case the cooler doesn't work, that would be a signal. Only a PGP2 owning a plum would be willing to offer this since we are assuming a 0% chance that the cooler wouldn't work. As such, they would be able to charge INR 5,000 for their cooler and provide a 100% (or greater) refund. The owner of a lemon wouldn't be able to offer this, since they would expect to earn INR 0 (or less), which is below their expectation for the cooler. Thus, signalling can help solve the issue of information asymmetry.

Another interesting scenario in which the effect of signalling arises is the case of formalised education. Your choice to read this book and learn as much as you can about business isn't signalling or is a very weak signal at best. No one cares what books you have read, much less whether you have read this book in particular. However, your choice to compete with lakhs of students to get into a prestigious business school, and complete your MBA is a signal to potential employers. It signals that you are smart, competent and hard-working, and would therefore make a good employee. This is a large part of the crux of the book, "The Case Against Education" by Bryan Caplan.

Recap

In our attempt to understand how to manage a business, we have thus far learnt:

- Management thinking. We have extensively been using convergent thinking, structuring in particular and divergent thinking along the way.
- We got started with 4 steps of business value creation so that we can capture value from customers in return. We are capable of understanding the marketplace, positioning our brand to target the right customers, designing an effective market mix and managing relevant relationships along the way.
- To understand the language of finance, we have understood:
  - The financial reporting process.
  - How to build and analyse the 3 key financial reports.
  - Basic concepts, accounting principles and nuances.
  - Metrics and ratios for financial analysis.

- What else can be learnt from financial markets to valuation of firms.
- To tackle any operational challenge, we had a look at:
    - The basics and terminology of operations.
    - The mathematical nature of operations.
    - The specific math managers need to know.
    - The scope of technology in business.
- So that our technical knowledge can practically be put to use, we learnt how to communicate better with anyone involved. We spent sometime understanding how individuals, groups and large organisations may behave at scale. And we understood the role that HR plays in managing the human element of business.
- To understand how our business fits into the outside world, we had a glance at some of the basics of business law, including:
    - Offers, acceptance, formation and breaking of contracts.
    - Special types of unilateral contracts.
    - The fundamentals of the companies act.
- To improve our understanding of any new situation we might find ourselves in, we learnt how to model and analyse:
    - The market, consumers, firms, prices, costs and profits.
    - Regulations, game theory, externalities, taxes/subsidies and information asymmetry.

Chapter 31
Macroeconomics: The Economy at Large

We are now nearing the end of this section, on understanding the world around us. We have a reasonable understanding of how to navigate business law, or at least how to interpret it. We have also started building up an understanding of economics, and how we can model all of the interactions in the market.

As managers, to be equipped with a more comprehensive and useful model of the world around us, we often want to model these economic interactions at scale. Of course, there is a lot of added complexity in trying to model the entire economy and understanding the impact that it will have on our own business. Luckily for us, economic experts have done the hard work. Through this chapter, we shall try to understand some of the useful theories that they have put forward. In doing so, we will be able to make sense of what the news tells us about our country and the national and international economy. To this end, we shall aim to develop an understanding of what the economy is, as well as what consumption, investment, inflation and unemployment mean. We shall learn how to use powerful models such as the IS-LM curve, and thus get introduced to the world of short-run macroeconomics and monetary policy.

Welcome to the economy

One might start by wondering what the economy is. As usual, we shall try to stay away from perfect and complex definitions. We shall think of the economy as a scaling up of what we have seen in microeconomics. Thus, the economy is the set of interrelated production, consumption and exchange activities. It thus tracks the flow of goods, services and money supply.

The next important question to ask is perhaps why this is important. Here, let's step out of our business shoes, and look at the lives of individuals in the country. We expect that at least some of these goods and services, and the flow of money has a defining impact on the quality of people's lives. So, the economy can be in a state which is good for the country, and it can also swing to devastatingly bad states. This should be reason enough to study the economy and understand how we can keep it in a good state.

There are, however, metrics other than just money which help us understand how well the country is doing. And even monetarily there are a few metrics that we could look at. Monetarily we could judge an individual's (or family's) well-being from their wealth or their income. Wealth is the sum of all of the assets (property, vehicles, financial assets etc) that they own. Some of these assets may themselves generate income, which is the sum of all monetary gains that they earn in a given period. Outside of monetary bounds, we may also try to study people's well-being through metrics of happiness, satisfaction, anxiety and so on. This is the motivation behind the introduction of metrics like gross national happiness or the human development index. That being said, within economics, we remain cognizant of the fact that there is a strong correlation between financial wealth and overall wellbeing.

We have already understood roughly what the economy is, what we measure and why. So, before we get to the crux of the economy, let's understand what some of our biggest concerns around the economy are. While this might not be the most intuitive way of exploring the topic at hand, it will certainly add some colour to what we are studying. A slowdown in the economy is when economic activity decelerates. This implies that goods, services and money don't change hands as quickly, and so at least some people would be left with less than they desire or even need. Sometimes slowdowns can get really bad. If the economy declines across sectors and geographies for 6 months or more, we call that a recession. The key implication is that a large number of people will end up with less money and essential goods and services than needed. When recessions get really bad, we have a depression. A depression is a particularly severe decline in the economy, which can last for years. In these situations, the economic activity usually declines to the point that a large chunk of the population is unemployed.

And now to the crux and most thrown around phrase in the context of the economy. The Gross Domestic Product of a country is the total market value of all final goods and services produced within a country in a given period of time. That definition should be rather intuitive from the term itself, gross being total, domestic referring to the boundary being drawn, and product referring to the value of all production. The important nuance to keep in mind is that only the value of final goods/services is counted, not the value of intermediate goods being sold. There are of course a whole lot of other details to be kept in mind to calculate the GDP fairly and effectively. Since we aren't calculating it ourselves, we shall skip some of the dirty details for now. Instead, we shall observe the levers driving GDP (Das, 2021).

$$Y_{(GDP)} = C_{(consumption)} + I_{(investment)} + G_{(government\ purchases)} + NX_{(net\ exports)}$$

The 4 key drivers of the GDP are:

- Consumption – A lot of goods and services being produced in the market are being consumed by someone else in the market. Thus, this is a bucket which is relatively easy to observe.
- Investment – Many of the goods or services being produced are not consumed, but rather are investments in the future of a business or of the country. These too are an important aspect of what is produced in our economy.
- Government Purchases – The single most powerful consumer in a country's economy is often the government. They can commission large infrastructure projects or even just purchase goods at scale and decide on how they need to be distributed. Thus, this is a really important lever in the economy.
- Net Exports – And finally, some of what is produced in one country are sold in another. The reverse is also true. Thus the net of what our country exports, minus what we import is the last component of our GDP.

I hope that this has thus far been a simple enough view of what is contained within an economy. But of course, there are a huge number of finer points. For example, there are a large number of other income metrics, each of which measures a slightly different aspect of the economy, with slightly different implications (Das, 2021).

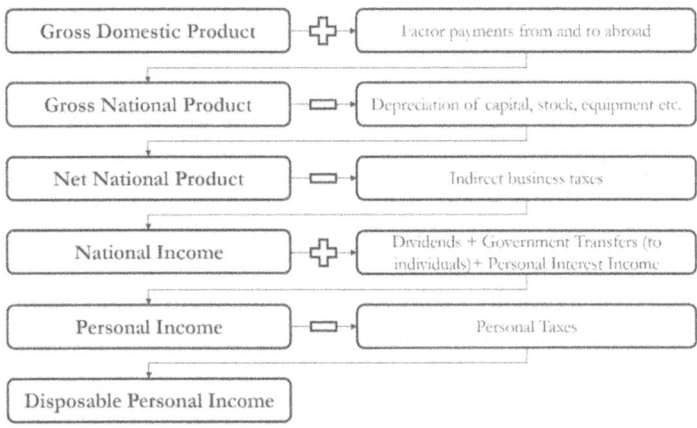

Consumption

We have seen how consumption is a major bucket that affects the GDP of a country. In fact, consumption usually has the largest impact of all. However, GDP essentially represents the country's output, which is the same as the country's total income. It is also true that income affects consumption. John Maynard Keynes proposed a simple, directly proportional relationship between the 2.

$$C_{(consumption)} = \overline{C}_{(subsistence\ consumption)} + c_{(marginal\ propensity\ to\ consume)} \times Y_{(income)}$$

Further, in an ideal world output and demand would both be equal, and would each be the sum of consumption, investment, government purchases and net exports. However, this isn't always the case. The aggregate demand of the country, after factoring in consumption as a function of income can be represented as:

$$AD_{(aggregate\ demand)} = \overline{C}_{(subsistence\ consumption)} + c_{(marginal\ propensity\ to\ consume)} \times Y_{(income)} + I_{(investment)} + G_{(government\ purchases)} + NX_{(net\ exports)}$$
$$AD_{(aggregate\ demand)} = \overline{A}_{(autonomous\ spending)} + c_{(marginal\ propensity\ to\ consume)} \times Y_{(income)}$$

Given that both consumption and aggregate demand fluctuate as a function of income, equilibrium with output will exist only at a certain point. However, when output is below the equilibrium point, firms will increase production, and when output is higher than equilibrium, firms will reduce production. Thus, there is a tendency for output and aggregate demand to reach equilibrium (Das, 2021).

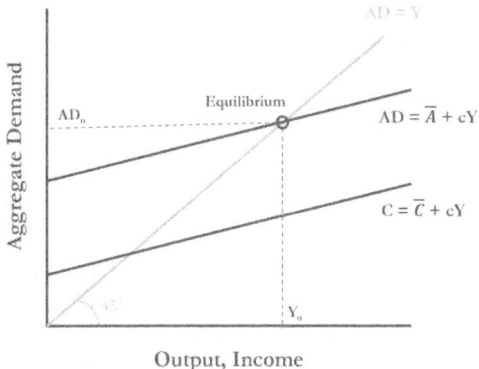

Output, Income

More interestingly, at the equilibrium, we can represent the equilibrium output as a function of autonomous spending (all the usual levers of GDP). Thus, we can represent how a change in autonomous spending will affect the equilibrium output. The interesting result is that with a larger marginal propensity to consume, any change in autonomous spending has a larger impact on equilibrium output.

$$Y_{0(\text{equilibrium output})} = \overline{A}_{(autonomous\ spending)} \big/ (1 - c_{(\text{marginal propensity to consume})})$$

This multiplier effect of autonomous spending on equilibrium output, however, is dampened by the effect of taxation (Das, 2021).

$$Y_{0(\text{equilibrium output})} = \overline{A}_{(autonomous\ spending)} \big/ (1 - (c_{(\text{marginal propensity to consume})} \times (1 - t_{(\text{tax rate})})))$$

What we have seen in some detail just now is John Maynard Keynes' theory of consumption and current income. While it is a very useful theory in predicting economic outcomes, like most theories it has some drawbacks. It predicts that as income rises, the proportion of income spent on consumption will reduce, but this doesn't always prove to be true.

There is a range of other theories of consumption. Irving Fisher's theory of intertemporal choice suggests that consumption is not a function of just current income, but of lifetime income, which can be spread through saving and borrowing. Franco Modigliani's life cycle hypothesis suggests that consumption will remain relatively stable over one's life and saving and usage of savings will be adjusted as a function of income, lifetime and retirement. Some of the other such theories which are relevant and interesting are:

- Milton Friedman's permanent income hypothesis
- Robert Hall's random walk hypothesis
- David Laibson's pull of instant gratification

Investment

When we talk about investment, in the context of economic output, there are traditionally 3 types of investment that we are referring to (Das, 2021):

- Business fixed investment – This involves the investment that firms make on equipment, structures or anything else used in the process of production.
- Residential investment – This investment refers to the purchase of new housing units. This investment may be made by the residents of the house, or by landlords.
- Inventory investment – This investment refers to the change in quantities or values of inventory which may be finished goods, materials and supplies, or work in process.

Any investment makes sense when the benefits from the investments outweigh the costs of the investment. We assume the market at large to be rational and to make investments when they tend to be more beneficial than expensive. Some of the major factors that determine the cost of investment are interest rates, depreciation and capital loss. Two of these don't fluctuate, or can't be controlled or timed for. Interest rates, however, tend to vary from one time to another. It, therefore, follows that when interest rates are lower, investment tends to be higher. Whereas higher interest rates lead to lower investments.

This can be understood through a simple model, where we assume that investments require the borrowing of capital, which in some way or form they do (at least from other activities). Thus, interest rates and investments are negatively correlated.

There are levers other than interest rates to drive up or dampen investment. For example, the provision of investment tax credit reduces the amount that firms spend on tax, as a function of investment. Thus, it effectively reduces the cost of capital and therefore encourages more investment. There is also a metric called Tobin's q.

This metric is the ratio of the market value of investments relative to their replacement costs. Higher Tobin's q also prompts higher investments.

It should therefore not come as a surprise that poor stock market performance, or even pessimism about future profitability of capital would (Das, 2021):

- Drive down stock prices.
- Cause Tobin's q to fall.
- Shift the investment function (profitability of investment) downward.
- Bring the aggregate demand down.
- Reduce household wealth and reduce consumption, once again bringing the aggregate demand down.

This close relationship between the stock market and investment, or more broadly economic performance is potentially concerning. On the one hand, one may take the view of the efficient market hypothesis. In this case, one believes stock prices perfectly reflect all the information available about a company. If investors have all the relevant information and are perfectly rational, there is nothing to be worried about. However, if one subscribes to Keynes' view that the stock market is like a beauty contest, where each investor is trying to guess which contestant others find most beautiful, we might be in trouble. This is concerning because then, with each investor trying to outguess the other, we may be subject to more random waves of optimism and pessimism, which have deeper ramifications (Das, 2021).

Inflation & unemployment

Both inflation and unemployment are reasonably unpopular terms. But there is much more that ties them together. For starters, there is the misery index, defined by Arthur Okun. The idea behind this index is to have a metric for the misery felt by everyday people, as a result of the fear of joblessness and rising prices. Understandably, this is simply defined as the sum of inflation and unemployment.

That's a pretty basic understanding of these 2 terms. It shouldn't be surprising that fewer people having jobs and prices being higher is a bad combination. However, Okun has given us a far more powerful law. According to Okun's law, for every 1 percentage point increase in the unemployment rate, the GDP will likely fall by 2 percentage points. This tells us 2 key things (Kenton, Okun's Law, 2021):

- Unemployment is bad for the country's GDP. This is hardly surprising. But more specifically, unemployment is directly proportional to the drop in GDP.
- The drop in GDP is double the increase in unemployment. The key implication is that increasing unemployment rates will very quickly lead to a cascading drop in GDP.

There is a similar concept called the sacrifice ratio, which is the number of percentage points of GDP lost for every percentage point increase in inflation. This number doesn't have as steady a value and varies from time to time as well as region to region.

Further, there is also a useful relationship which exists between unemployment and inflation. According to the Phillips curve, unemployment is indirectly proportional to the inflation rate. The Phillips curve is in itself far more complex than this simple relation. However, for simplicity, the implication that they're inversely related is the key takeaway from the Phillips curve (Das, 2021).

IS-LM curve

The IS-LM curve is yet another model, where we look at 2 curves, how they intersect, and how various decisions will impact certain equilibria. But before we get ahead of ourselves, the reason that this is a useful model to get acquainted with is that we have thus far not yet factored in interest rates or monetary policy. Surely, we have heard these phrases being thrown around before, so it would be interesting to see how they fit in. This is far from the end of macroeconomics and how it can be used to analyse our economy. But for the purpose of this book, this is as advanced as we will be able to get before I am way out of my depth.

So, let's begin with the fact that we have seen that interest rates and investment move in opposite directions. We can show this relationship through the following simple equation.

$$ I_{(investment)} = \bar{I}_{(autonomous\ investment)} - (b_{(responsiveness\ to\ interest\ rate)} \times i_{(interest\ rate)}) $$

We have already seen how we can calculate aggregate demand in our section on consumption. Just as we had complicated the consumption variable, we will now do the same with the investment variable. Thus, we can now calculate our aggregate demand through the following equation.

$$AD_{\text{(aggregate demand)}} = \overline{A}_{\text{(autonomous spending)}} + C_{\text{(marginal propensity to consume)}} \times (1 - t_{\text{(tax rate)}}) \times$$
$$Y_{\text{(income)}} - (b_{\text{(responsiveness to interest rate)}} \times i_{\text{(interest rate)}})$$

And once again, we shall use the aggregate demand equation to represent the income/output as a function of autonomous spending. This result is what we call the IS (investment savings) curve. At the moment, we haven't seen why this is useful. So, let's start by noting that what it tells us is that as the interest rate goes up, the output comes down. Further, it tells us that the output's sensitivity to the interest rate is a function of the coefficient. The coefficient in this equation is the same as in the consumption section. So, a higher marginal propensity to consume and lower tax rates make the output more sensitive to changes in the interest rate (Das, 2021).

$$Y_{\text{(output)}} = \alpha_{G\text{(coefficient)}} \times (\overline{A}_{\text{(autonomous spending)}} - (b_{\text{(responsiveness to interest rate)}} \times i_{\text{(interest rate)}})$$

The IS curve is one downward sloping curve, as a part of our model. If you have been paying attention to the chapters on economics, you might have guessed that we will now add an upward-sloping curve. This is the LM (liquidity preference – money supply) curve.

Let's first try and understand what shapes the demand for real money. We say real money because we don't mean only the nominal value of cash, but rather the value of money, after factoring in things like inflation. One might guess that greater income and output would lead to a greater demand for real money to purchase more. This is an easily observable trend as one looks at countries in order of their GDP per capita. Further, you might notice that with higher interest rates, people are less inclined to hold cash in hand, preferring to deposit it in a bank. You can think of this as a preference to earn interest, rather than allow their money to sit idle. You can also think of this as a preference to borrow less real money at higher interest rates. Either way, when these 2 factors are combined, the demand for real money may be modelled as:

$$L_{\text{(demand for real money)}} = (k_{\text{(coefficient)}} \times Y_{\text{(income)}}) - (h_{\text{(coefficient)}} \times i_{\text{(interest rate)}})$$

The supply of real money is a function of only the total volume of nominal money in supply and the price levels.

$$\text{supply of real money} = \overline{M}_{\text{(nominal money supply)}} / \overline{P}_{\text{(price level)}}$$

When we reach an equilibrium between the demand and supply of real money, we end up with another relationship. As per this equation, we can see how the interest rate is determined as a function of income, money supply and price levels (Das, 2021).

$$i_{\text{(interest rate)}} = (1/h)_{\text{(coefficient)}} \times ((k_{\text{(coefficient)}} \times Y_{\text{(income)}}) - (\overline{M}_{\text{(nominal money supply)}} / \overline{P}_{\text{(price level)}}))$$

Here also, we may note that a steeper LM curve would imply that the demand for money is more sensitive to income and less sensitive to interest rates. The position of the LM curve is itself a function of the amount of money in supply.

More interestingly, when we put the IS and LM curves together, we can learn a lot about what actions would impact the economy and how. And at this stage, I will leave you at a bit of a cliffhanger. I am not equipped to go into the details of how each economic activity impacts this model, and how to read the after-effects.

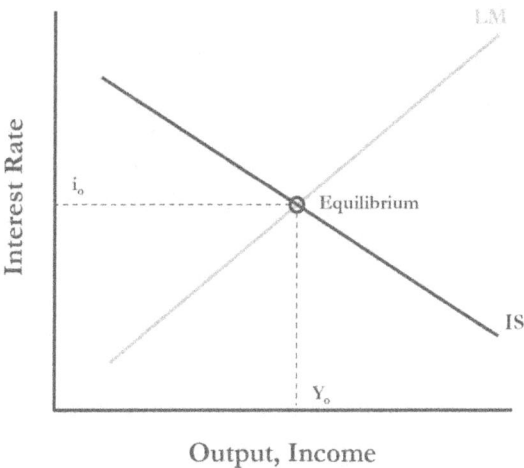

Output, Income

But, I hope that from what we have seen throughout this book, with this model in hand, you will be able to make sense of any economic news through this model. One only needs to understand how the underlying equations and curves shift and then understand how the equilibrium is impacted, and what that will mean for the variables of interest. This should be enough to understand the opinions of experts while reasoning out their arguments on one's own.

Recap

In our attempt to understand how to manage a business, we have thus far learnt:

- Management thinking. We have extensively been using convergent thinking, structuring in particular and divergent thinking along the way.
- We got started with 4 steps of business value creation so that we can capture value from customers in return. We are capable of understanding the marketplace, positioning our brand to target the right customers, designing an effective market mix and managing relevant relationships along the way.
- To understand the language of finance, we have understood:
  o The financial reporting process.
  o How to build and analyse the 3 key financial reports.
  o Basic concepts, accounting principles and nuances.

- Metrics and ratios for financial analysis.
- What else can be learnt from financial markets to valuation of firms.
- To tackle any operational challenge, we had a look at:
  - The basics and terminology of operations.
  - The mathematical nature of operations.
  - The specific math managers need to know.
  - The scope of technology in business.

- So that our technical knowledge can practically be put to use, we learnt how to communicate better with anyone involved. We spent sometime understanding how individuals, groups and large organisations may behave at scale. And we understood the role that HR plays in managing the human element of business.

- To understand how our business fits into the outside world, we had a glance at some of the basics of business law, including:
    - Offers, acceptance, formation and breaking of contracts.
    - Special types of unilateral contracts.
    - The fundamentals of the companies act.

- To improve our understanding of any new situation we might find ourselves in, we learnt how to model and analyse:
    - The market, consumers, firms, prices, costs and profits.
    - Regulations, game theory, externalities, taxes/subsidies and information asymmetry.

- To take our economic understanding a step further, we introduced ourselves to:
    - The concept of the economy and GDP.
    - The 4 key levers of economic output.
    - The ideas of inflation and unemployment.
    - The IS-LM curve as a powerful economic model.

Chapter 32
That's All Folks!

After 6 sections, each absolutely packed with information and frameworks, you have reached the end of the book. You might still find yourself wondering what exactly it is that you have learnt and whether you have learnt anything that you can use. You might find yourself asking yourself whether you are now equipped to be a manager. At least these were some of the questions on my mind, by the time I completed my MBA. So, as a closing note, allow me to share some of the insights that I have found for myself in the process of writing this book. If I had done a good job of writing this book, none of these insights would be new to you. But alas, I'm sure that I have made hundreds of mistakes along the way. Therefore, this is my last-ditch effort to try and impart some enlightenment in the last minute.

- A business school programme is an opportunity to develop one's knowledge, as well as one's self.
- **Knowledge** – This book, much like any business school programme targeted the 6 major areas of study in business. Over the course of a 2-year MBA, you will undoubtedly be taught a lot more than I have been able to cover in this book. However, there are the limitations of:
  o What one can absorb in the rush of an MBA programme.
  o What one will retain once the programme is complete.
  o What one is interested in pursuing after the programme.

  Because of these limitations, I believe that the average student should aim to retain a basic level of understanding of management, across these 6 subject areas. I also believe that each of us can and should strive to go above and beyond in at least one area that we hope to become experts in. Because life is long, and memory is not, creating one's own references and indices to supplement their learning is a great long-term plan. That is what I have tried to create through this book. If you are just now entering business school, or if you have the time on hand, I would encourage you to create something better than I have been able to.

- **Self** – What my book cannot do, and what no programme will hand you on a platter is self-development. That being said, there is no place like college to pause, look around and look within. It is a luxury to have the time to ask one's self tough questions about what they want, where they see themselves and how they plan on getting to their goals. It is a privilege to be surrounded by talented individuals from whom one can quietly learn, or openly ask for help. What one will do with this good fortune, and what they will retain from it is entirely up to them.

References

Akerlof, G. A. (1970, August). *The Market for "Lemons": Quality Uncertainty and the Market Mechanism.* Retrieved from The Quarterly Journal of Economics: https://www.jstor.org/stable/1879431

Alderfer, C. P. (1969, May). *An empirical test of a new theory of human needs.* Retrieved from Organizational Behavior and Human Performance: https://www.sciencedirect.com/science/article/abs/pii/003050736990004X

Allport, G. W. (1954). *The Nature of Prejudice.* Retrieved from https://faculty.washington.edu/caporaso/courses/203/readings/allport_Nature_of_prejudice.pdf

Amblee, N. (2021). Marketing Services Course at IIM-A. *Marketing Services.* Ahmedabad: IIM-Ahmedabad.

Ansoff, H. I. (1957). *Strategies for Diversification.* Retrieved from Harvard Business Review: https://www.mindtools.com/pages/article/newTMC_90.htm#:~:text=The%20Ansoff%20Matrix%20was%20developed,about%20the%20risks%20of%20growth.

Anthony, R., Hawkins, D., & Merchant, K. A. (2017). *Accounting : Text & Cases 13th Edition.*

Borah, S. (2020). Marketing 2 Course at IIM-A. *Marketing 2.* Ahmedabad: IIM-Ahmedabad.

Chandwani, R. (2022). Leading and Managing Sales Forces Course at IIM-A. *Leading and Managing Sales Forces.* Ahmedabad: IIM-Ahmedabad.

Chatterjee, C. (2020). Microeconomics Course at IIM-A. *Microeconomics.* Ahmedabad: IIM-Ahmedabad.

Cherry, K. (2021, February 20). *The Big 5 Personality Traits.* Retrieved from verywellmind.com: https://www.verywellmind.com/the-big-five-personality-dimensions-2795422

Daniel, D. (2021, October). *Poka-Yoke*. Retrieved from Tech Target: https://www.techtarget.com/searcherp/definition/poka-yoke#:~:text=A%20poka%2Dyoke%20is%20a,%22avoid%20blunders%22%20in%20Japanese.

Das, A. (2021). Macroeconomics Course at IIM-A. *Macroeconomics*. Ahmedabad: IIM-Ahmedabad.

Desai, N. (2021). Costing and Control Systems Course at IIM-A. *Costing and Control Systems*. Ahmedabad: IIM-Ahmedabad.

Dolan, R. J. (2014, June 30). *Marketing Reading: Framework for Marketing Strategy Formation*. Retrieved from Harvard Business Publishing: https://hbsp.harvard.edu/product/8153-PDF-ENG

Gandhi, S. (2020). Financial Reporting Analysis Course at IIM-A. *Financial Reporting Analysis*. Ahmedabad: IIM-Ahmedabad.

Gopakumar, K. V. (2021). Interpersonal and Group Processes Course at IIM-A. *Interpersonal and Group Processes*. Ahmedabad: IIM-Ahmedabad.

Griffiths, N. (2010, May 14). *Brand Key Workshop*. Retrieved from slideshare.net: https://www.slideshare.net/NGA2010/understanding-brand-and-developing-a-brand-key

Gupta, P. (2020). Individual Dynamics Course at IIM-A. *Individual Dynamics*. Ahmedabad: IIM-Ahmedabad.

Hersey, & Blanchard, K. H. (1972). *Situational Leadership*. Retrieved from Sage Journals: https://journals.sagepub.com/doi/abs/10.1177/107179199300100104

Herzberg, F., Mausner, B., & Snydermann. (1959). *The motivation to work*. Retrieved from New York : Wiley: https://www.lifesciencesite.com/lsj/life140517/03_32120lsj140517_12_16.pdf

Hirschman, A. O. (1970). *Exit, Voice and Loyalty*. Retrieved from Harvard University Press: https://core.ac.uk/download/pdf/288379219.pdf

Housel, M. (2020). *The Psychology of Money : Timeless lessons on wealth, greed, and happiness.*

Humphrey, A. (1960). *What is SWOT Analysis.* Retrieved from lucidchart.com: https://www.lucidchart.com/pages/what-is-swot-analysis#:~:text=SWOT%20analysis%20was%20invented%20in,that%20was%20executable%20and%20reasonable.

Investopedia. (2022, April 7). *Pareto Principle.* Retrieved from Investopedia: https://www.investopedia.com/terms/p/paretoprinciple.asp

Kanbanize. (n.d.). *What is a Kanban board.* Retrieved from Kanbanize: https://kanbanize.com/kanban-resources/getting-started/what-is-kanban-board

Kenton, W. (2021, May 11). *Demand Curve.* Retrieved from Invetopedia: https://www.investopedia.com/terms/d/demand-curve.asp

Kenton, W. (2021, November 11). *Okun's Law.* Retrieved from Investopedia: https://www.investopedia.com/terms/o/okunslaw.asp

Kinnison, A. (2019, April 26). *How to Conduct a 5c Analysis: Templates, Examples, and What to Ask.* Retrieved from Volusion: https://www.volusion.com/blog/situation-analysis-the-5-cs/

Kotler, P. (2010). *Principles of Marketing : A South Asian Perspective 8th Edition.*

Kulkarni, V. (2020). Workshop on Interviews and Presentations Course at IIM-A. *Workshop on Interviews and Presentations.* Ahmedabad: IIM-Ahmedabad.

Maslow, A. H. (1943). *A Theory of Human Motivation.* Retrieved from psychclassics.york.ca: https://psychclassics.yorku.ca/Maslow/motivation.htm

McClelland, J. L. (1988, April). *Connectionist models and psychological evidence.* Retrieved from Science Direct: https://www.sciencedirect.com/science/article/abs/pii/0749596X88900691

McGregor, D. (1960). *Theory X and Theory Y*. Retrieved from https://static1.squarespace.com/static/60bddec1a93337235ecfdbcf/t/620 5165bca24ea4adc4943df/1644500572175/McGregor_Thinker.pdf

Miecznikowski, G. (2016, April 20). *Shape Your Brand With This Exercise*. Retrieved from medium.com: https://medium.com/@gmiecznikowski/shape-your-brand-with-this-exercise-4645ac3ea26d

Mohan, M. P. (2020). Legal Aspects of Business Course at IIM-A. *Legal Aspects of Business*. Ahmedabad: IIM-Ahmedabad.

Moses, A. C. (2020). Human Resources Management 2 Course at IIM-A. *Human Resources Management 2*. Ahmedabad: IIM-Ahmedabad.

Pandey, A. (2020). Financial Markets Course at IIM-A. *Financial Markets*. Ahemdabad: IIM-Ahmedabad.

Parasuraman, Zeithaml, V. A., & Berry, L. L. (1985, September 1). *A Conceptual Model of Service Quality and Its Implications for Future Research*. Retrieved from Sage Journals: https://journals.sagepub.com/doi/10.1177/002224298504900403

Peters, T. J., & Waterman, R. H. (1970s). *The 7S Framework*. Retrieved from McKinsey Quarterly: https://www.mckinsey.com/business-functions/strategy-and-corporate-finance/our-insights/enduring-ideas-the-7-s-framework

Pindyck, R., & Rubinfeld, D. (2017). *Microeconomics 8th Edition*. Pearson.

Porter. (1980). *Competitive Strategy*. Retrieved from New York Free Press: https://www.jstor.org/stable/256040?seq=22

Porter, M. E. (1979, March). *How Competitive Forces Shape Strategy*. Retrieved from Harvard Business Review: https://hbr.org/1979/03/how-competitive-forces-shape-strategy

Ready, D. A., Hill, L. A., & Conger, a. J. (2008, November). *Winning the Race for Talent in Emerging Markets*. Retrieved from Harvard Business Review: https://hbr.org/2008/11/winning-the-race-for-talent-in-emerging-markets

Richard, L. (2006). *Integrated Marketing Communications: Creativity, Consistency and Effective Resource Allocation*. Retrieved from Harvard Business Essentials: Marketer's Toolkit: The 10 Strategies You Need to Succeed: https://www.carnegiehighered.com/blog/the-6-ms-of-mastering-your-integrated-marketing-campaign/

Sadwick, R. (2020, June 22). *How To Price Your Product: A Guide To The Van Westendorp Pricing Model*. Retrieved from Forbes: https://www.forbes.com/sites/rebeccasadwick/2020/06/22/how-to-price-products/?sh=2d09490955c7

Schien, E. H. (1984, January 15). *Coming to a New Awareness of Organizational Culture*. Retrieved from MIT Sloan Management Review: https://sloanreview.mit.edu/article/coming-to-a-new-awareness-of-organizational-culture/?use_credit=fecf2c550171d3195c879d115440ae45

Sharma, R. (2020). Marketing 1 Course at IIM-A. *Marketing 1*. Ahmedabad: IIM-Ahmedabad.

Sinha, A. (2021). Operations Management 2 Course at IIM-A. *Operations Management 2*. Ahmedabad: IIM-Ahmedabad.

Sinha, S. (2021). Corporate Finance Course at IIM-A. *Corporate Finance*. Ahmedabad: IIM-Ahmedabad.

Soman, C. (2020). Operations Management 1 Course at IIM-A. *Operations Management*. Ahmedabad: IIM-Ahmedabad.

Sreekumar, A. (2022). Marketing for Startups Course at IIM-A. *Marketing for Startups*. Ahmedabad: IIM-Ahmedabad.

Theory, C. (2021). *The Johari Window Model*. Retrieved from Communication Theory: https://www.communicationtheory.org/the-johari-window-model/

Ulrich, D. (1997). *Human Resource Champions*. Retrieved from Harvard Business School Press: https://books.google.co.in/books?hl=en&lr=&id=qTxz6I7tNSEC&oi=fnd&pg=PR7&dq=david+ulrich+hr+model+1997&ots=Nq1t-exldk&sig=F64qh27m2_XaWxigRaYkh1KrV1M#v=onepage&q=david%20ulrich%20hr%20model%201997&f=false

Varkkey, B. (2020). Human Resources Management 1 Course at IIM-A. *Human Resources Management 1*. Ahmedabad: IIM-Ahmedabad.

Vijayalakshmi, A. (2021). Business Research Methods Course at IIM-A. *Business Research Methods*. Ahmedabad: IIM-Ahmedabad.

Zakon, A., & Henderson, B. (1970). *What Is the Growth Share Matrix?* Retrieved from bcg.com: https://www.bcg.com/about/overview/our-history/growth-share-matrix